A Modern Guide to Economic Thought

In memory of David

A Modern Guide to Economic Thought

An Introduction to Comparative Schools
of Thought in Economics

Edited by
Douglas Mair and Anne G. Miller

Edward Elgar

Published by
Edward Elgar Publishing Limited
Gower House
Croft Road
Aldershot
Hants GU11 3HR
England

Edward Elgar Publishing Company
Old Post Road
Brookfield
Vermont 05036
USA

British Library Cataloguing in Publication Data

A modern guide to economic thought: an introduction to
  comparative schools of thought in economics.
  1. Economics
  I. Mair, Douglas *1939–* II. Miller, Anne G. *1941–*
  330.15.

Library of Congress Cataloguing in Publication Data

A modern guide to economic thought: an introduction to comparative
  schools of thought in economics/edited by Douglas Mair and Anne G.
  Miller.
      p. cm.
  Includes bibliographical references and index.
  1. Comparative economics. 2. Economics. 3. Economics—History.
  4. Economics—History—20th century. I. Mair, Douglas.
  II. Miller, Anne, 1941–
  HB90.M63 1991   91–18139
  330.1—dc20   CIP

  ISBN 1 85278 323 0
       1 85278 640 X (paperback)

Printed in Great Britain by
Billing & Sons Ltd, Worcester

Contents

Figures

Contributors

Sheila C. Dow received her higher education at the Universities of St Andrew's, Manitoba, McMaster and Glasgow. Between degrees, she worked at the Bank of England and in the Department of Finance of the Government of Manitoba. She has taught at Stirling University since 1979 (with periods of leave at Toronto and Cambridge, England) and now holds the position of Reader in Economics. She is author of *Macroeconomic Thought* (1985), *Financial Markets and Regional Economic Development* (1990), and (with Peter Earl) *Money Matters* (1982), and of articles in the fields of monetary theory, regional economics, methodology, history of thought and Post-Keynesian economics.

John Foster is a graduate of Manchester University. He is currently a professor in the Department of Economics at the University of Queensland. He is author of *Evolutionary Macroeconomics* (1987). He has published papers on a variety of topics, including modelling UK housing markets, macroeconomic modelling, and money and credit, in a number of academic journals.

J.M. Alec Gee is a senior lecturer at Dundee University in the Department of Economics. His articles and books are on the theory of market structures and the history of economic thought.

Frank Harrigan is a senior research fellow at the Fraser of Allender Institute at the University of Strathclyde. He has written extensively on various aspects of economy-wide modelling, particularly on input–output and general equilibrium analyses, and has also written on labour market issues. He is co-editor (with Peter McGregor) of *Recent Advances in Regional Economic Modelling* (1988), and is author of articles in *Demography, Environment and Planning, Journal of Regional Science*, and *The Economic Journal*.

Brian J. Loasby studied economics at Cambridge, and held appointments in the Universities of Aberdeen, Birmingham and Bristol before joining the University of Stirling for its opening in 1967. He became

Professor of Management Economics in 1971 and though taking early retirement in 1984 remains active in the University. He was President of the Scottish Economic Society from 1987 and 1990. His main interests are in organizational behaviour and the evolution of economic ideas; his publications include *The Swindon Project* (1973), *Choice, Complexity and Ignorance* (1976), *The Mind and Method of the Economist* (1989) as well as articles in a variety of journals and contributions to books.

James Love is a senior lecturer in the Department of Economics at the University of Strathclyde. He is a co-editor of *Understanding the Scottish Economy* (1983), and has published regularly in the *Oxford Bulletin of Economics and Statistics*, *Journal of Development Studies*, *Journal of Development Economics*, *Journal of Economic Studies*, *World Development* and *Journal of Developing Areas*.

Peter G. McGregor graduated from the University of Stirling, and is currently a Senior Research Fellow at the Fraser of Allender Institute at the University of Strathclyde. He is co-editor (with Frank Harrigan) of *Recent Advances in Regional Economic Modelling* (1988). He has written on macroeconomic, financial, labour and general equilibrium issues. He has published papers in *Applied Economics*, *European Economic Review*, *History of Political Economy*, *Journal of Regional Science*, *The Manchester School* and the *Oxford Economic Papers*.

Douglas Mair graduated in economics from St Andrew's University in 1960 and with a PhD from Heriot-Watt University in 1975. Since 1975 he has been a senior lecturer, and is now Reader, in the Department of Economics at Heriot-Watt. He is the editor of *The Scottish Contribution to Modern Economic Thought* (1990). His main interests are in property taxation, Post-Keynesian economics and the history of economic thought. He has published papers in the *Economic Journal*, *Scottish Journal of Political Economy*, *Cambridge Journal of Economics*, *Government and Policy*, *Urban Studies* and *Journal of Post Keynesian Economics*.

Anne G. Miller obtained a Master's degree in economic theory and econometrics from Southampton University, after completing a science degree (Reading), and a Diploma in Public and Social Administration (Oxford). She is currently a lecturer in the Department of Economics at Heriot-Watt University in Edinburgh. Her main academic interests comprise economic methodology, comparative schools of economic thought, and the sociological and psychological foundations of economics, particularly the specification of needs in utility functions. She has contributed papers to the *Quarterly Economic Commentary, Urban Studies*, and has edited the proceedings of the first *International Conference on Basic Income*.

Andrew G. Scott is a lecturer in the Department of Economics at Heriot-Watt University. He is the author of books on EC trade flows and European integration, and has published in the *Journal of Common Market Studies*.

Thomas S. Torrance is a graduate of the Universities of St Andrew's and of Edinburgh. He is currently a lecturer in the Department of Economics at the University of Aberdeen. His main academic interests are in the areas of the economics of financial management, monetary economics, the history of economic theory, and the philosophy of economics. He is the author and co-author of various papers, including articles in *Economica, Oxford Bulletin of Economics and Statistics, Oxford Economic Papers, The Manchester School* and *The Scottish Journal of Political Economy*.

1. Introduction

Anne G. Miller and Douglas Mair

WHY WE WROTE THIS BOOK

Without giving too much away about our ages, we learned our economics as students in the late 1950s and early 1960s. Like most postwar English-language economists, our introduction to economics was essentially the conventional mainstream neoclassical–Keynesian synthesis. We were taught by a generation of economists who had been brought up to believe that 'It's all in Marshall' and we, in our turn, were brought up to believe that 'It's all in Samuelson'. The economic conditions in the UK at that time seemed to justify the belief in the efficacy of Keynesian demand management policy – growth by previous standards was high, unemployment was virtually non-existent and inflation was something that might have happened in Germany in the 1920s but was totally unknown in the UK. There was consensus over economic policy; this was the era of Butskellism and, as Harold Macmillan was to remind us just after we left university, we had never had it so good. The Cold War was at its peak; the Hungarian uprising of 1956 had been ruthlessly suppressed, so that teaching of Marxist economics was strictly taboo. The MV ≡ PT relationship, if we were taught it at all, was a historical curiosum associated with the name of some obscure early twentieth century American economist called Irving Fisher (or was it Irving Berlin?). Perhaps we knew the names of some prominent Austrian-born economists like Böhm-Bawerk or Schumpeter, but we certainly were not aware of the existence of any distinctive Austrian school of economics which offered an alternative to the Marshallian microeconomics that we were taught. There is always a tendency among the older generation to remind the younger generation that they are having it easy by comparison with the rigours we experienced, but in the case of economics it is probably fair to say that we were exposed to a science which was much less contentious and much more unified than it is today.

This consensus started to break down in the 1960s, and the 1970s saw the debates between the monetarists of the Chicago school, led by

1

Professor Milton Friedman, and the Keynesians and then, somewhat later, the emergence of the Chicago-inspired new classical macro-economics. A clearly discernible post-Keynesian school began to emerge in the 1960s and 1970s, led in the UK by Lord Kaldor and Professor Joan Robinson, and the publication in 1960 of Sraffa's 'Production of Commodities by Means of Commodities' paved the way for a return to economic analysis in the then almost defunct tradition of David Ricardo. In the US, Baran and Sweezy were challenging a number of the basic tenets of orthodox Marxism and arguing that traditional Marxist analysis was inappropriate to an understanding of mid-twentieth century monopoly capitalism. Also in the US, J.K. Galbraith was performing in the 1960s and 1970s much the same role that Thorstein Veblen had played 50 years earlier of reminding economists of the importance of institutional factors in the determination of events. Also from the University of Chicago, Professor Friedrich Hayek, after spending a quarter of a century working on issues of constitutional philosophy, re-emerged as a trenchant critic of Keynesianism and provided the stimulus for a resurgence of interest in Austrian economics.

By the early 1980s, there was a growing ferment of debate in the literature on the crisis of economic theory, with criticisms of mainstream economics arising from within and outwith its own ranks (Ward, 1972; Blaug, 1980; Bell and Kristol, 1981; Eichner, 1983; Thurow, 1983; Wiles and Routh, 1984; and Lutz and Lux, 1988). This provided an impetus to the study of methodology in economics, deriving from the work in the philosophy of science of Popper, Kuhn and Lakatos (Caldwell, 1982; Boland, 1982). Economists have long been chary of issues in methodology but the emergence of a number of competing schools of thought has made it necessary to return to a consideration of certain fundamental philosophical and methodological issues. There has emerged an enormous literature on these various schools (see, for example, the series 'Schools of Thought' published by Edward Elgar), yet there is no easy access to this extensive material.

There are plenty of relatively advanced texts written by members of each school for its own adherents. There are books which criticize neoclassical or orthodox Keynesian economics from the perspective of a particular school of thought, usually written by professional economists for each other. Backhouse's (1985) excellent comprehensive text, suitable for more advanced undergraduates, compares the development of the different schools of thought as they affect the mainstream schools. But there are no simple, comprehensive introductions to the different schools of economic thought. There is certainly none which presents the current state of each school on its own terms, indicating its *raison d'être*, why each school thinks as it does, and the questions to which it is trying to find answers. There is none which tries to facilitate comparisons between the schools. As teachers, we feel the lack of such a book, as do, we think, our students.

This book does not go so far as to provide a textbook on each school of thought, but it does aim to fill this perceived need in an easily accessible manner. Its purpose is to explain in straightforward terms the current state of development of each of the main schools of economic thought, comparing their ideologies, methodological practices and the main questions they are exploring, their preoccupations, assumptions, evidence and conclusions. It is aimed at first- and second-year undergraduates who have had some introduction to economics, but we hope that it will also be helpful to the pre-college student who is trying to decide whether to study economics at tertiary level. We hope it will provide a useful introduction to the alternative schools for our professional colleagues and for anyone for whom it is important to have a broad view of the current state of economics.

Each chapter, one for each of the seven main schools of economic thought, has been written by an economist with specialist knowledge of that school. Each writer presents the ideology, methodology and the main content of a particular school. The tone of each chapter is intended to be constructive, not merely criticizing what the other schools are doing. Each attempts to find the common ground and to indicate what a textbook by that school might be like, if it were written for the beginning student. Each chapter concludes with suggestions for further reading. But because we think that it is not possible to develop an adequate understanding of what each school is trying to achieve without some basic appreciation of the underlying philosophical and methodological issues, we begin the book with a chapter on philosophy and methodology.

Only the seven most prominent schools of economic thought are presented here. Within each school there are varying shades of opinion and at the margins it is sometimes difficult to draw very precise lines of demarcation between them. This means that one cannot be dogmatic in defining each school; one can merely convey the flavour of the main part of it. Also, it can often be misleading to attach particular labels to people as, for example, is the case with Professor G.L.S. Shackle, whom many regard as the Grand Old Man of British economics, who is claimed with equal enthusiasm by the British chapels of both Austrian and post-Keynesian economics as their leading guru.

The purpose of this introduction is to give an overview or perspective, to provide a framework within which to fit the main schools, to guide the reader by anticipating what is to come, and indicating how the schools may be compared and related. A useful method of comparing them is provided by placing them into the context of the paradigms of Kuhn and the Scientific Research Programs (SRPs) of Lakatos. Kuhn and Lakatos are philosophers of science, who put forward theories about the growth of knowledge. Their ideas are introduced in the next section, but they are explained in greater detail and placed in the context of philosophy of science and methodology by Torrance in Chapter 2. At the end of each of Chapters 3 to 9 is given a summary of the school, based on a series of standard headings derived from Kuhn's and Lakatos's theories. The following section explains the purpose of these summaries and gives the meanings of the headings in more detail. In the fourth section, a vignette of each school is presented, providing an entrée to the following chapters, outlining the ideological values of the researchers in that school, their goals and methodological practices, and finally an indication of the substantive content of the schools. The subject matter of economics, which essentially is society itself, is too vast and complex for any one school to encompass it all, and each school tends to specialize in different aspects of the subject matter. Thus, although some of the subject matter of the schools is overlapping, much of it is not, and the schools should be regarded as complementary, rather than rival. In the last section, we discuss the question of why, since the schools are complementary, the neoclassical school is currently so dominant in the English-speaking world.

KUHN AND LAKATOS

Anyone who studies economics has to develop a thick skin. There are any number of 'jokes' about the apparent inability of economists to agree on anything. Prime ministers from Winston Churchill to Margaret Thatcher have cried out in despair for the one-armed economist or indeed for the extermination of the entire species. To a certain extent, these criticisms are justified, as many economists have tended to be dogmatic about the particular brand of economics they espouse, tending to be rather dismissive of any other school or denying that any other discipline, with the possible exception of mathematics, has a useful contribution to make the creation of the 'Compleat Economist'. What we hope to do in this book is to show that far from being a matter for ridicule, the diversity of present-day economics is a sign of scientific maturity and a cause for some optimism.

There are two ways in which one can justify the diversity of present-day economics. One is the line of argument developed by one of the UK's Nobel prize-winning economists, the late Sir John Hicks (1983). Hicks argues, and here he is very close to the positions of Professor Shackle and of another Nobel prize-winner, Friedrich von Hayek, that the facts we study in economics are changing incessantly and without repetition. What we as economists must do is to try to detect repeating patterns from the mass of absorbing detail and to do this we must simplify. For this we need theories, our tools of analysis, which Hicks regards more as rays of light which, we hope, illuminate at least part of our target, leaving the rest of complex reality in darkness. But we must be sure to choose our theories well, otherwise they may illumine only irrelevant objects. And because the world in which we live is changing, a theory which illumines the right things now may illumine the wrong things at another time. There cannot be, as Hicks rightly says, an economic theory which does everything we want of it all the time. Hicks's analogy of economic theories as rays of light brings to mind the old joke about the drunk who spent a whole night looking for his latchkey under a streetlamp because that was the only place where it was bright enough for him to see. Without wishing to suggest that all economists are drunkards, a lot of them have spent a great deal of time in fruitless search with the aid of irrelevant or redundant theories.

The second way is that, in the history of economic thought, there are certain well recognized periods when a prevailing mode of thought has been rejected in favour of what was deemed to be a more satisfactory paradigm. Examples are the marginal revolution of the 1870s and Alec Gee in his chapter on neoclassical economics (Chapter 4) discusses how one branch of the 'revolution' has subsequently matured to fruition, while Brian Loasby in Chapter 3 discusses the way in which Carl Menger, one of the three architects of that 'revolution' developed what has come to be known as Austrian economics on a set of principles fundamentally different from those of the previous classical school and also in important respects different from those of the neoclassical. Another was the Keynesian revolution of the 1930s which James Love analyses in Chapter 6, where he brings out the reasons why Keynes's *General Theory* was such a radical departure from the previous classical approach to macroeconomics. More recently, we have witnessed the widespread and rapid abandonment of Keynesian economics in favour of the macroeconomics of the Chicago school for the reasons discussed by Frank Harrigan and Peter McGregor in Chapter 5, coming as it did shortly after President Nixon had told the world 'we are all Keynesians now'.

But these 'revolutions' occur only relatively infrequently and for long periods of time economics has proceeded with only minor ripples on its surface. It is then that we have the problem of how economists are to choose between competing schools of thought when there may be no compelling empirical or theoretical reason to prefer one in favour of another. Hicks does not give us any real guidance on this issue. What economics needs, therefore, is some rational or 'scientific' way of choosing between schools, or between theories from different schools. This is why we asked Tom Torrance to write the opening chapter on the philosophical foundations of economics. And this is why the authors of each of the chapters on the various schools have quite deliberately emphasized the methodology of each school, its assumptions and its criteria for acceptance or rejection of a particular proposition. As Torrance indicates, there is no clear or unambiguous way in which we can compare theories from different schools, or even accept or reject any theory in economics with complete confidence. Popper's test of falsification runs into difficulties when we try to use it in practice and this is one reason why many economists have been attracted by Kuhn's ideas of 'normal' and 'revolutionary' science.

Kuhn argues that scientific development can be divided into two phases: long periods of what he calls 'normal science' which are characterized by step-by-step advances within the framework of the ruling paradigm; and much shorter periods of 'revolutionary science' when the ruling paradigm has gone into decline and there is a struggle for supremacy with some new and ultimately victorious paradigm. The attraction that Kuhn has had for the social sciences generally and for economics in particular is his argument that science is not validated by 'objective' positivistic norms but by the collective judgement of communities of scientists. It is the peer group approval of these 'invisible colleges' that confers the stamp of scientific respectability which is ultimately rewarded in economics, as in other sciences, with the award of a Nobel prize.

Kuhn's is essentially a sociological approach to the growth of knowledge and Torrance compares his ideas with those of another well known philosopher of science, the Hungarian-born Imre Lakatos (1970), who argues that what scientists should be concerned with is the 'logic of appraisal', that is, by what objective criteria can we judge the progress of science? In Lakatos's opinion, what scientists ought to be appraising are constellations of theories or 'scientific research programmes'. These research programmes are characterized by a 'hard core' of what the scientists in that research programme regard as irrefutable axioms, surrounded by a 'protective belt' of auxiliary hypotheses in which the scientific work of testing and refuting is carried out. The 'hard core' contains a 'positive heuristic' which is a set of suggestions or guideposts as to the directions in which work in the protective belt should proceed. A research programme may be 'progressive', that is, the work in the protective belt leads to the explanation of a wider set of phenomena or to increasing empirical corroboration: or it may be 'degenerative', that is the research programme can only be kept alive if its practitioners have to resort to ever-restrictive assumptions to sustain it and where it is no longer capable of generating new empirical corroboration. (For a discussion of Lakatos's ideas see Blaug and Leijonhufvud in Latsis (ed.), 1976.)

So when should economists switch from one research programme to another? Lakatos's answer is given in his 'First Criterion' for choosing between models, which states that Model 1 should be replaced by Model 2 if, and only if, Model 2 has excess empirical content over Model 1 which is at least partly corroborated and all the unrefuted content of Model 1 is contained in Model 2. This implies that a research programme cannot be progressive for all time, that it may change from being progressive to being degenerative. But the reverse may also be true, that a hitherto degenerative research programme may acquire a new lease of life as a result of some new development in its protective belt. Lakatos's central message is that scientists should never abandon a research programme too rapidly. Newly emergent research programmes should be given the opportunity to establish themselves; otherwise there will never be any scientific progress: but mature programmes should be kept under constant review for signs of degeneration or regeneration. No research programme can have a monopoly of the truth at all times.

It is not simply as a result of the faddiness or inherent contentiousness of economists that present-day economics is characterized by a number of schools of thought. No subject which aspires to the status of a science can be dominated exclusively by a single research programme because then it lacks the means by which its propositions may be evaluated objectively. What economics must have, therefore, is two or more competing research programmes so that the opportunity is always available for economists to switch *rationally* between them and not on the grounds of ideology or fashion or expediency. (For an interesting account of how Lakatos's method of scientific research programmes can be used to explain the Marginal Revolution, see Fisher 1986.)

What economics lacks, then, is not alternative research programmes and we discuss the more important of the contemporary contenders in this book. Where economics has been at fault in our view is in not giving enough thought to questions of methodology or philosophy as these relate to how we define and measure scientific progress in economics. As Alec Gee comments in the opening paragraph of his chapter, in most universities and colleges in the West, neoclassical economics is the *only* brand of economics that it is deemed necessary or even desirable to teach undergraduates. Until recently, the same could also be said of the status of Marxist economics in Eastern Europe and the Soviet Union. What economists in general have failed to do adequately is to provide students with the critical ability to make rational choices between competing research programmes. This failing is cogently described by Blaug (Latsis, 1976, pp. 159–60).

> Analytical elegance, economy of theoretical means and generality obtained by ever more 'heroic' assumptions have always meant more to economists than relevance and predictability. They have in fact rarely practised the methodology to which they have explicitly subscribed and that, it seems to me, is one of the neglected keys to the history of economics. The philosophy of science of economics, ever since the days of Senior and Mill is aptly described as 'innocuous falsificationism'.

THE SUMMARIES

In this book we attempt to assimilate these important ideas of Kuhn and Lakatos and each author has consciously sought to adopt the same approach in what he or she has written. After each chapter that presents a school of economic thought there is a summary of the school, with details usually abstracted from the text of the chapter, laid out under a set of standard headings. This has two purposes. First, it is intended to provide a convenient summary of the contents of that chapter. It comes at the end of the chapter because its compact keywords are more relevant for an *ex post aide memoire* than an *ex ante* guide. But, second and more importantly, it should make it easier for the reader to make direct comparisons between the schools both from the standpoint of their methodological approaches, and also in terms of their substantive content. We must emphasize, however, that as is inevitable with any process of summarizing, there is the risk of oversimplification and the important and subtle features of a particular school's stance may not be adequately captured in these summaries.

The headings we have chosen are significant. They derive from the 'growth of knowledge theories' of Kuhn and Lakatos. As we have seen above, Kuhn argues that choice between paradigms (schools in our case) has less to do with the scientific merits of theories and more to do with extraneous sociological or political factors influencing the researchers. For example, the success of monetarism in the US or the UK would not have been possible had there not been in power in these two countries a President and a Prime Minister each with a strong ideological belief in the effectiveness of markets and a commitment to a reduction in the role of the state. Or, as in the Soviet Union and Eastern Europe, where orthodox Marxism is now in retreat as these countries attempt to restructure their economies along Western market-oriented lines, the economists who will prosper both academically and financially will be those with the ability to offer policy advice relevant to the demands of *perestroika* and *glasnost*. Economists who wish to influence policy can only do so if the economic arguments they put forward are in tune with the political climate of the day.

Lakatos put forward his theory of scientific research programmes as a development of Popper's falsificationism and as a modification of Kuhn's theory. In fact it is complementary, rather than rival, to Kuhn, since the SRP can exist within a paradigm determined by sociological factors. Thus, the headings derived from Kuhn's theory highlight the *raison d'être* of the school (that is, its 'why' and 'how'), its general approach or paradigm, and the headings derived from Lakatos's methodology of SRPs translate this into the substantive content (the 'what') of the school.

Under each heading is provided an illustrative sample of relevant statements. They are not intended to be definitive, and nor could they be, given that the schools are heterogeneous entities, comprising many branches or intertwining strands. Sometimes we have not felt able to give examples for all the headings for some schools. Sometimes they are irrelevant to a particular school. For instance, protective belt assumptions are likely to be less relevant to the Austrian school because objective empirical evidence plays a very low-key role in its methodological practices. In other cases, no clear indications for the heading were given, or they were contradictory or ambiguous. This was particularly true of the mainstream schools, where the methodological issues are generally perceived to be of less importance, and are less explicit than for the alternative schools.

We have identified Kuhn's sociological or political factors as the

World View, Ideological Values and **Goals** of the researchers. These help to determine the **Methodological Practices** adopted for the analysis, and the **Criteria** used to choose between competing theories. These comprise the first five standard headings used in the summaries and help to fulfil our objective of indicating the motivation of the schools and why they are different.

Until recently, it was popularly assumed that perception through our five senses was infallible and totally reliable. Now we are aware of illusion in perception, and of the fact that our central nervous systems receive far more stimuli that they can possibly process satisfactorily, and on account of this very simple fact, our brains are subconsciously selective in what they choose to let through and in what they filter out. Each individual develops a view of the world that is unique, influenced both by societal and cultural factors, and by his/her personal experience. Each person's ideological values are similarly affected, and it is likely that his/her world view and values interact throughout a lifetime. Both **World View** and **Ideological Values** help to define each economist's subject matter of interest, determining what is selected and emphasized, and more importantly, to exclude what they feel is not relevant to them. They identify what is a 'problem' and thus what is a 'solution'.

A simple example of different world views is that the 'cell unit' of the neoclassical microeconomics school is the commodity, whilst that of the Austrian school is the individual human. Another occurs by noting that it is possible to look at economic activity at different levels of society. The Austrians are interested in economic activity as the result of the decisions of individuals, the institutionalists look at both individuals interacting within an organization, and at organizations interacting with each other. The Keynesian school is concerned about macroeconomic aggregates and Marxians look at the whole of capitalist society divided into two classes.

World view also refers to an individual's perception of reality, for instance, the extent to which one considers the relationship between one's perception and the external world as something subjective, or whether one thinks that absolute truth may be reached and identified. Thus, world view also influences one's ideas about what knowledge it is possible to achieve, and the methodological practices that one adopts to achieve it. Whether one can achieve a value-free analysis of economics (or any social science) is another aspect of world view.

The seven schools encompass a wide range of **Ideological Values**. The order in which they are presented corresponds roughly to this, and starts with the most right-wing and ends with the most left-wing.

'Right-wing' and 'left-wing' here refer to the degree to which their adherents recognize the collective, organic phenomenon of 'society', and the roles both of different types of human relationship, and of social or economic obligation by individuals to other individuals, in creating the type of society that pertains, and of societal structures in affecting individuals' choices and the distribution of resources, incomes and consumption. The schools also differ in the extent to which they would like to change society.

Ideological values are extremely important in determining the type of questions that an economist asks, or perhaps more pertinently, carefully does not ask, thus defining the subject matter to be investigated.

It is not always recognized that there is a wide variety of **Goals**, or reasons why economists, or any other researchers, choose to study their subject. Not all of their motivations are strictly scientific, concerned with the search for knowledge, and even within the scientific goal there is a range of possible objectives from mere description, classification, and association, through various degrees of explanation and causality to the anticipation of novel phenomena. Other types of goal include personal ones such as career advancement and the application of techniques for personal gain or political ends, and ideological (or religious) ones, such as to prevent poverty. Frequently, the researcher will have several goals and their order of priority is important. The goals, or their priorities, may change over time or according to circumstance, but each set may be valid. The search for scientific knowledge, while a very important goal, is not the only valid one. Ideological values comprise one set of factors which may determine a researcher's goals.

The goals themselves are an important influence on the **Methodological Practices** of, or the processes adopted by, the different schools, and these in turn influence the type of **Criteria** that each school adopts to validate its own work, and to choose between theories (where appropriate).

World view, ideological values, and goals of the researchers, their methodological practices and selectivity criteria – all these concepts are difficult to pinpoint accurately, and their influences are interrelated. These sociological factors, while not objective, are perfectly valid and very compelling reasons for taking very different stances towards the common subject matter of economics. These differences partly help to explain why the schools are frequently unsympathetic to each other, even before they are aware of the substantive content of their theories.

Lakatos emphasized the components of an SRP, which comprises a series of encompassing theories. He defined its **Hard Core** as a set of statements which provide a fundamental theoretical framework within which scientists can work, and which contains definitions of its most central **Concepts**. As one would expect, the hard core is explicitly influenced by the world view and the ideological values of the school.

The negative heuristic is a guideline which warns against altering the hard core statements, since these define the SRP. The **Positive Heuristic** is a set of directives which sets the **Agenda** for the SRP, that is, the type of questions asked. Not surprisingly, the positive heuristic of an SRP is strongly influenced by the goals of its researchers.

The **Protective Belt** is a set of auxiliary hypotheses which protect the hard core, because they, rather than the hard core, can be tested, and possibly refuted by empirical evidence. Each school has a set of **Themes** which it develops. Each school relies on a specific type of **Evidence**, which is appropriate to the criteria applied by the adherents of the school in choosing between competing theories. Each school has a body of **Conclusions**, of as-yet-untested, or not-yet-refuted, theories.

THE SEVEN MAIN SCHOOLS

In this section, a vignette of each school is presented, providing an entrée to the following chapters, outlining the ideological values of the researchers in that school, their goals and methodological practices, and finally an indication of the subject matter of the schools. Each school tends to specialize in different aspects of the subject matter; some explore the historical processes of time, and some take account of ignorance and uncertainty as experienced by agents. Similarly, the extent to which the different schools allow for social complexity, or explore a variety of motivations in their agents, differs widely. Thus, although some of the subject matter of the schools is overlapping, much of it is not, and the schools should be regarded as complementary, rather than rival.

The Austrian School

The Austrian school is the most right-wing, or libertarian, of the seven schools. Austrians are not noted for their concern for other people's welfare, although the possibility of altruism is recognized. Austrians have the vision of a society where there is less state intervention in economic activity, because of the threat to individual liberty which they consider is posed by the existence of the state. These values are reflected in the subject matter of the school, which typically only considers exchange relationships between individuals.

This school has the scientific goal of aiming to explore and explain economic activity, but its subjective deductivism is often unacceptable to other schools. Its initial premises are derived *a priori*, often subjectively, and Austrians then apply very systematic and rigorous logic to deduce a continuous chain of causation, the consequents of which are rarely tested empirically.

The Austrian school is a microeconomic school in which the self-interested individual is the cell unit. Its emphasis is on the evolutionary market processes that arise through the exchange interactions between individuals. The changing market processes are the source of information upon which individual behaviour is based. The Austrian school stresses the roles of imperfections in information, uncertainty and surprise in the decision-making process. It also explores the concept of intentionality, recognizing that individuals do not just react to their situations, but act for the purpose of achieving quite explicit objectives, and may do so in very creative ways.

The Neoclassical School

The neoclassical microeconomics school claims to be value-free. It does not question that its criterion of Pareto optimality, which gives primacy to the *efficiency* of the allocation of resources given their underlying distribution, is a value statement. Thus, neoclassicists accept the prevailing distributional features of society. Their work is not geared towards understanding societal or economic processes better, nor to posing probing questions about distributional issues. The neoclassical theory of welfare economics reflects this restricted attitude, and is consequently limited in its relevance to understanding the political and social processes at work in society.

This school's principal objectives are, first, to derive the necessary and sufficient mathematical conditions for a hypothetical general equilibrium in the allocation of resources by well informed individuals and, second, for a Pareto-optimal market economy which, if it existed in real life, would imply a spontaneous economic and social harmony. This process of deducing (often strange, unrealistic) assumptions in order to indicate the conditions in which some desired outcome could be feasible, is known as retrodiction, and does not lead to the anticipation of any novel phenomena. The school uses deductive processes,

frequently involving sophisticated mathematical techniques, and claims
that its motives are scientific. Much of its empirical work is directed
towards estimating elasticities in a variety of situations.

It is interesting to compare the Austrian and the neoclassical
schools, both being microeconomic schools, deriving from similar roots
in the marginal revolution of the early 1870s, and yet they have
developed in very different ways, due to their different goals and
methodological approaches. The cell unit of the neoclassical school is
the commodity, and the guiding force which determines economic
outcomes is, again, the self-interested behaviour of individuals, who
place marginal valuations on alternative feasible outcomes in determining their courses of action. The dynamics and changes that occur in
the process are glossed over. The analysis is static in the sense that
hypothetical changes at a point of time are examined. The neoclassical
school, which is the mainstream microeconomic school, although technically accomplished and aesthetically pleasing, is the least sophisticated of all when it comes to dynamic analysis, the implications of
poor quality information, the exploration of intentionality, or the
complexity of social relations and institutional structures.

The Chicago School

The Chicago school is also a right-wing, libertarian, but macroeconomic school, which recognizes only exchange relationships, and
abhors government intervention, especially fiscal policy. The new
classical branch has spent considerable time and effort in demonstrating that government fiscal policy is immediately counteracted by private individuals using their rational expectations and, therefore, is
ineffectual or, even worse, destabilizing. Since the Chicago school has
developed through the neoclassical tradition and accepts the assumptions of neoclassical microeconomics, it too is geared towards demonstrating that market systems unfettered by constraints or directives
imposed by government will lead to market clearing in the long run.

The Chicago school openly eschews the search for truth, regarding
theories as merely instruments for forecasting the future, and adopts
a pragmatic approach to spotting associations of variables which might
be useful for its policy-oriented objectives, using a methodological
practice known as instrumentalism.

It is mainly a macroeconomic school, which emphasizes the supply
side of market systems. The differences between the Chicago and
Keynesian schools are mainly ideological and methodological. The
Chicago school accepts much of orthodox Keynesian theory, but differs

in its empirical perceptions. The main theoretical contributions of the Chicago school are in its monetary theory, and its new classical theories, which have replaced the adaptive expectations of monetary theory with the rational expectations hypothesis, and combined it with a vigorous optimism about the ability of markets to clear given enough time. This has led to a new theory of business cycles to explain how fluctuating economic activity could still be in equilibrium.

The Keynesian School

The orthodox Keynesian school is a liberal, macroeconomic school. Its principal aim is to show that an unfettered market system will not necessarily achieve a full employment equilibrium and, therefore, government has an important role to achieve it by influencing aggregate demand.

The orthodox Keynesian macroeconomic school has similar goals to its sister microeconomic neoclassical school, except that it wishes to show that market clearing in the labour market will not be achieved in an unfettered market. It contrasts with the neoclassical school in adopting mainly inductive procedures, so that Keynesians' methodological practice emphasizes the role of empiricism in deriving and developing, rather than in testing, theories.

The Keynesian school is an aggregative macroeconomic school. Keynes's main concern, arising from the depression of the 1920s and 1930s, was to explain how involuntary unemployment can occur. Keynes's theories emphasized the role of uncertainty and expectations about the future, but many of his most innovative ideas were lost in the subsequent neoclassical–Keynesian synthesis, the IS–LM analysis, since they were difficult to integrate with neoclassical microeconomic theories. The resulting orthodoxy of Keynesian economics, as opposed to the economics of Keynes (Leijonhufvud, 1968), is a static analysis of macroeconomic aggregates, with few concessions to social complexity; to poor quality information and ignorance; or to intentionality.

The Post-Keynesian School

The post-Keynesian school is mainly left of centre, concerned with unemployment, and the distribution of income and economic power. It adopts an interdisciplinary, realist approach, searching for causal processes. Its adherents recognize a strong role for government in a mixed economy, and policy considerations override theoretical ones.

They are reformist, rather than revolutionary, seeking to make a capitalist economy more just and equitable.

The post-Keynesian school also concentrates mainly on macro-economic aggregates, but pays close attention to its microeconomic foundations, particularly as developed by Kalecki. There are three main strands in post-Keynesian thought, a first which explicitly develops Keynes's original ideas, another which builds on the work of Kalecki, and a third based on the theories of Sraffa. The post-Keynesian school eschews the static analyses of the mainstream, and emphasizes dynamic processes in historical time. The roles of ignorance and uncertainty also figure prominently, and the motives of agents are widened to include more than just optimization of utility or profits. Social complexity is acknowledged by recognizing the roles of institutions. These extensions of economic theory into difficult and complex areas do not necessarily lend themselves to traditional mathematical economic analysis. The post-Keynesian school shares with the institutionalists a recognition of the role of institutions, and the institutionalists extend a regard for the post-Keynesians. Keller (1983) suggests that there are many points of complementarity between the two, the post-Keynesians having developed their theories more fully, whilst the institutionalists have concentrated more on policy.

The Institutionalist (Evolutionary) School

The institutionalist school claims not to have any specific ideological values, but seeks the implementation of the collective values of a particular culture. However, the fact that they recognize 'collective values' immediately puts them on the left rather than the right, according to the definition we have used.

The objectives of the institutionalist school are mainly policy-oriented, to implement the collective values of a particular culture, and institutionalists do not claim scientific goals. They eschew theories, but rather use case studies to describe the formation, development, maintenance and demise of particular institutions. Their methodological practices are interdisciplinary, qualitative, non-technical, inductive empiricism, and they share with the Chicago school a pragmatic approach to their work, judging it by how well it serves the task in hand.

The institutionalist school is not so individual-based as the Austrian or the neoclassical school. It takes a holistic and evolutionary view of society. The society as a whole determines, and is in part determined by, the working of the economy through societal institutions. Thus, the neoclassical procedure of taking wants and tastes as given is regarded as unsatisfactory because these wants are themselves a function of the social, political and power relationships that determine individual actions. Technological change and the ability of firms to manipulate tastes, as well as the influence that social status and power have on tastes, are incompatible with the notion that the consumer is sovereign and that wants implicitly spring from original and innate personal characteristics. Also, the market itself is a nexus of evolutionary institutions, and does not behave in the allocatively efficient and distributionally neutral manner assumed by neoclassicists. The institutionalists specialize in the exploration of social relationships within and between institutions, and in developing an evolutionary approach to the subject.

The Radical and Marxian Schools

The Marxian school, in many senses, is the most ambitious of the seven schools. Its declared aim is to build a decent and just society of fulfilled human beings. Its theory is not just that of an economic system, but a theory of society, in which a set of social structures is determined by the material conditions of production.

The Marxian school aims to combine scientific enquiry with political activity. It wishes to identify the causal mechanisms underlying economic processes in a capitalist society, and especially to expose the exploitative basis of capitalism, in which the class that owns the means of production extracts surplus value from the wealth-producing labouring class, and to overthrow capitalism. However, the methodological practices adopted were those developed by Marx more than a hundred years ago. His dialectical materialism was a laudable attempt to recognize the interactive, conflictual relationships within society. Dialectical materialism has not been recognized as a valid methodological practice by mainstream economists. Marxians have been known to employ retrodiction, too, especially in their claim that capitalism essentially contains the seeds of its own destruction.

The Marxian school was the earliest to develop as a distinct school if one dates it from Marx's first volume of *Capital* (1867). Marxians are very aware that social structures, particularly the class system of capitalist society, frame and constrain economic decisions, but social complexity has not been developed much beyond class relationships and conflicts. Marxians are very aware of dynamic processes in historic time. They emphasize that the primary motivation of capitalists is capital accumulation over time, rather than optimization of utility or profits at a point of time. Marx's purpose was to expose the disadvantages of the capitalist system, emphasizing its inherent conflicts between capitalists and workers, its discrimination, exploitation, injustice and inequalities, the way it alienates workers from their work, its inherent inefficiencies, and instabilities as expressed in the volatility of business cycles. Its whole perception is the antithesis of the mainstream schools, which are trying to demonstrate the benefits, and prove the harmony, of the capitalist system at its best.

The radical school is an offshoot of the Marxian school, which started in the 1960s in the US, developing the ideas of Baran and Sweezy (1966) about monopoly capitalism, and in the protest movements opposing the role of the US in the Vietnam War. It is concerned about injustices, such as discrimination, sexual and racial inequalities, and the exploitation of the third world by developed countries (Backhouse, 1985).

CONCLUSION

The main message from this volume is that there is a range of schools of economic thought which are not necessarily rival to each other, in the sense that if one were true then the others are necessarily false. Each has something to contribute to our understanding of economic decision making. The schools are complementary to each other.

This, then, raises the interesting question of why the 'mainstream' schools, the neoclassical, Chicago and orthodox Keynesian schools of thought, are the only ones that are taught as core subjects in any depth in most Western educational establishments. This is especially puzzling in the light of the crisis in mainstream economic theory which erupted in the 1970s and 1980s. So why is there a neoclassical hegemony? Several theories have been put forward to explain this.

It may be argued that it is the elegance of the mathematical techniques applied in these schools, or the coherence of their theories, which seduces their researchers. However, Arouh (1987) argues that the main reason is that most economists agree or concur with the implicit ideological values of the schools. Earl (1983) gives a convincing account of the sociology of the economics profession, which explains how economists' investment in the neoclassical schools over their lifetimes prevents established economists from switching to other schools, where they would no longer have a comparative advantage. Colander (1988) claims that researchers' incentives, and needs for topics which yield impressive research articles, and for theories which are easy to teach in a coherent textbook form, determine which theory they use, and that this has played a key role in macroeconomic thinking. Thus, a paradigm will be chosen on account of its 'article criterion', and its 'teachability criterion'. Lastly, McCloskey (1986) suggests that rhetoric could be the determining factor in whether a theory is accepted, or a paradigm shift takes place, and that the forcefulness of the argument may be at least as important as the empirical evidence in persuading one's colleagues to accept one's point of view.

Each of the theories above emphasizes the goals, or the ideological values of the researchers, or other subjective aspects of the community of economists, as the reasons for the current dominance of the mainstream schools, rather than citing any objective evidence to demonstrate their superiority. This book seeks to redress the balance, and to present all the main schools of economic thought with equal weight, and to stress that the schools are complementary.

We have emphasized earlier that no school is homogeneous, that each comprises different strands of thought, and that it is sometimes difficult to draw very precise lines of demarcation between the different schools. The newly founded European Association for Evolutionary Political Economy, for example, welcomes economists from the non-mainstream schools, and provides a unique opportunity for them to develop their common themes cooperatively. In addition, there are other nascent schools, which have not yet achieved the same status as the main schools. It is not possible in an introductory text to discuss these, but those who wish to pursue their comparative studies further could peruse the volumes of readings in the 'Schools of Thought in Economics Series' (Edward Elgar) to explore the experimentalists (Smith, 1990), Sraffian economics (Steedman, 1989), and the Behaviouralists (Earl, 1988).

Given the diversity of factors which contribute to the particular flavour of any school, it would be inappropriate to judge all schools by a single set of criteria; each must be judged on its own internal criteria (Caldwell, 1982). Each school is developing new areas and pushing back the frontiers of the discipline. The diversity amongst the schools is to be welcomed as a sign of maturity and a cause of some optimism. If there is a message that the authors of this book would like to leave with their readers, particularly those who are just embarking on their study of economics, it is to beware of false prophets. No individual, no school of thought has a monopoly of the truth in economics.

FURTHER READING

Backhouse's scholarly work (1985) provides a comprehensive history of modern economic analysis, and indicates how the alternative schools have developed and affected the mainstream schools. It is easy to dip into, but may be heavy going for the beginning student.

Hunt (1979) looks at the history of economic thought from a Marxian point of view.

Pheby (1988) presents both a clear account of economic methodology, including the philosophy of science theories of Kuhn and Lakatos, and examines in more detail the methodology of Friedman's instrumentalism, of the Austrians and of Marx.

Hodgson (1988) also combines a clear presentation of the methodological issues with a wide view of the field, but from the alternatives point of view, and he attempts a synthesis of the alternative schools under the institutionalist banner by emphasizing their common evolutionary strands.

2. The Philosophy and Methodology of Economics

Thomas S. Torrance

The origins of modern economics lie with the writings of the two giants of the eighteenth century Scottish enlightenment, David Hume (1711–76) and Adam Smith (1723–90). During their lifetimes both Hume and Smith were considered to be philosophers rather than economists. Economics, as we are familiar with it, developed from within philosophy and only gradually came to be recognized as a distinct scientific discipline during the course of the nineteenth century. If science is the systematic study of a domain of real-world events, how today should we understand philosophy and its relationship with individual sciences such as economics?

At the risk of oversimplification, we can say that philosophy is the subject which concerns itself with revealing and appraising the key presuppositions of the various sciences. Among the more important branches of philosophy are epistemology and metaphysics. The former, known also as the theory of knowledge, studies the grounds for claims to knowledge of any kind. It looks at the question of when we can be said to possess knowledge rather than mere beliefs. Metaphysics, on the other hand, is interested in examining the results of searches for ultimate principles of order and for basic entities. Most philosophical enquiries will be partly epistemological and partly metaphysical, and it should not be thought that these two types of philosophical interest can be pursued wholly independently of each other.

Philosophy cannot be entirely uncontroversial: as a subject, it is pluralistic in character, and consists of many competing schools of thought, each tending to be critical of the others. And though itself not free of presuppositions, it is, perhaps, more critically aware of the nature of its own assumptions than is commonly the case throughout the sciences.

'Methodology' is often used in an extremely narrow sense to denote technical research methods in use within scientific enquiry. The word, however, has a broader sense in which it means the most general kind of examination of scientific theories and their particular methods of investigation. In this latter and wider sense, methodology is the theory of scientific method and has as its objective the epistemological and metaphysical appraisal of the theories researchers use in pursuit of knowledge and other aims.

SCIENCE AS SYSTEMATIC EXPLANATION

What are the aims of science? There is more than one way to reply to this question, as we shall see in a later section. But for the moment let us note that among the most important aims of those who engage in scientific research is the desire to obtain explanations of phenomena which have attracted their curiosity or attention. (An explanation in any science, it should be emphasized, is always an answer to the question 'Why did this happen?' An explanation, in other words, is what reveals the underlying reason, or network of reasons, why an event occurred rather than did not occur. Hence, to refer solely to the prior observation of concomitant events is not, on the usual understanding of the word, sufficient to provide an explanation.)

Given this interest, it is natural that a central issue for methodology is the problem of what constitutes an authentic explanation. The answer that many in the twentieth century have defended was first given in a modern form by the philosopher John Stuart Mill (1806–73). In Book V of his *A System of Logic* (1843), Mill states (p. 305): 'An individual fact is said to be explained by pointing out its cause, that is, by stating the law or laws of causation of which its production is an instance'. This causal law theory of explanation is also known as the 'covering law' theory, because the event in question is explained by being 'covered' by a causal law. As a theory of what constitutes a genuine explanation, it is exceedingly demanding. Unless we are able to derive a description of the event to be explained from causal laws (and statements of particular conditions), we have simply not explained the event.

The requirement that events are only adequately explained by reference to causal laws creates an enormous problem for economics and the other social sciences. The explanations given by these subjects do not appear to involve laws of this kind, which feature so crucially in the explanations provided by the physical sciences. The social sciences are concerned with human actions and their intended and unintended repercussions in society. In neoclassical economics, for instance, an explanation usually functions in the following fashion. First, we discover what bundle of preferences is held by agents acting within an institutional framework (which involves various types of constraint, including opportunity costs attached to all choices concerning alternative courses of action). Second, the agents are assumed to be rational in the sense that they will pursue their preferred objectives in recognition of the opportunity costs entailed. And then, finally, the social consequences are sought when different groups of agents attempt at the same time to realize their respective goals. This type of explanatory structure in no way gathers its force by appeal to law-governed events; rather, it relies on the quite different framework of discerning human intentionality and the meaningfulness of actions. In fact, the concepts of 'action', 'aim', 'purpose', 'rationality' etc. are not notions that have a place in a science which studies events of the sort which occur according to causal laws. In contrast, the concepts typically used in a social explanation entail the ideas of choice, decision, and acting on reasonable grounds, and these ideas belong to a realm of concepts on which the sciences that do examine law-determined events are utterly silent.

THE ROOTS OF SCIENCE IN PHILOSOPHY

From what we have just said it should be clear that methodological discussion tends quickly to run into the area where underlying metaphysical beliefs become exposed. The topic of the nature of social explanation is no exception to this.

Several lines of action are open to the methodologist when faced with the claim that the causal law theory of explanation seems grotesquely inappropriate when applied to the sorts of events that the social sciences are interested in explaining. One option is to advance the metaphysical view that, in the final analysis, the universe does consist of purely physical and chemical events and that, on this basis, it is indeed the case that nothing is genuinely explained unless it is presented in terms of the underlying causal laws that have been discovered to hold in the purely physical realm. This sort of philosophical view is known by a number of names, the most common being 'physicalism', 'behaviourism', 'naturalism' or, the preferred description of the Austrian economist F.A. Hayek (1955), 'scientism'. It is also known as 'reductionism', on account of its insistence that the explanation of social events be shown to be reducible to the explanation of events that are purely physical in character.

If this particular philosophical approach is taken, the inevitable conclusion is that economics does not offer proper or 'adequate' explanations: this must be so, if only for the reason that there is nothing in economics that corresponds to the causal laws of sciences like physics and chemistry. It is true, of course, that in economics we do meet propositions in universal form which are often called 'laws'. An example is Jevons's Law (also known as the Law of the Consumer's Equilibrium): each consumer balances his or her consumption of different goods to ensure that the ratios of the marginal utilities to prices for each good are equal. But this so-called law and others like it do not refer to invariant connections of causal necessity, but rather to something very different: outcomes that habitually occur as the result of intelligent decision making by rational individuals, acting of their own free will, in certain common types of social or institutional settings.

Obviously, the causal law theory of explanation and the metaphysical views behind it do not reign unchallenged. A rival approach starts from the idea that in every science the concepts and terms employed by an explanation must be appropriate to the nature of the subject matter under investigation. Thus in economics where we study human behaviour and its societal repercussions, the use of concepts that imply end seeking by conscious agents is appropriate. It is plausible to argue that it is as fundamentally misguided to attempt to expel all such notions from economics in favour of laws describing law-determined connections (in which free choice has no role), as it would be to attempt to explain events in the inanimate world by attributing end-seeking behaviour and consciousness to the purely physical entities whose attributes are the proper study of physics and chemistry.

Something very like this alternative philosophical approach is persuasively argued by the philosopher Peter Winch in his book *The Idea of a Social Science* (1958). Winch claims (p. 108ff.) that attempts to explain social events by means of theories that use only the concepts to be found in theories of inanimate events must end up by actually destroying the social character of social phenomena. His argument is that individual events and objects can only be identified as instances of particular kinds: in other words, an entity can only be identified as an object of reference by virtue of its classification as a thing of a certain kind. When it comes to the social sciences, the chief criteria that enable us to say of single events that they are of the same kind are those that allude to meaningful and purposive behaviour. To give an example: economic reasoning often involves the notion of price, and comparing the price of one thing with the price of something else. Yet a price is a ratio of exchange defined in terms of a numeraire, and the notion of exchange only makes sense if it could be analysed in terms of the meanings placed on certain types of behaviour by the agents participating in the activity. And so, if we attempt to describe or identify exchange activity solely by reference to the physical characteristics that may belong to such actions, then the intrinsic nature of the event as something social is lost completely.

To those sympathetic to the tenor of Winch's argument, the starting point for an economic theory is the recognition that the overall structure of explanation should be appropriate, given the type of events and phenomena of interest. Thus, at the outset, economics should advance theories about human activity that treat it as goal-directed and springing from the knowledge, expectations, beliefs, ethics and traditions of single agents or groups of agents. Other economic phenomena can then be explained as the intended or unintended social consequences of the interaction of rational behaviour at the micro-level. But even in situations where regular types of behaviour regularly produce certain kinds of large-scale societal repercussions, there is nothing in economics, it should be emphasized again, that can with philosophical propriety be called a 'causal law', if this expression is understood to entail the sort of causal determination that exists in the sphere of purely inanimate objects. To frame an explanatory theory of events of one kind in terms of the concepts and categories appropriate to the explanation of events in a quite different realm, is the antithesis of good scientific procedure.

THE PROGRAMME OF INSTRUMENTALISM

At the start of this chapter we asked what the aims of science were, but at that point we postponed further discussion and just proceeded on the assumption that an important part of the answer was that scientific enquiry aims at truth and hence is concerned to obtain explanatory theories.

Other aims for science are undeniably held. Of these, perhaps the most important is linked to the fact that scientific knowledge is of great assistance in achieving the many objectives that human beings entertain: scientific knowledge is capable of yielding political and military power, and can be used in a vast number of directions to aid the material and living conditions of humankind. Whatever may be the motives, the view that the main aim of science is not to uncover truths about areas of reality, but to produce results that enable the social and physical worlds to be manipulated and controlled to serve certain human goals, is referred to as the instrumentalist conception of science (or instrumentalism for short). It should be mentioned that in the family of philosophical views, instrumentalism is a sub-species of pragmatism: the notion that what makes any idea or doctrine worthwhile is purely its effects on what is held to be important.

A well known and frequently quoted expression of the instrumentalist view in economics is that presented and defended by Milton Friedman in his paper 'The Methodology of Positive Economics' (1953). Friedman here argues (p. 8) that 'the only relevant test of the validity of a hypothesis is comparison of its predictions with experience', and then, a little further on, he writes (p. 14):

> The difficulty in the social sciences of getting new evidence . . . and of judging its conformity with the implications of the hypothesis makes it tempting to suppose that other, more readily available, evidence is equally relevant to the validity of the hypothesis – to suppose that hypotheses have not only 'implications' but also 'assumptions' and that the conformity of these 'assumptions' to 'reality' is a test of the validity of the hypothesis different from or additional to the test by implications. This widely held view is fundamentally wrong and productive of much mischief.

Friedman then elaborates an 'as if' type of methodology: on this, provided good predictions can be obtained from a theory, it is not a matter for concern that its assumptions are false (if that is what they are). High-quality predictions indicate that the theory can be used to good practical effect on the basis that the phenomena in question behave as if the assumptions were correct.

To illustrate this approach, Friedman gives an example of predicting the behaviour of an expert billiard player (p. 21):

> It seems not at all unreasonable that excellent predictions would be yielded by the hypothesis that the billiard player made his shots as if he knew the complicated mathematical formulas that would give the optimum directions of travel, could estimate accurately by eye the angles, etc., describing the location of the balls, could make lightning calculations from the formulas, and could then make the balls travel in the direction indicated by the formulas. Our confidence in this hypothesis is not based on the belief that billiard players, even expert ones, can or do go through the process described; it derives rather from the belief that, unless in some way or other they were capable of reaching essentially the same result, they would not in fact be expert billiard players.

This example illustrates well what is involved in accepting a theory on an instrumentalist basis. The theory contains only such components as are required to enable it to function as a good producer of predictions. Under this conception, a successful theory is not viewed as something that explains phenomena but as a device that works, at least to the extent required by those that wish to make use of the theory for their own purposes.

Since instrumentalism as a goal of scientific analysis is born of the decision to regard science as of primary value when its theories function well as prediction generators, it cannot, as a bare choice, be criticized. However, it is legitimate to question whether, even given the aim of explicitly fashioning theories in order to yield useful predictions, it is a sound move to be indifferent to the truth or falsity of their 'assumptions'. Is it just as satisfactory if predictions come from a theory, some or all of whose elements are known to be false, as from a theory none of whose elements are presently suspected of being false?

The answer to this last question must depend on what exactly it is that we wish to achieve by means of our theories. If the objective is to predict the routine occurrence of events of a sort that is already familiar, and nothing more is demanded of a theory than that it perform this limited task competently, then there can be little quarrel with the instrumentalist approach. But, on the other hand, if one of the purposes is to use a theory to make predictions of events of an unencountered and novel kind, then an instrumentalist-devised theory is ill-equipped to serve this objective. The central principle of sound logical reasoning is that from premises, some or all of which are false, either true or false conclusions can be validly deduced; and from premises all of which are true, only true conclusions can be drawn. Obtaining a prediction from a theory is the same thing as deriving a conclusion from a set of premises. If a theory contains known falsehoods, then, no matter how well these may have functioned under circumstances of narrower predictive tasks, there can be no basis for credence in its predictive implications once these are made to refer to events in hitherto uninvestigated areas. But, in contrast, if a theory contains elements that are not known to be false, then its implications can be viewed as the most reliable indicators available of what to expect in these unexplored regions. Such expectations may, clearly, turn out to be unfounded, in which case we would have to accept the incorrectness of our starting belief that no part of the theory was false. But this would be something that we would learn only *ex post*, that is, only after we had actually made the predictions and found them not to be in conformity with subsequently observed phenomena.

A theory constructed along the lines permitted by instrumentalist methodology and which contains propositions known to be false cannot, then, operate as a successful predictor where the predicted events lie outside the range of phenomena with which we are already familiar. If our aim is to make useful predictions of unknown areas of reality, then the most sensible means to achieve this end is to rely on theories whose 'assumptions' have to date not been shown to be false. We conclude, therefore, that an economist who specifically sets out to obtain useful predictions should studiously avoid theories containing palpable untruths, and should seek instead to build on well tested theories from which, to the best of current knowledge, all falsehoods have been expelled.

THE POSITIVE – NORMATIVE DICHOTOMY IN ECONOMICS

At the start of his essay, Friedman quotes with approval a triple distinction made by John Neville Keynes (father of John Maynard Keynes) in his book of 1891, *The Scope and Method of Political Economy*. Keynes's work is one of the earliest discussions to be devoted specifically to methodological issues in economics, and near the beginning he distinguishes between the following (p. 34):

(1) a body of systematic knowledge concerning what is;
(2) a body of systematic knowledge concerning what ought to be; and
(3) a system of rules for the attainment of a given end.

Under this classification, (3) is dependent on (1) and also, in part, on (2). A rule for a given end is not intelligent unless, first, its application is actually capable of obtaining the end in question and, second, that end is itself desirable.

J.N. Keynes refers (p. 34) to economics under category (1) as a 'positive science' and under category (2) as a 'normative or regulative science'. The task of positive economics is to discover true explanations of certain classes of goal-directed activity by individuals and by groups, and of the wider repercussions on society of such behaviour. Normative economics, on the other hand, involves the study and ethical appraisal both of the goals agents set themselves and of the features of the social outcomes that actually result from the attempts of many individuals and groups to bring about their own chosen goals.

Positive economics is frequently viewed as a more important and worthwhile discipline than normative economics. This view comes partly from the realization that actions cannot be fully judged in a moral sense solely on consideration of their motives and goals: to judge actions fully requires knowledge of their actual effects, intended and unintended, and such knowledge has to come from economics as a positive discipline.

But attitudes to normative economics are not shaped solely by the insight that the subject cannot be pursued in the absence of the conclusions of positive economics. There is a tradition of intellectual prejudice against a serious consideration of moral and ethical matters on the grounds that views in this area are merely the expression of subjective emotions and are hence about nothing 'real'. This tradition in modern thought can be traced back to David Hume. In Book III of his *Treatise on Human Nature* (1740) he contends (pp. 468–9): 'morality . . . consists not in any matter of fact, which can be discovered by the understanding . . . it lies in yourself, not the object . . .'

Immediately following these comments, Hume argues that a proposition involving the word 'ought' can never be derived from propositions involving instances of just the verb 'is'. This point subsequently has become known as the is–ought dichotomy, and under its influence it has come to be accepted by many that moral judgements are merely subjective, generated by reflections on objective matters of fact.

We cannot here pursue all the ramifications of this important debate in moral philosophy. It is, however, striking that the relegation of all evaluative and normative claims to the domain of subjective emotions does not sit easily with the practical development of explanatory theory in economics or elsewhere. The reason for this is that we pursue scientific enquiry, in large measure at least, because we consider that truth and knowledge ought to be preferred over falsity and ignorance, and that truth and knowledge are worthy of pursuit as ends in themselves. We also believe, as scientific enquirers, that rationality and coherence are desirable while their opposites should be avoided. But all of these are choices made in accordance with normative standards of greater intellectual compulsion than would be possible were they wholly subjective in character.

It does thus seem clear that without unambiguous normative preferences for truth, rationality and coherence, the enterprise of creating and testing positive theories in science could never even begin. In this light, disparagement of ethical and other normative propositions as mere descriptions of subjective preferences as though they were not at the same time statements concerning some realm of fact, amounts to a demeanment of scientific enquiry itself.

THE METHODOLOGY OF FALSIFICATIONISM (AS PHILOSOPHICAL THEORY)

Perhaps the most interesting part of the methodology of economics is that concerned with the critical analysis of suggested accounts of theory development. For large areas in this topic, what can be said about economics applies equally to other sciences, both social and physical. Although social and purely inanimate events have distinct characteristics that should be reflected in the general features of explanations offered of them, there is, nonetheless, considerable common ground between social and physical theories when it comes to appraising the manner of how they are best to be tested against the occurrence of the real-world phenomena they purport to explain.

One of the twentieth century's best known philosophers of scientific method is Austrian-born (Sir) Karl Popper, whose first work in this field, *The Logic of Scientific Discovery*, was initially published in German in 1934. His methodological theory, known (for reasons that will become apparent) as 'falsificationism', originated when he first examined a philosophical conundrum raised by David Hume. In Book I of his *Treatise*, Hume argues (pp. 89–94) that any attempt to found a scientific theory purely on the supposedly secure basis of the testimony of the human senses is doomed to failure, because of the inescapable need to rely on a key principle that cannot be justified by reference to evidence gained by investigation. Hume contents (p. 69ff.) that all reasoning about the nature of reality has to be reasoning about causes, but causal reasoning can only be rationally justified on the basis of the assumption of an immutable causal order. But since this cannot be established or even made probable by factual enquiry, the method of science, factual or causal reasoning, rests on an unjustifiable supposition. Hume then moves to a startling conclusion: since both the results of scientific method and the results of fanciful philosophical speculation depend on what is unjustifiable, scientific knowledge cannot be superior to traditional thought, inherited from as far back as the ancient world. This epistemological scepticism, the doubt whether there does indeed exist any genuine knowledge about factual and causal matters, formed the basis of a long-lasting philosophical tradition in English-speaking countries well into the present century: Bertrand Russell is perhaps the most influential twentieth century philosopher vigorously to uphold both Hume's argument and conclusions.

The originality of Popper's methodology lies in his acceptance of Hume's main argument coupled with his rejection of the consequential scepticism. Popper's position is based on the disanalogy (p. 41ff.) between a scientific theory, which refers to a realm containing a potentially infinite number of events of some kind, and a spatially and/or temporally circumscribed proposition, which refers unambiguously to a realm of a finite number of events. With statistical sampling, a probability value can be placed, within confidence limits, upon propositions about events within the latter sort of realm. But no number of positive or confirming instances entitles us to place any such value on propositions about events within the former sort. Popper avoids Hume's sceptical conclusions by denying that the impossibility of obtaining scientific knowledge through an accumulation of positive confirmations puts all such claims to knowledge on the same level. And, above all, Popper disagrees that Hume's conclusions mean that there cannot be any rational criterion for establishing a preference between rival explanatory accounts.

Popper's basic insight is that tests for truth and falsity are asymmetric in character. What does this mean? It is the claim that however many positive or confirming instances we may observe, we can never establish as proved a hypothesis in universal form such as, for example, 'All Fs are G'. But, and this is the crucial point, given a theory in this form, a single sound observation of an F that is not a G is enough to establish it as false.

The powerful methodological implication from this asymmetry is that even though all theories (in purely universal form) are equally unprovable, it is nonetheless possible to show such a theory to be false. And our ability to do this provides a criterion for establishing a preference amongst a number of competitor theories. The rule of method that emerges here is thus: a theory that has not been shown to be false is preferable to a false theory. Adherence to this prescriptive methodological rule lies at the very heart of falsificationism.

At this juncture it should be pointed out that falsificationism is firmly allied to the stance of realism, that is, the metaphysical position that there is a realm of events that exists 'objectively', or independently of the opinions of those that seek to undertake scientific enquiry. In this context, falsificationism is one theory about the best way to secure knowledge about particular realms of independent reality. Chapter 9 of this book is devoted to the theory of Marxism, which too is wedded to realism in that it holds that there is a universe of objects and events whose actual characteristics are in no sense a function of what enquirers may imagine them to be. And it is as a type of realism that Marxism makes the distinction between the 'essence' (intrinsic nature) and the 'appearance' (superficial features) of social reality. Needless to say, Marxism differs radically from falsificationism on the critical epistemological matter of precisely how researchers ought to proceed to develop theories about the events it seeks to explain.

   Those who engage in scientific research naturally expect methodology to be concerned with appraising the actual procedures, and the rationale behind them, of theory development. But the account we have given of falsificationism has been confined to the sphere of philosophical theory: what we have outlined is a methodology based on a logical relationship between propositions of one type and those of another. An appraisal of a scientific method, however, cannot be content to remain just in the domain of philosophical theory; it should also be of relevance to the actual business of research. The task falsificationism faces, therefore, is to demonstrate that the conclusions that arise on the basis of a philosophical theory do indeed transfer well into the practical arena. If a particular methodological stance cannot do this, it remains nothing but a philosophical toy.

THE METHODOLOGY OF FALSIFICATIONISM (AS PRACTICAL PRESCRIPTION)

It is in the transition from philosophical theory to practice that the shortcomings of falsificationism as a workable methodology become visible. Although this prescription of method is on solid ground in stating that an effective test of a theory can only occur as a result of attempting to uncover potential refuting instances or disconfirmations, this advice by itself provides no useful guidance on a crucial issue. This is the question of precisely how disconfirming instances can be compellingly deployed against an existing theory. Consideration of this question leads to the realization that to try to apply the methodology of falsificationism runs into at least the following three significant hurdles:

1. It is nearly always possible to reject a single purported disconfirmation as an experimental, observational or statistical error (and this is especially true for theories in economics and the other social sciences).
2. Because most scientific theories are a complex bundle of components (and are hence not expressible in the form of a solitary proposition), even if a disconfirmation is accepted as genuine,

there is no straightforward way of knowing which particular element of the theory is at fault.

3. In certain cases, it is in fact impossible in principle to solve the problem raised at (2) by subjecting each separate component of a theory to independent test.

We shall now comment on these points in turn.

On the first, there is no science, where any purported disconfirming evidence is automatically accorded priority over the expected implications of a prevailing theory. If this were to happen, few theories would be likely to reach the stage of full development and their potential explanatory strengths would thus never reach the stage of telling tests. Any workable methodology, therefore, must permit an existing theory to possess a degree of staying power and some ability to resist attacks upon it. The trouble is, however, that there is no completely unambiguous way to distinguish prudent dismissals of erroneous evidence from a 'reactionary' refusal to countenance inexplicable findings of a noteworthy kind.

The second problem with falsificationism arises because theories in all areas of science do not typically consist of just a single proposition in universal form like 'All Fs are G'. The more usual situation, conforming to what is normally found in economics, is that a theory is a complex conjunction of propositions of different kinds: those in universal form, those stating the existence of certain entities or properties, and those of mixed universal and existence form. (We shall have more to say later about propositions of a mixed form.)

A conjunction is false if just one of its conjuncts is false, but the practical problem for falsificationism is that it offers little or no general direction as to how to assign responsibility for the breakdown of a theory to any one particular component or group of components. Yet, to be useful in practice, this is part of the guidance that ideally a methodology should provide. For unless such responsibility can be assigned in a non-arbitrary manner, a researcher will be unable to make progress by adapting the theory in the light of the lessons gained from the results of submitting the theory to tests.

A partial resolution of this problem in a way consistent with the prescriptions of falsificationism, is to attempt to undertake an independent test of each separate element contained within the overall theory. But is it possible, on all desired occasions, to conduct independent tests on each separate component of a theory? This question carries us conveniently to a discussion of the third problem we identified with falsificationism as a workable methodology.

This third problem concerns the extent to which it is open to a researcher to arrange an independent test for each separate component of a theory. At this point, we need a short digression to explain that there are at least three distinct senses in which it is impossible to undertake an action.

First, there is the weak sense, in which the impossibility relates to the current state of technology (as in: 'It is impossible to integrate the tax system with the welfare benefit system'); second, there is the semi-strong sense in which the impossibility relates to the functioning of social or physical reality as currently conceived (as in: 'It is impossible to produce real income growth along with zero inflation with a rapid expansion of the money supply,); and third, there is the strong sense in which the impossibility alludes to an incoherence of some kind (as in: 'It is impossible to return to June 1314 and observe the victory of the Scots over Edward II of England at the Battle of Bannockburn').

With respect to these very different types of impossibility, any of the three can be responsible for preventing the individual components of a theory from being given an independent test. In many cases in the history of science the reasons are technological: for example, up to the beginning of modern times many sophisticated physical theories could not be adapted after testing because the equipment required to make the observations to test its components was lacking (in many instances because the further theories required to manufacture the requisite equipment were unavailable). In other cases the impossibility involved is of the semi-strong kind: an example here would be of a social or biological phenomenon where the various sub-systems were not sufficiently isolable in reality to enable their separate functioning to provide the data required for an accurate test of each of the separate parts of the wider theory.

In yet other cases, the impossibility involved is of the strong kind. It is possible to test universal propositions within a theory because although these cannot be confirmed they are, in principle, falsifiable. Also, it is possible to test statements that assert existence, because although these are not falsifiable they are, in principle, confirmable. (An existence proposition, e.g. a proposition of the form 'There is an F that is a G', cannot be overthrown by factual investigation but can be established if investigation discovers such an entity.) So with both universal and existence propositions we have elements that are open to test, at least in principle.

As well as being composed of universal and existence propositions, complex scientific theories will also usually contain those of mixed universal–existence form. This point will be clearer if we give several examples of propositions that conform to this pattern. Take the following:

1. For every change, there exists a prior set of physical circumstances which causally necessitated its occurrence.
2. With all objects where agents prefer to consume more rather than less, there exists a point beyond which increments to consumption yield diminishing benefit.
3. For the quantity demanded and the quantity supplied of every good, there exist respective functions related to price.

Propositions of mixed universal–existence form have the following features. The universal element (i.e. 'For all x, . .') ensures that proof is impossible, while the existence element (i.e. 'There exists a y, . .') ensures that refutation is impossible. It then follows that since a mixed universal–existence proposition can neither be proved nor refuted, an independent test of such a proposition is impossible, with the impossibility being of the strong kind.

As constituents of theories, whether these be of economics or any other science, mixed universal–existence propositions give, or make reference to, the skeletal outline of what is presupposed to be a basic pattern of order in the phenomena under investigation. Within a theory, their relation to universal propositions is that they lay down for the latter the overall structure in terms of which specific testable components should be framed. When we remark that mixed universal–existence propositions state what is presupposed to be a basic pattern of order in the relevant area of events, what lies behind this presupposition is, of course, a metaphysical view as to the appropriateness of the particular explanatory structure, given the type of events in question. Thus, again, we return by another route to our argument presented earlier in this chapter that metaphysical stances are crucially relevant to scientific enquiry: it is from these that we draw our (often implicit) criteria as to what should count in a given realm as an appropriate structure for an explanatory hypothesis.

A theory's components that consist of particular hypotheses in universal form are, at least in principle, testable and open to refutation. However, what may be wrong with a theory is not merely that its portrayal to date of specific connections and functional relationships has been mistaken, but that a part of it rests on an unsuitable or faulty metaphysical conception of the nature of the underlying system of order. But since, as we have argued, it may be impossible to subject the constituent elements of such a theory to independent test, this must mean that there is an important feature missing in falsificationism as a practical methodology. For it cannot offer straightforward guidance on the matter of whether a theory's failure under test is due to a mis-specification of its testable constituents or of its metaphysical basis. An informal escape from this impasse can, nevertheless, be indicated. When a theory appears to be repeatedly disconfirmed, although it is always open that some as yet undiscovered adjustment could be made to its testable components, an alternative answer is to devise a new theory on a modified or different metaphysical foundation. The two theories could then be viewed as rivals. But in such a situation, can it be shown, by non-arbitrary arguments, that one theory does indeed have superior explanatory ability to that of its competitors?

PARADIGMS AND RATIONALITY

All sciences at some time in their development reach a stage where a new theory is created and supplants all that preceded it. With economic theory, an example of this is given by the marginalist revolution of the 1870s. An excellent account of the emergence of marginalism as a revolution in the history of economic theory is given by R.M. Fisher (1986), *The Logic of Economic Discovery*. Up to then, economists had sought to account for the 'value' of goods and services in terms of their 'natural prices' (namely, by reference to the costs of the factor inputs used to supply them). But after the pioneering work of Stanley Jevons in his *The Theory of Political Economy* (1871), which emphasized the distinction between total and marginal utility (pp. 105–21), a radical alternative to the traditional analysis of the functioning of product markets was created. At the heart of this alternative (p. 139ff.), was the idea that the appropriate way to explain prices and quantities sold was to view them as part of the outcome of an exchange in which buyers, acting on the motive of utility maximization in a setting of income constraint and subject to diminishing marginal utility, attempted to equalize the benefits to be gained from the last pound spent in each of the various directions in which money could be expended.

Following Jevons, the marginalist conception of the operation of markets became the foundation stone of modern microeconomic theory. This transformation came about not as the result of any particular failure under test of the old theory of markets, but because the marginalist approach, once created, convinced economic researchers that theories formulated within its overall terms of reference were more fruitful in their explanatory scope and depth. In other words, a change in the underlying metaphysics of the theory of markets enabled the new theory to provide systematic explanations of a wider range of phenomena and to yield a greater number of testable implications than the old theory; and as a consequence, the pre-marginalist theory, rather than being formally refuted, simply faded away.

In 1962 the philosopher and historian of science Thomas S. Kuhn wrote a book, *The Structure of Scientific Revolutions*, in which he drew attention to the prescriptive vacuum that often occurs when aspects of a theory's metaphysical assumptions are called into question. With Kuhn, a sharp distinction is made between '*normal science*' (p. 23ff.) and '*revolutionary science*' (p. 92ff.). The former exists when tests lead to the modification of the detail of existing theories, while 'revolutionary science' involves the collapse of credibility of a theory associated with one metaphysical outlook and its replacement by a theory based on another. The word used by Kuhn to describe a system of foundational ideas, in accordance with which a theory's testable components are framed, is 'paradigm' (p. 10ff.). The kernel of his theory is that the shift from one paradigm to another is essentially something that occurs outside any formal system of methodological prescription (p. 111ff.).

As well as Kuhn's concept of a paradigm, it is worth noting that methodological literature also makes extensive use of the notion that a theory (or a cluster of related theories, which together as a group constitute what is called a scientific research programme) possesses a hard cord of basic ideas. The hard core of a theory, or group of theories, consists of all the components which, during periods of 'normal science', lie largely unquestioned. We owe both the concepts of scientific research programme and hard core to the philosopher of science Imre Lakatos (1970, p. 132ff.).

If Kuhn is correct that 'revolutionary science' involves the replacement of one theory by another on grounds that are not wholly formalizable, does this discredit the intuitive idea that theory development is an essentially rational process? Is scientific development a process that at crucial junctures rests just on the force of what is considered to be 'acceptable' or 'thought to be desirable' within the working ethos of the current community of researchers?

The answer to this question is in the affirmative, but this does not mean that choices between theories in a situation of metaphysical turbulence are necessarily arbitrary or in any sense non-rational.

Although decisions in such circumstances cannot be made according to concise methodological prescriptions, they can and should be made informally within the context of adherence to a number of very general and self-evident principles of rationality. No arguments giving grounds for the acceptance of these principles can be advanced: any such grounds could only possess the ability to produce intellectual conviction on account of the fact that they themselves already presupposed such principles. Among such principles, we find precepts such as the following: a proposition and its contradictory should never be entertained together; an incoherent proposition should never be considered to describe an existing entity; other things being equal, theories that explain a wider range of phenomena should be preferred to those that explain a narrower range; and, other things being equal, simpler theories (i.e. those involving fewer variables and fewer constituent propositions) should be preferred to more complex.

It is not in dispute that all sciences at some time in their development pass through intervals when the results of formal test procedures (such as those recommended by falsificationism) are unable to provide unambiguous indications of which of two or more rival explanatory theories should be supported. At these times, although the choice of preferred theory may not be able to be made by reference to a set of clear-cut methodological prescriptions, the business of choosing still occurs within an intellectual framework that presupposes certain core principles of rational thought. And during these periods, it is up to researchers within the science to act in the most sensible way open to them; 'sensible' here is to be understood as being congruent with those precepts of rationality that continuously underline and uphold all scientific enquiry, including the more formal methodological approaches deployed during periods of what Kuhn describes as 'normal science'.

CONCLUDING REMARKS

It may seem unsatisfactory that at critical turning points in a science's evolution, recommendations as to procedure from methodological theory seem indeterminate, perhaps even 'vague'. But times of acute scientific controversy merely bring to light that there can be no absolute prescriptions offered by theories of scientific method. Since there cannot be an infinite regress of rules, there cannot be, ultimately, rules for the application of rules. Given this, the application of rules must, in the final analysis, depend on what we discern, self-evidently, to be rational for a given context. And, furthermore, although we may certainly be able to display examples of what we generally consider to be rational (and hence effective) research procedures, there can be no definitive set of criteria uniquely identifying, for all times and occasions, what precisely constitutes such courses of action. If the study of scientific method teaches us anything, it should teach us to be cautious, and not to expect even the most profitable of methodological prescriptions to be mechanically applicable in every particular set of circumstances.

FURTHER READING

Three books are especially recommended as initial reading for students. Blaug's *The Methodology of Economics* (1980) gives an account of the methodological debates and then examines particular areas of neoclassical economics to see how the approaches used to develop those topics compare with the ones recommended. John Pheby's more recent *Methodology and Economics* (1988) also gives a clear account of the debate, and goes on to examine the methodological approaches adopted in Austrian and Marxian economics. Ian Stewart's *Reasoning and Method in Economics* (1979) has a more nuts-and-bolts approach, and points out many of the pitfalls along the way when one tries to apply scientific method (hypothetico-deductive method) to economic subject matter.

There are many other interesting books on methodology and economics at a more advanced level. Among these are Caldwell (1982) and Boland (1982). It is also worth reading some of the original works, such as Popper (1957), Popper (1963), Popper (1972), and Quine and Ullian (1970). Knight (1956) gives a useful historical perspective, and Shackle (1972) is a delightful read.

3. The Austrian School

Brian J. Loasby

THE AUSTRIAN SUCCESSION

The creation of the Austrian school can be clearly attributed to one man – Carl Menger (1841–1921). His ideas were first propagated and extended by his near-contemporaries, Friedrich von Wieser (1851–1926) and Eugen von Böhm-Bawerk (1851–1914). The outstanding figures of the second generation were Ludwig von Mises (1881–1973) and Joseph Schumpeter (1883–1950) – though Schumpeter's work is too individual and too expansive to be confined within any one school, except perhaps the school which may now be coalescing around his own ideas. The members of the third generation, born around the beginning of this century, were the last to be educated in Austria, which most of them left in the disturbed 1930s; for a time it also seemed likely that they would be the last with distinctively Austrian ideas, since those ideas were apparently being assimilated into mainstream economics. Indeed, Gottfried Haberler (1900-), Fritz Machlup (1902–83), Oscar Morgenstern (1902–77), and Paul Rosenstein-Rodan (1902–85) are usually, and quite reasonably, included in the mainstream. However, no-one would now so regard Friedrich Hayek and Ludwig Lachmann; their later work marks a clear reaction to the apparent submergence of Austrian ideas. The reasons for this reaction will be explained later; it gave rise to a new generation, based in the US, whose most significant representatives are Israel Kirzner and Murray Rothbard. Not surprisingly, the new Austrian school emphasized its distinctiveness – almost its exclusivity; but though the objections to neoclassical orthodoxy have not been muted, Austrians have shown a growing interest in other alternatives to mainstream economics. Among the best-known of the younger Austrian economists are Roger Garrison, Don Lavoie, Gerald O'Driscoll, and Mario Rizzo; but there are many others (such as James Buchanan and Stephen Littlechild) who would perhaps be reluctant to accept a simple Austrian label but who approach economic questions in a similar way.

In this chapter we shall attempt to display the principal characteristics of the Austrian approach by considering some of the main Austrian contributions. The treatment is selective and generally brief – with one exception: since so much Austrian thinking can be traced back to Carl Menger, whose work is so poorly understood by most economists, he receives priority in space as well as time.

CARL MENGER

It was not Menger's intention to establish a particular school. On the contrary, the purpose of his first book (1871, 1981), translated as *Principles of Economics*, was to provide a secure basis for all economic theory. He did hope for a particularly ready welcome from the German economists, headed by Wilhelm Roscher (to whom the *Principles* was dedicated) who, he thought, shared his objections to the prevalent orthodoxy; but in this he was sharply disappointed. The Germans ignored Menger's work; and he came to interpret their emphasis on historical study as a rejection not just of bad theory but of all theory.

His second book (1883, 1963), translated as *Problems of Economics and Sociology*, was primarily inspired by the need to combat this fundamental error – as he saw it – committed by those whom he had expected to be natural allies. Thus, instead of producing the three further volumes in which he had originally intended to expand and apply his basic ideas, he turned back to provide a methodological basis for his first book. What he had designed as foundations apparently required further underpinning. A willingness – or indeed a perceived necessity – to engage in methodological issues is a distinguishing characteristic of modern Austrian economists; it is typically the assumptions and procedures – not just the conclusions – of other economists which they question.

Within the English-speaking community of economists, it has become standard practice (except among specialists) to identify Jevons, Menger, and Walras as independent authors of the marginal revolution – which thus appears to be a notable instance of multiple discovery. Though this practice may be an acceptable first approximation, it conceals the distinctiveness of their contributions (Jaffé, 1976).

Jevons exploited the strong British tradition of philosophical utilitarianism to develop a value theory which was based on a unified principle of marginal utility instead of disparate categories of cost; and by clearly specifying the central economic problem for individuals and society as the efficient allocation of known resources to given ends he helped to shift the focus of attention in economic theory from growth and change to optimization within a well defined system.

For Walras, the most important task was to demonstrate the coherence of an economy which was propelled by independent action. This he sought to achieve by formulating a general equilibrium of perfectly competitive markets, in which marginal utility provided the means of specifying demand. Walras's strategy has dominated microeconomics for the last 50 years.

Menger, however, was neither a utilitarian nor a theorist of equilibrium. It is not difficult to adapt his analysis to make it compatible with the formulations of Jevons and Walras, or with modern microeconomics; and indeed the possibility of such adaptation is often used as the justification for including Menger among the pioneers of modern economics. Those who now call themselves Austrian economists do not accept this view of Menger; in this chapter neither shall we. Instead we shall interpret his work in ways which emphasize its distinctiveness.

The Scope of Menger's Principles of Economics

In his *Principles*, Menger attempts to provide a systematic exploration of economic activity, proceeding carefully – sometimes laboriously – step by step along a continuous chain of causation. His universal principle, stated in the opening sentence of his first chapter, is that of cause and effect; and his originating cause is human needs. That Menger consistently writes of needs rather than wants perhaps reflects his view that some of them – food, clothing and shelter – are physiologically determined; but, like almost all modern economists, he does not consider it his business to explain them. Needs are personal; subsequent Austrian economists have increasingly emphasized that they are subjective.

Menger explains how individual perceptions of needs, and of the ways in which they might be met, cause some objects to be classified as goods, how some goods become economic goods, and how value is ascribed to economic goods. He then goes on to explain how goods which have value to individuals may become the subject of exchange; this leads to an analysis of the factors which influence the terms of exchange. The prospect of meeting one's needs more effectively by way of exchange than by the direct use of the goods in one's possession encourages people to produce or to hold goods for sale. How likely it is that any particular good will thus be used as a commodity depends on its marketability, to which Menger devotes a chapter. A commodity which is exceptionally marketable may come to be used as an intermediary of exchange between two which are much more difficult to market; and if it is widely used in this way, then it acquires the characteristics which we associate with money. Thus Menger concludes his analysis of the consequences of people's needs by explaining the emergence of money, which is such an aid to exchange, as a consequence of the process of exchange itself.

Human needs and human knowledge

We shall now follow the course of Menger's analysis in more detail, emphasizing those aspects which may be considered particularly Austrian. The primary orientation is not towards the wealth of nations, or the coherence of a system of markets, but individual human action. Everything to be considered is a consequence of human needs, and of the attempts by conscious and reasoning beings to meet those needs. The subject matter of economics is purposeful human action and its consequences; its analytical basis is methodological individualism. These principles were most comprehensively expounded by Mises (1949, 1962).

For Menger and his followers needs are basic, goods are not. Whether any particular object – or human skill – becomes a good depends, first, on the perception of a particular individual that it is capable of meeting a need and second, that individual's power to employ it for that purpose. Thus economic analysis does not begin with a list of goods, as in standard textbooks; such a list is a consequence of the working of the economic system, not one of its initial conditions. Nor can needs, though basic, be specified in detail by the analyst. Each individual's needs can be thoroughly known only to that individual; there is no objective procedure for compiling a publicly agreed list. Therefore, say Austrians, analysts should not pretend that it is possible.

This feature of Austrian doctrine received increasing emphasis as a consequence of the debate on the possibilities of economic planning, and of the fashion for welfare economics, which will be considered later; for the practice of treating individual human needs as data encourages the assumption that such data are readily accessible to governments, and may be used for the public benefit. Austrians have never been ready to assume that governments work for the public benefit (though Menger was much less critical than some of his successors); but their suspicion of governmental motives is less distinctive than their denial of governmental capability.

Individuals, it is assumed, know their own needs; but they do not necessarily know how best to satisfy them. Since an object or skill cannot become a good unless it is recognized as a means of satisfying a specific need of a specific individual, such recognition is a condition of goods-status; and it is not to be taken for granted. Goods are a consequence of knowledge; and knowledge is personal, local and incomplete. Thus at any time some potentially useful objects will not be goods; and, as Menger points out, some goods will be imaginary, because their use is based not on knowledge but on error. Error is inseparable from human knowledge, and its consequences are part of the subject matter of economics.

Knowledge changes over time; and it is the increase of knowledge – especially knowledge of the causal connections between things and human welfare – which Menger identifies as the principal cause of economic progress. In Menger's exposition, the growth of knowledge assumes the crucial importance which Adam Smith assigned to the effects of increasing the division of labour. (We may note that Adam Smith listed improvements in technique among the beneficial consequences of division of labour, while Menger included methods of achieving a more effective division of labour among the kinds of knowledge which foster progress.) Menger never developed the theme of knowledge and progress, as Marshall (1920) did in Book IV of his *Principles*, and Schumpeter (as we shall observe) used it in a very different way; but knowledge is an important, and sometimes troublesome, theme among modern Austrians.

Value in use

To be counted as a good, an object must be recognized as useful; to be valuable, and thus an economic good, it must also be scarce. In the first instance, value is related to use, not to exchange; for without value in use, Menger insists, a good cannot be worth exchanging. Though he does not use the phrase, Menger explains that value is determined at the margin of use for each individual. Menger assumes that people's consciousness of their needs includes the ability to rank them – though in discrete units rather than a continuous gradation – and therefore to construct an order of priority among the uses to which each good may be put. The value of each good to each person is not a property of that good, or of the resources required to produce it. It rests on two judgements by that person: the importance of the lowest-ranked need which the good satisfies, and the dependence of that satisfaction on the last available unit of the good. If there is enough to satisfy every need which the individual believes it can meet, the good has no further use – and therefore no value in use. Menger thus rejects the distinction between value in use and value in exchange as a means of explaining why the price of water is so often zero; when the price of water is zero that is precisely because it has no value in use. Indeed, he uses water to construct some detailed examples, showing how a period of drought or a diminished flow from a spring may confer value on what had previously been valueless.

Since value is the consequence of unsatisfied need, Menger observes that measures of value are likely to be very inadequate measures of welfare; and Austrians have generally been sceptical about the possibility of measuring welfare. He also notes that when some needs must remain unsatisfied, we usually have allocation problems at two levels: each person must decide how to use what he or she has available, and (except for isolated individuals) some means must be found of distributing the total supply among them. Both problems might be handled by government allocation; but private property rights allow decisions to be decentralized to those with the most localized information about individual needs and the ways of satisfying them. The emergence of private ownership of resources, instead of being included in the original specification of the economic problem, is thus incorporated into Menger's chain of cause and effect; though Menger himself offers no detailed explanation, it is a favourite theme of some contemporary economists (e.g. Demsetz, 1988) who have been influenced by Austrian ideas.

When the quantity of any good which is at the disposal of an individual is insufficient to satisfy all the needs which it appears to be capable of serving, he or she allocates it between needs so as to maximize the benefits obtainable. In stating this principle, Menger joined Jevons in providing the basis for the logic of choice, which has become central to economic theory – a development which Hayek, for example, first welcomed but later regretted. For Austrians, the logic of choice is the logic of the individual chooser, which depends not only on subjective preferences (as in standard neoclassical theory) but also on subjective perception – which may be incomplete or erroneous – of the alternatives available and of their relative effectiveness in satisfying these preferences. It is on this basis that the individual selects what appear to be the most attractive opportunities and relinquishes the rest. That the cost of any choice may be measured by the value attributed to the most attractive of the opportunities forgone is an Austrian idea which has been widely adopted; but for

Austrians this opportunity cost is in the mind of the chooser – it is not public or objective knowledge.

Menger examines the usefulness of goods in considerable detail. His observation that among the units of a particular good, such as timber, there may be variations in quality, and that these variations may sometimes be measured by the differences in the degree to which they allow particular needs to be satisfied – some qualities perhaps being excluded from the category of economic goods – foreshadows the analysis of goods in terms of their characteristics which has emerged in the last 25 years. It was not, however, an idea developed either by Menger or his successors.

Capital and time

Another elaboration of the basic conception of goods as ways of meeting needs, and ways which are continually being extended by the growth of knowledge has, by contrast, become a prominent and distinctive theme of Austrian economics. This is the concept of a structure of production, in which the goods that satisfy needs are themselves produced by other goods – a process which often extends over many stages. Increasing roundaboutness of production is an indication of a greater control over the human situation, based on an increased understanding of the less obvious connections between things and human welfare. If the stages of production can be clearly distinguished, then as we proceed further and further back from the point of consumption we encounter goods of higher and higher order. The value of such goods is imputed sequentially from the final satisfactions to which they contribute. Inputs derive their value from outputs, rather than the reverse as in cost-based theories of value. But, as Menger points out, we must not attribute the order of any particular good to its inherent properties; it is a consequence of human knowledge and human action. (To take a simple modern example, a personal computer may function as a first-order good if it is used to play games, or as a good of very high order if it is used to work out a detailed specification for a laboratory dedicated to research into the behaviour of fundamental particles.) Thus the classification of goods into their various orders, or even a simple division – which, as Austrians are likely to point out, is not so simple – between capital and consumption goods, cannot be a proper starting point for analysis; it is an outcome of the process to be analysed.

Menger's exploration of the complex structures which emerge as a consequence of human efforts to achieve greater satisfaction may be compared with Walras's attempts to construct a general equilibrium. Walras's system makes claims for comprehensiveness which Menger's cannot match; on the other hand, Menger's system has a depth of structure which Walras never attempted. This contrast of emphasis between breadth of coverage and depth of structure still differentiates Austrian economists from the great majority of neoclassical theorists.

Modern Austrians, like Menger, believe that homogenizing capital stultifies analysis. What matters is not the quantity of capital – a concept which they reject – but its heterogeneity and its structure. Each multi-stage process of production employs a particular collection of capital goods arranged in a particular way; moreover the goods and their arrangement within this process embody a particular configuration of knowledge, which should not be assumed to be publicly available. This insistence on the complementarity of capital goods does not imply fixed technological coefficients (as is assumed in input–output analysis). Other arrangements are usually possible; but what alternatives are actually available in any situation depends, first, on what the decision makers know (or think they know, for there can be imaginary goods of any order) and on the prospects of finding a means of putting a chosen structure in place.

The principle of methodological individualism carries over into the analysis of production methods. Austrians do not assume that technology is given (or that it can be bought ready-made). Knowledge is problematic; and it may be difficult to transfer, even if both parties are well motivated. Thus Austrians are not surprised to find differences in practice between firms which seem to face the same objective conditions; they are still less surprised when attempts to transfer methods of production between countries lead to unexpected results.

Two consequences deserve attention: the significance of time and of expectations. Complex processes take time, and each stage must be undertaken in its appropriate sequence. But of even more importance than the time required for the complete sequence of operations which is embodied in an established production process is the time needed to install that process. Any theory which attempts to explain the coordination of economic activities should be able to cope with problems of adjustment; and the development of a new pattern of production cannot be instantaneous, but requires a particular sequence of modifications. Time is not a reversible dimension, as in so much modern theory: it provides the context in which people must act. For Austrians, exercises in comparing positions of equilibrium are likely to be inadequate, or even misleading, since they ignore the complexity and the time-scale of adjustment, and the possibility that the process of change may itself be an important determinant of the final position.

Among the problems of change, not least is the difficulty of forming reliable expectations. To undertake any adjustment (including, of course, the first establishment of a multi-stage process of production) requires an ability to judge future possibilities, and to plan an appropriate series of actions in order to take advantage of them. Thus Austrian economists, who are opponents of comprehensive economic planning, have generally paid much more attention than most other economists to the need for planning by individuals. This is no paradox; for it is their recognition of the complexities of planning, and its dependence on knowledge of particular facts and circumstances – including future facts and circumstances which must always be doubtful – which has helped to persuade Austrian economists of the enormous difficulties facing even the best-intentioned and most assiduous government in attempting to produce a sensible plan for a whole economy. Nor will they be surprised at the mistakes of large corporations which attempt to centralize decision making.

Exchange

Hitherto, we have (like Menger) considered only the ways in which goods provide value in use: first, as direct means of satisfying wants, and second, as part of more complex structures which, after due time, deliver greater satisfactions. Not until the fourth of his eight chapters is Menger ready to discuss exchange. In Menger's sequence of cause and effect, founded on individual needs and individual action, exchange is one step beyond using an object as a good of higher order in a production process, as an indirect means to a desired objective; for whereas a roundabout method of production may be controlled by a single individual, exchange necessarily entails interaction with others.

We begin with direct exchange, in which both parties are simultaneously buyers and sellers: each is willing to dispose of an object which has relatively little value in personal use, if by so doing it is possible to acquire an object which can be used either directly or indirectly to meet a more important need which is currently unsatisfied. (We must not forget that such willingness depends on a subjective assessment of need and a judgement about the means of satisfying it.) If trade is to take place, both parties must gain; each must therefore exchange a lesser use-value for a greater. This may not be possible; many objects are not exchanged. If it is possible, that will be the result of differences between the two parties in needs, the collection of goods possessed, or ideas about the ways in which goods might be effectively used – or some combination of these.

Exchange will take place as long as opportunities are perceived by both parties for personal gain. Menger emphasizes the mutual gains from each transaction, and makes no attempt to establish marginal equalities of the kind that are now standard. As with use-values, he thinks in terms of discrete units. But more significantly, he directs attention to the process of exchange and the economic sacrifices which it entails, especially when (as at this stage of the analysis) all exchange is by direct barter. From a present-day perspective, he seems to be providing the basis for a transactions–cost theory of the firm; but his conscious intention is to prepare the way for an explanation of money. (Conceptually, money and the firm have more in common than is usually appreciated.) However, before turning to money Menger examines price.

It may be said that Menger had no theory of price in the modern sense – no theory which in principle yields a single value. That is partly because of the difficulties and costs of arranging suitable trans- actions. He points out, with examples, that exchanges are not revers- ible; there is a gap between the lowest price at which any person is willing to sell and the highest price at which the same person is willing to buy. It is also partly because he declines to take competition as his basic case. On the contrary, he begins with isolated exchange, and then examines monopolistic pricing, before introducing elements of competition; perfect competition is never reached. This mixture of monopolistic elements, transactions costs, and – once again – limited knowledge, leaves price within a region of bounded indeterminacy, which Menger appears to think marks also the bounds of economic analysis. (Morgenstern, an Austrian economist who was concerned with these issues, became von Neumann's collaborator in developing game theory as a way of coping with such problems.) Here, too, we see a characteristic difference between the Austrian tradition and conventional microeconomics. Whereas the latter may invoke some simple process story – or, more rarely, a formal analysis of stability conditions – in order to support a theory of equilibrium price, for Austrians it is the process which demands priority, and equilibrium (if it is recognized) is characterized as the end-state of that process.

Commodities

So far we have traced the consequences of human needs in identifying certain objects and actions as goods, of first and higher orders, and then as instruments for the acquisition of more highly-valued goods through exchange. With the development of regular patterns of exchange, and therefore of some reasonable basis for price expectations, it becomes possible to contemplate not merely the exchange of what one happens to have to hand but the deliberate acquisition or production of goods for the express purpose of exchange. Goods which an individual intends to exchange are – for that individual – commodities. Once again, what matters are the needs and perceptions of the individual; and these, as Menger points out, are likely to change with age and situation.

Adam Smith had attributed the division of labour to the human propensity to exchange. Menger sought to incorporate exchange into his causal sequence, and he enquired what goods were likely to become commodities – and thus likely to be subjected to increasing division of labour. He therefore focused on the obstacles to exchange previously discussed, and considered the factors which affect the marketability of particular goods, in an analysis which, with some changes in style, could be incorporated in modern textbooks of marketing. It leads into a discussion of organized markets which, however, are not associated with perfect competition.

Money

Direct exchange works well when each party is willing to offer precisely those goods which the other requires; but achieving such a match is not always easy. However, the emergence of highly marketable commodities opens up possibilities of indirect exchange: the costs of accepting a readily marketable commodity, and subsequently trading it for what is required for use, may be less than the costs of finding a suitable but elusive direct bargain. Here too, roundabout methods may be more productive. Anyone who begins to use a commodity in this way increases its marketability, and thus increases its attraction as an intermediary for other sellers. A cumulative process of intermediation is therefore likely to develop, with increasing concentration on a very few commodities – perhaps only one – for this purpose. If the use of a commodity as a medium of exchange comes to predominate over its use to deliver satisfactions, either directly or as a good of higher order, then it acquires the status of money. From a medium of exchange it easily becomes a unit of account, and also – if it is durable – a store of value.

The development of money brings us to the end of Menger's causal chain, which begins with human needs and the attempts of reasoning human beings to find ways of meeting them. But two features of Menger's treatment deserve comment. The first is the link which he provides between the use of money as a store of value and uncertainty. Though people attempt to predict the future, they are subject to unknown or uncontrollable influences. Thus, as a necessary part of their attempts to provide in advance for their future needs, sensible people make whatever provision they can against unpredictable events, by way (in Menger's examples) of a fire extinguisher or a first aid chest. A more versatile form of provision is the accumulation of a stock of money. It was this recognition of the variety of ways in which people seek to accumulate reserves against unforeseeable contingencies which led Hicks (1982, pp. 287–8) to declare that Menger had a deeper insight into such issues than Keynes displayed with his exclusive (though much more conspicuous) concentration on financial liquidity.

No follower of Menger is likely to support the attempts by other theorists to introduce money into an otherwise unchanged general equilibrium system, because such a system requires a complete listing of contingencies. It is not surprising that general equilibrium theorists have repeatedly found that money has no value in such a system; people hold money to cope with unpredictable hazards or opportunities. However, financial reserves are not the only, and often not the most effective, means of making provision against the unknown. One cannot therefore produce a comprehensive treatment of money without considering alternatives – and that, in one way or another, includes a wide range of human activity and of human institutions. It is a range much wider than even Austrian economists have generally shown any enthusiasm for tackling.

Institutions

The other feature of Menger's treatment which requires comment has just been signalled by the phrase 'human institutions'. Though Menger's *Principles* trace out a continuous chain of cause and effect, based on purposeful human action, he makes no claim that what happens in an economy is always and only what people intended. People make mistakes, and there is much that they do not know. In particular (as Keynes also observed), we are often ignorant of the less direct consequences of our acts. Thus human institutions – conventions, practices, informal (and sometimes formal) organizations – are not to be explained solely as purposeful creations, though many of them may be. Money is a very effective institution, though not without its problems; yet it developed as the unintended consequence of individual attempts to make particular exchange transactions more efficient, and thereby to satisfy individual needs more effectively.

The significance and development of institutions is a main theme in Menger's second book. In his controversy with members of the historical school, who argued for the study of historical circumstances rather than the construction of theory which, they believed, ignored context, Menger was thus able to accept, and indeed emphasize, the importance of the historical evolution of custom and practice, and also to argue that this evolution could – and should – be explained by theory. The idea that some institutions might be the result of human action but not of human design was not new, and the argument that individuals pursuing their own interest could unintentionally promote the public good was a central (though not the only) feature of Adam Smith's theory of social coordination; but Menger drew attention to the great variety of institutions and the importance of a theoretical basis for studying them. He was careful not to deny the importance of what he called pragmatic institutions – deliberately created, and working roughly as intended – nor to claim that what had evolved without an overall plan must be good. The explanation of an institution should be kept distinct from its appraisal – an early example of the distinction between positive and normative economics.

On the whole, despite Menger's advocacy, Austrian economists have done rather little to develop theories of institutions. Neoclassical economists have done less, being content merely to invoke or assume institutions (such as the auctioneer or a complete system of commercial law) as required. The modern emphasis on fully rational behaviour has allowed some economists (e.g. Williamson, 1975, 1985) to explain particular organizational structures (such as divisionalized or vertically integrated firms) as the products of optimization; and the rationality of the law has also attracted much attention. What inhibits neoclassical economists from following Menger's programme is that it depends on incomplete rationality. People act in a way which is intended to promote their own interests, and usually succeed in doing so, at least in the short run; but their actions may have other consequences which were not part of their intentions – indeed which were simply not recognized as possibilities. Optimality, as defined by modern theorists, requires a complete specification of the problem; therefore optimal choices, as understood by such theorists, can have no consequences which were not foreseen at the time of the decision. Unfortunately, an insistence on rational choice equilibria deprives us of an explanation for many institutions.

Theory and method

Austrian economists, however, have never been fascinated by optimality. For some, such as Menger (who appears to have had a substantial acquaintance with mathematics), this has been a reason for not using mathematical techniques; for others, perhaps, limited mathematical skills have encouraged them to avoid optimizing formulations. Their philosophical approach, studying the attempts of people to improve their situation on the basis of knowledge which is limited and incomplete, in circumstances where important factors are usually beyond their power to control, to predict, or even to recognize, is very similar to that of Herbert Simon and his supporters. Partly, no doubt, because Simon has given much of his attention to human behaviour in formal organizations, while Austrian economists have generally shown little interest in such organizations, this compatibility has not been acknowledged on either side until very recently; but we may see a convergence between Austrian economists and the followers of Simon, focused on the analysis of both formal and informal institutions. Whether this will persuade Austrian economists to use mathematics in the style of Simon and his followers is an open question.

Menger's principal objective in his second book was to defend the priority of theory. In response to the claim of the historical school that we must study the facts in their complexity, which is beyond the capacity of any theory to represent, Menger insists that we need a theory to help in studying the facts. Theories are essential precursors of empirical studies; but they are not a substitute for them. Menger's argument appears to be a version of the now familiar case for abstraction in order to generate a clear chain of reasoning, which will need to be supplemented, and sometimes modified, in its application to individual cases.

It is, however, a characteristic of Menger's position, and that of subsequent Austrian economists, that the laws of economics, generated by logical argument, are not hypotheses to be tested, but established truths. That view was far more generally accepted in Menger's time than it is today. It is now likely to be dismissed as '*a priorism*'; however tightly the conclusions of a chain of reasoning are entailed by the premises, we cannot be sure that they are true, because we cannot be sure that the premises are true. But it is the view of Menger and his successors that we should take care to start with premises which are indeed known to be true; and that in the social sciences it is possible to do this, because we have direct personal knowledge of our own human situation. Our chains of reasoning should be founded on a secure empirical base. This was what Menger had attempted in his first book; by repeatedly and somewhat laboriously applying the principle of cause and effect, he had sought to deduce a chain of logical consequences – what he called 'exact laws' – from the basic situation of human beings attempting to find ways – and then to find better ways – of meeting their needs. Along this chain, it may be necessary to make certain simplifications or assumptions in order to produce exact laws, and these may need to be withdrawn when dealing with a specific problem; but finding that the exact laws do not apply to that problem neither invalidates those laws nor undermines their base.

This view is open to criticism, but it is not naive. If one makes the obvious contrast with Friedman's (1953) position, that predictions must be tested, but that the assumptions from which they are derived are typically false, we can see that attention is directed to opposite ends of the causal chain. For Austrian economists, the truth of assumptions is essential; and they believe that the truth of the assumptions which they use is well established. Like the people whose actions they study, their theories are based on what they know – or perhaps one should say of both, on what they think they know. That knowledge is substantially based on introspection; it was therefore automatically suspect during that lengthy period in which economists and psychologists, in their desire to follow the purest scientific methods, would accept only the evidence of observation – forgetting that observation is likely to be contaminated by some of the very factors which they were trying to exclude. Perhaps Austrian economists are too reluctant to re-examine what they believe they know, and the adequacy of its basis; but they do not operate on principles which are obviously unscientific.

AUSTRIAN ECONOMICS SINCE MENGER

Choice and equilibrium

The Austrian conception of scientific method was adopted by Lionel Robbins in his very influential work, *An Essay on the Nature and Significance of Economic Science* (1932). There is an Austrian tone also to his famous definition of economics as the study of the relationship between ends and the scarcity of the means available for achieving them. Robbins's definition, in turn, has encouraged the tendency to envisage the core of economics as the pure logic of choice. This might indeed appear to be the apotheosis of Menger's research programme – the formulation of exact laws based on the attempts of human beings to find the best available ways of satisfying their needs. But modern Austrian economists are not comfortable with this view of economics, for two principal reasons.

The first reason is that the pursuit of rigour in rational choice theory has entailed ever tighter specification of the choice situation, with the result that what began as spontaneous human action emerges as fully programmed behaviour in which all problems of knowledge are expunged. There is some ambivalence about Menger's own position: his recognition in the *Principles* of uncertainty and error, of the importance of providing for the unpredictable, and of the indeterminacy of price, leave us in some doubt about how exact we should want our economic laws to be. However, there are clear signs in modern economics that the relentless pursuit of rationality may cause more, and deeper, difficulties than it resolves. The reluctance of Austrians to accept what might appear to be the neoclassical implications of Menger's work is therefore not unreasonable.

The second reason for Austrian disquiet is the symbiotic relationship which has developed between the logic of choice and the concept of equilibrium. At first, choice theory was used to build up a model of equilibrium; and Austrian economists (notably Hayek) envisaged general equilibrium as a situation in which the individually chosen plans of all those within an economy turned out to be mutually compatible. Mises made use of a similar concept of an evenly rotating economy. Here too, a convergence between Austrian and neoclassical ideas seemed to be in progress. Around 1930 it seemed reasonable to expect that the Austrian school would fade away, its work completed. But neoclassical economists concentrated on the logical possibilities of general equilibrium as a solution set for a system of equations, and showed little concern about the practical possibilities of achieving it.

Indeed, the more closely the properties of equilibrium were examined, the more economists were forced towards the conclusion that if an economy were not in equilibrium then at least one of its members could not be optimizing; therefore the analysis of behaviour out of equilibrium was not compatible with the logic of choice. The strategy for dealing with what looked like disequilibrium was then to find a suitable redefinition of the constraints so that their apparently irrational behaviour would be rational after all.

Austrians, by contrast, have preferred to take processes seriously, ignoring the claims that all scientific economics must be equilibrium economics. In so doing, it may be said, they can claim support from Walras, who believed that the analysis of general equilibrium must be followed by the study of behaviour out of equilibrium (Walker, 1989). Walras did not believe that a real economy would often, or perhaps ever, be in equilibrium, since there were too many sources of change; though it was appropriate to start by constructing a model which assumed that it was, this was not the end of economic theorizing. (What view Walras would take of modern microeconomics no one can know.) The insistence of high theorists on equilibrium (which is no longer universal) has probably encouraged most modern Austrian economists to avoid even rather simple equilibrium models; but it should be noted that the use of equilibrium concepts as an aid to analysis is not alien to the Austrian tradition.

The Coordination of Economic Activities

The problem to which Walras was trying to find a more satisfactory answer than had hitherto been provided was whether it was possible for a large number of independent, self-interested decision makers to constitute a coherent economic system; and this problem, usually under the title of the coordination of economic activities, is of central interest for Austrians too. Indeed, as later generations of Austrians have become increasingly opposed to state activity, it has become more crucial for them to demonstrate, if they can, that successful coordination can be achieved without state action. However, for many years they were satisfied – like many other economists – that this task had already been accomplished; what remained was to examine the causes of possible failures of coordination, and to discover how such failures might be remedied or prevented.

Money, Credit and Cycles

The Austrian concern with coordination failure may be traced back to Menger's treatment of the emergence of money as an unintended consequence of individual attempts to reduce obstacles to exchange. Menger had insisted on the need to appraise such unplanned institutions in relation to current circumstances. There was, of course, a very long tradition of public concern about the consequences of money, including its effects on production and trade; and the new methods of economic analysis being developed in the last third of the nineteenth century offered new ways of formalizing the issues. Menger's emphasis on the complex structure of production, with its time-related complementarity between goods of higher order, provided a particular example – and an example of growing importance – of coordination which depended both on the time-pattern of cash flows and on the costs of borrowing and lending.

The banking and credit system, and even the means of regulating it, were also, in large part, the undesigned result of private decisions and therefore, according to Menger's programme, required both a theoretical explanation and an investigation of their current effects. (The Bank of England, as regulator of credit, and readily marketable public debt, as the prime instrument of its regulation, originated as joint expedients for financing war.)

Böhm-Bawerk had attempted to simplify the analysis of complex production systems by introducing the concept of 'the average period of production' of such a system, and sought to use time as an invariant measure of capital (Böhm-Bawerk, 1884, 1889, 1959). The rate of interest could then be regarded as the price of time, and a fall in that price would lead to the adoption of more complex (or roundabout) processes of production. Though Böhm-Bawerk, in Menger's view, had undervalued the complexity of capital structures, he had emphasized the relationship between the time-span of production and the rate of interest, and therefore the importance of interest rates as a factor for coordination or disruption. Moreover, by his association of increasing roundaboutness with economic progress, he had raised the question of the appropriate role of interest rates in a progressive economy.

Böhm-Bawerk's theory of capital and interest was taken up by Wicksell (1898, 1936), who sought to combine it with Walrasian general equilibrium. Wicksell's concern for neutral money, which would simply transmit, without distortion, the impact of the real forces to which the economy should adjust, was a natural consequence of this combination. Wicksell's influence was widespread. In addition to stimulating the Swedish school which rose to prominence in the interwar years, it reinforced Dennis Robertson's (1926) fears that the normal working of the banking system could not be relied upon as a neutral transmission mechanism, and it was a significant inspiration (along with Mises's (1912, 1953) work) of Hayek's (1931) theory of the trade cycle.

In Wicksell's theory, money was neutral when investment was equal to voluntary savings. Hayek recognized that, in an economy where productivity was increasing through continuing net investment, the equality of investment and voluntary savings was not compatible with a stable price level – a natural, and traditional intepretation of neutral money. There was thus some doubt as to what should be meant by monetary neutrality. But Hayek's principal concern, like that of Mises before him, was with the disruptive consequences of credit. Wicksell had shown how an excess of credit could set in motion a cumulative process of rising prices until a new equilibrium was reached. But by considering the structure of production, Hayek identified differential effects which could cause serious trouble.

Excess credit entailed lower interest rates, as Wicksell had argued; but lower interest rates encouraged more roundabout methods of production, because the opportunity cost of waiting for output was reduced. If the fall in the rate of interest reflected a change in economic fundamentals, such an adjustment was to be welcomed; but if it was a mere product of excess credit (because of a failure of monetary control, or deliberate action by government), then the longer processes were unjustified. The value of the new goods of higher order being installed by producers depended on consumers' increased willingness to postpone consumption, as apparently indicated by lower rates of interest. But if the fall in interest rates was the result only of credit creation, there was no such increased willingness. Producers were being misled by false signals; and the consequences were much worse than a Wicksellian cumulative process.

Hayek, like Wicksell, began with a fully employed economy, and traced out a sequence which began with a credit-inspired boom in the production of capital goods, at the expense of consumption. This diversion of resources imposed an immediate loss on consumers, whose preferences had not changed; and their attempt to maintain their patterns of consumption caused the prices of goods for present consumption to rise. Schemes for increasing future supplies of consumption goods therefore became less attractive in relation to meeting immediate demands; and as prices began to catch up with expanded credit, interest rates also began to rise. The relative rise in the prices of goods for present consumption and the rise in interest rates together invalidated the producers' assumptions behind the capital boom. Their schemes for more roundabout methods of production could not be justified; the resources embodied in them were wasted; and instead of becoming richer through the use of more productive methods, the community found itself poorer. The boom was inevitably followed by a slump, in which the capital structures based on false expectations were abandoned, and the population had to come to terms with its reduced circumstances. Since the distress and unemployment of the slump directly reflected the breakdown of intertemporal coordination of supply, it could not be remedied by any stimulus to demand – which indeed would generate further distortions.

It seemed possible for a time that Hayek's theory of the trade cycle would be widely accepted among economists; but it was swept aside by Keynes's *General Theory* (1936). Hayek himself turned to more philosophical and political issues, and within economics has given more attention to basic problems of knowledge (though continuing to warn of the disruptive consequences of inflation through its effects on intertemporal coordination). But the new business cycle theory which has emerged from rational expectations macroeconomics (see Chapter 5) is sometimes labelled by its advocates an Austrian theory.

What appears to be Austrian about it is its dependence on systematic error in people's interpretation of price information. Just as Hayek's trade cycle is initiated by the false signals given by an interest rate forced below its equilibrium level by excess credit, so equilibrium business cycles are initiated by misperceptions of relative prices. What differentiates this class of theory from Austrian theories is that these misperceptions drive rational choices which define an equilibrium sequence, whereas Hayek attempted to chart the sequential process by which people made plans which could not be realized and then had to abandon them as the consequences of their decisions became apparent. Nor are the explanations which are offered by rational expectations theorists for these misperceptions very plausible – perhaps because their authors accept Friedman's view that assumptions need not be true and therefore do not take them very seriously. The paradox of modern business cycle theory is that it depends on systematic errors, for which no adequate explanation is given, and of which no-one has any inkling, but which are made by people who are otherwise astonishingly well informed.

If Keynes had not produced the *General Theory*, we might have had a different story. In attempting to resolve some of the issues left unsettled by Wicksell, Swedish economists during the 1930s developed the method of sequence analysis, with its contrast between the *ex ante* view, on which plans were based, and the *ex post* view, in which the outcomes of those plans were reviewed, as a preliminary to formulating new plans. As has already been noted, the Swedish school had an Austrian ancestry, and it is possible that Swedish sequence analysis might have been assimilated to Austrian concerns with economic processes.

Creative Destruction

Hayek's theory of the trade cycle was based on monetary failure; yet it would be misleading to call it a purely monetary theory, since the course of events is critically dependent on the real structures of the economy. It may nevertheless be contrasted with another Austrian theory of the trade cycle which also fell out of favour, but which has recently attracted greater interest: that of Joseph Schumpeter (1934). Schumpeter, it might be said, extended Menger's causal chain by showing how, in a world of increasingly complex structures of production, cycles could result from attempts to take advantage of the growth of knowledge in order to satisfy human wants more effectively. The important innovations made possible by new knowledge entailed the construction of novel interconnected structures which would sweep away the old in a process which he labelled creative destruction. This process, he argued, necessarily produced a cycle.

These innovations came in waves, not because great improvements in knowledge came in waves but because of the special circumstances needed to encourage innovators to act. In Schumpeter's theory, innovators are calculating visionaries. They have a conception of a new class of products, new markets, new technologies, or new methods of organization. Their motivation, however, is not social welfare but their own benefit: they will not attempt to realize their vision without an assurance of profit. But no such assurance can be found if the economy is already undergoing large-scale disturbances of any kind, since in such circumstances there is no rational basis for expectations. Though it may be envisaged much earlier, an innovation will therefore be launched only in a period of tranquillity – in an evenly rotating economy, to use Mises's phrase. Into this tranquillity the innovator injects a new source of demand for goods of higher order, required for the new structures of production. The consequence is a boom, which looks rather like a Hayekian boom: the critical difference is that new Schumpeterian structures are destined for use, not abandonment.

That difference, however, is not enough to prevent a slump, though its causes and effects are different. The Shumpeterian slump results from a combination of three factors. First, the additional investment is intended to put a new structure in place, after which no more than replacement is required; at the same time even the demand for replacement investment disappears where old structures have been superseded. Thus the initial impulse is self-liquidating. Second, the flow of new goods and services which emerges from the new structures as the investment is completed, accompanied by substantial changes in the demands for particular kinds of labour and of material inputs, disrupts old patterns and expectations; and in Schumpeter's view, most businessmen are capable only of following established routines, and therefore when faced with such disruption either abandon their activities or are driven out. Finally, even if other potential innovators have their own schemes already prepared, they cannot calculate their prospective profits until conditions have settled down. Thus the new structures not only destroy the old; they also destroy the conditions for further innovation. A process of adjustment, by trial and error, is therefore necessary in order to find a new balance of activities which will constitute an evenly rotating economy, and permit the entrepreneurial calculations which will trigger the next innovatory cycle.

The cyclical swings in prices, output and employment are exacerbated by the influence of credit; but Schumpeter is not prepared to agree with Hayek on the desirability of avoiding any credit expansion which does not reflect a change in consumers' willingness to forgo current consumption – for the simple reason that innovators normally require an increase in credit to finance their beneficial operations. Whereas in Hayek's theory credit expansion, by driving interest rates below their equilibrium level, creates a false vision of profitable investment, in Schumpeter's theory credit expansion allows true visions of profitable investment to be realized. The investments undertaken in Hayek's cycle are based on old knowledge, subverted by the false signals generated by excess credit; the investments undertaken in Schumpeter's cycle are based on new knowledge, and lead to an increase in human satisfactions. But at first, this new knowledge is confined to the entrepreneur; without it, others are not ready to relinquish their claims on present resources, and therefore have to be outbid by the entrepreneur's new credit.

Modern Austrian economists have not always been comfortable with Schumpeter's analysis, because they have shared the underlying concern of neoclassical economists with the coordination of economic activity. Schumpeter's emphasis is on progress through discoordination; the establishment of a new balance necessarily takes some time, but did not seem to him problematic. He was as ready as any neoclassical theorist to take equilibration for certain, though he insisted that it could not be hurried. Demand management does no good in a Schumpeterian slump. For Austrian economists, however, coordination needs to be explained.

Planning, Welfare and Equilibration

Walrasian general equilibrium, either as the terminal state of an Austrian process (which, as Walras himself recognized, would never be
reached), or as a kind of exact law from which empirical laws might
be constructed, was acceptable to Austrian economists in the early
part of this century. Indeed, for a time they believed that their own
theoretical contributions were being adopted and absorbed. But this
convergence did not continue. On the contrary, further exploration of
the properties of equilibrium by neoclassical theorists exposed differences; and for Austrian economists – primarily Mises and Hayek –
these differences had disturbing implications for policy. The principal
issues were economic planning and welfare economics.

Adam Smith argued that markets could be expected to work more
effectively than government regulation. More elaborate and more
formal analysis of market systems encouraged some economists to
claim that only market systems could work: in particular that socialist
planning could not produce a well ordered economy. Mises so argued,
and some economists who were sympathetic to planning tried to
answer him. Eventually they believed that they had succeeded in
demonstrating that planners could replicate a perfectly competitive
market system by the use of planners' prices, based on a set of initial
endowments which could be decided by the planners or their political
masters. To many economists (including some who did not favour a
planned economy), the issue of principle appeared to have been
resolved; but to Mises and Hayek the debate showed how far neoclassical economists had gone astray (Lavoie, 1985).

Neoclassical economists had formulated the planners' problem in
the same terms as general competitive equilibrium: the optimal allocation of given resources to meet given needs, using given technology.
This was Jevons's definition of the economic problem; but it was not
Menger's. Needs were indeed given – to each individual; they were
certainly not public knowledge. But knowledge of resources and technology was not given to anyone: such knowledge was a matter of
individual perception, continually changing, and in part a product of
the economic process.

The data that were assumed in the statement of the planning problem had to be collected by the planners, or on their behalf; and they
had to be collected from a multitude of individuals, with no prior
knowledge of who knew what, or indeed what was known at all.
Moreover, it was far from obvious what incentives people might have
to disclose what they knew. (These problems of knowledge and incen-

tive occur, in greater or smaller degree, within every formal orga_
ation; since Austrian economists have generally paid little attenti_
to organizational behaviour, they have naturally had little to say abo_
them in that context.) Hayek, in particular, was persuaded by this
development that neoclassical economics was seriously flawed by its
use of a misleading conception of the economic problem: it ignored
the question of *how* equilibrium was to be achieved, and of the
importance of knowledge in that process (Caldwell, 1988). A market
system, Hayek (1949) argued, offered the best means of discovering
relevant knowledge and of putting it to use, as properly directed
theory would demonstrate.

These dissatisfactions were reinforced by the development of welfare
economics, in which the concept of a perfectly competitive economy
was employed as a welfare ideal, and all departures from perfect
competition were designated as market failures, providing at least
prima facie scope for beneficial government intervention. But the
heterogeneity and complexity of goods, reinforced by the processes of
change as people discovered new possibilities, which were part of
Menger's tradition, were not compatible with perfect markets; and to
expel them by government action was as likely to reduce as increase
welfare (as Chamberlin, 1933, also pointed out).

Neoclassical theory, which many Austrian-trained economists had
been prepared to accept as a close relation of their own analysis of
market systems, was thus generating policy advice which seemed to
them clearly misguided; and the source of the trouble was the theory
itself. Neoclassical theorists had failed to follow Walras's advice and
analyse behaviour out of equilibrium; and Austrian economists had
neither emphasized the need for this nor developed their own theories
sufficiently. The lead was now taken by Mises (1949) and Hayek; but
the main part of the work has been done by one of Mises's students,
Israel Kirzner. Kirzner's (1973) model is built on a concept advanced
by Walras himself, of the entrepreneur as the agent of coordination
(Walker, 1989); but Kirzner has worked out the implications in detail,
against a Hayekian framework (which can be traced back to Menger)
of problematic knowledge.

Competition and Entrepreneurship

A common way of characterizing a market equilibrium is that it is a
situation in which there are no unexploited gains from trade. Models
of optimization on the basis of given data do not leave any gains
unexploited. If, however, we start from the Austrian position of per-

sonal and incomplete knowledge, it is natural to suppose that at any time people will forgo many opportunities which would be readily seized if only their existence were known. In order to focus his criticism of neoclassical theory, Kirzner first develops his analysis in relation to the most obvious kind of failure in a price system: a situation in which a commodity is being exchanged at different prices in different parts of a single market.

A simple way of generating such a price disparity is to assume that an additional customer turns up in one part of the market, and that the price there rises in response to this additional demand. In the standard model such local variations are impossible, because it is assumed – or rather taken for granted – that everyone knows of the increased demand. But why should we make such an assumption? Is it not more reasonable to suppose that only those people making use of the particular trading post (to use a familiar neoclassical metaphor) will be aware of the change? If so, then the price disparity will persist until someone takes action to change it. That person Kirzner designates as an entrepreneur.

As Kirzner makes plain, his entrepreneur is very different from Schumpeter's. Each entrepreneur is a normal person looking for simple ways of achieving greater satisfactions – and being a normal person, looking in particular places. Looking may include a certain amount of deliberate search (if for example, there has been some report of immigration into the locality, it might seem a good idea to seek evidence of increased demand for particular goods) or it may simply entail sensitivity to particular clues in the normal course of activity. If the world is full of individuals each trying, with varying amounts of skills and diligence, to find opportunities for gains from trade, it is not unlikely that many opportunities will be found. In general, these will be different opportunities, because each person has special advantages and limitations. Contrary to the inferences drawn from neoclassical theory, it is important that competition for specific opportunities should not be so intense as to eliminate the possibilities of gains before they can be exploited; for if this is what people expect, such opportunities will not be sought, and therefore – except by accident – they will not be found.

On the other hand, the very act of exploiting an opportunity – which in the case of a price discrepancy between parts of the market is most simply done by arbitrage – will provide information to others, and thereby lead some of them to change their behaviour. We are familiar with the information content of prices; Kirzner draws attention to the information content of changes in price. The entrepreneurial initiative which shifts prices towards equilibrium reveals further opportunities to those who are alert; in attempting to profit from these newly recognized opportunities such people move prices yet closer together, and thereby accentuate the movement towards equilibrium. The approach to equilibrium is inseparable from the spread of knowledge; both are unintended consequences of entrepreneurial attempts by individuals to satisfy more of their own needs through exchange.

Austrian economists have no objection to the common association of perfect competition with perfect knowledge (nowadays often expressed in the form of well defined probability distributions). But to focus on formal solutions to the allocation problems of an economy which is completely specified is simply to ignore the problems of achieving coordination. That was the fundamental Austrian objection to the apparent demonstration that planning was perfectly feasible. It has become an increasingly strong objection to theories of market equilibrium also; such theories cannot provide a satisfactory explanation of how markets work. Such explanations, Austrian economists believe, can be found only by studying market processes.

Knowledge in Austrian Economics

Austrian economists continue to follow Menger's basic precepts. All analysis is to be based on the individual, who is attempting to use knowledge to satisfy his or her needs. These need not be selfish, though Austrians have not been distinguished for their analyses of behaviour directed towards the welfare of others. The knowledge which is emphasized is that of particular skills and circumstances; it is normally far from complete, and may be wrong – though in Austrian analyses this is usually because it is out of date, not because it embodies positive error. That is true in the very different – but not rival – analyses of Kirzner and Schumpeter. The opportunities for Kirzner's entrepreneurs arise because other people do not appreciate that circumstances have changed; but the entrepreneurs do not make new mistakes. Kirzner (1985) carries over these features of his theory when extending it to planning for future opportunities; the opportunities arise because people fail to foresee future developments – or at least, their implications – but the entrepreneur who acts gets it right. In Schumpeter's model, people have learnt the most efficient routines for an economy in equilibrium, but are simply unable to adjust to the upheavals caused by innovation; such innovation is based on entrepreneurial vision, but on a vision which proves correct. Schumpeter evades the problem of entrepreneurial error by specifying correct intuition as an attribute of entrepreneurship.

This treatment of knowledge ensures that the market process works well. In Kirzner's scheme it continually promotes the effective coordination of economic activity in response to a continuous flow of externally generated change. In Schumpeter's much grander theory coordination regularly breaks down, but this is an inevitable part of a highly efficient process of economic development – the breakdowns are a direct consequence of inherent human limitations. To most Austrian economists, the market 'failures' discussed in neoclassical theory are simply the theoretical results of inappropriate assumptions and irrelevant criteria; unobstructed market processes do not fail.

Not everyone who may be called an Austrian economist entirely shares this view: Lachmann (1986) observes that even simple Kirznerian arbitrage is, like Schumpeterian innovation, destructive as well as creative, since it disrupts some plans which were based on the old situation; and he is not convinced that the repercussions can necessarily be absorbed. If competition is not, as in neoclassical theory, an equilibrium state, but a procedure for making discoveries, then its results cannot be predicted. Indeed, that is its virtue. Lachmann's question echoes the traditional doubts expressed by general equilibrium theorists about the adequacy of partial equilibrium models. His recommendation, in the Austrian tradition of concern for complex structures, is to explore intermarket effects. O'Driscoll and Rizzo (1985), too, do not commit themselves to the view that market processes always result in successful coordination; they recognize similarities between their view and subjective Keynesianism. Indeed, by admitting particular, incomplete, and developing knowledge into their analytical system, Austrians have inevitably deprived themselves of any logical proof of success; the specification of the system being analysed changes as the analysis proceeds, and changes in ways which cannot be entirely foreseen.

The Austrian insistence on taking knowledge seriously in theories of both coordination and development distinguishes them clearly from neoclassical theory, in which the mechanical treatment of information sets simply avoids the problems of knowledge. The price which they necessarily pay is the loss of determinism, which is valued so highly in neoclassical theory. But neoclassical proofs of equilibrium are not proofs of its attainability. Moreover, the strategy of deriving equilibrium configurations from axioms of rational choice breaks down when the interdependence of choices is recognized – most obviously in oligopoly, but also in macroeconomics when agents and governments are required to form rational expectations about each other's actions. Thus the opportunity cost of the Austrian conception of economics may be less than it seems. It may have advantages in studying the implications of both the limitations and the growth of knowledge – especially the consequences which were not deliberately chosen.

FURTHER READING

O'Driscoll and Rizzo (1985) provide an exposition of modern Austrian economics organized around the themes of individual choice, subjectivism, incomplete and dispersed knowledge, and the effects of time. A particular virtue of their treatment is its exploration of links with other approaches to economics, as well as the contrasts with neoclassical analysis. It concludes with a chapter on unsolved problems. Lachmann (1986) also discusses problems, and the ways in which they might be tackled in alliance with other economists. Kirzner's (1973) *Competition and Entrepreneurship* is clearly written, and already a classic. Finally, everyone should read Schumpeter. His *Capitalism, Socialism and Democracy* (1943, 1976) ranges far beyond the scope of this chapter; like his vision of capitalist evolution, it is a work of creative destruction, written with the audacity and vigour which he attributes to his hero entrepreneurs.

SUMMARY OF THE AUSTRIAN SCHOOL

World View

Individual purposive human action, with incomplete knowledge.
Processes through time.

Values

Libertarian. Not known for their concern for others' welfare.
Opponents of comprehensive economic planning.
Suspicion of government's motives and capabilities.

Goals

Systematic exploration of economic activity.
Implications and consequences of human needs and human action.
Explanation rather than prediction.

Methodological Practice

Methodological issues are regarded as very important.
Methodological individualism.
The deduction of a continuous chain of causation.
Very systematic and rigorous.
Theories are essential precursors of empirical studies; abstraction.
Deductivism, subjectivism (introspection), *a priorism*.
Anti-mathematical formalism.

Criteria

Impeccable logic.

Hard Core

Subjective needs, perception and knowledge – data not publicly available.
Individual purposeful spontaneous human action to meet needs, known thoroughly to individual (only), and its consequences.
Other knowledge, re action, can be accurate or incomplete or erroneous.
The future is uncertain. Environment changes continually.

Processes are not deterministic.
Economics includes unintended consequences.

Concepts

Needs, goods, economic goods, value in use, opportunity cost, capital
and time, exchange, commodities, marketability, transactions costs,
intermediary of exchange.

Positive Heuristic (Agenda)

How do custom and practice evolve historically?
How are economic activities coordinated?
Demonstrate that a large number of independent, self-interested
decision makers constitute a coherent economic system.

Themes

1. Individual purposive action to meet needs (rationality).
2. Knowledge (of skills and circumstances):
   – problematic, difficult to transfer, incomplete, out-of-date,
   – uncertainty re future,
   – human beings able to discern causal relationships.
   – important factors are often beyond their control.
3. Capital (heterogeneous) and time (irreversible):
   – complex structures of production, time scale of adjustment,
   – process of change, expectations, planning by individuals.
4. Process (means), rather than outcomes (ends) or equilibrium states:
   – how economic activity is continuously coordinated,
   – role of entrepreneur, and knowledge,
   – concept of general equilibrium mainly avoided (does not explain
     anything),
   – dynamic processes of disequilibrium.
5. Interaction of individuals through markets:
   – little interest in organizational behaviour,
   – markets studied, but not perfect competition.
6. Money, credit and trade cycles:
   – the importance of interest rates as a factor for coordination, or
     disruption, of production – and for economic progress.
   – Hayek: trade cycles based on monetary failure.
   – Schumpeter: trade cycle is mechanism for progress (creative
     destruction).

7. Planning and welfare:
    – serious flaws in planners' information;
    – government intervention is likely to reduce welfare.

Evidence

Early work based on introspective evidence for axioms.
Later work prepared to expose consequences to external empirical testing.

Conclusions (examples)

Economic activity is not deterministic.
The future cannot be forecast.
Money is an unintended consequence (a social institution), of the satisfaction of human needs.
Central planning is not superior to market processes.
Growth of knowledge is the principal cause of economic progress.
Welfare is not the same as wealth.

4. The Neoclassical School

J.M. Alec Gee

There can be no doubt that the neoclassical school of economics is the dominant school of economics in the western world. University courses that major in economics are overwhelmingly grounded on neoclassical principles, especially for microeconomics. In fact, the orthodox economist would regard the type of economics taught as being definitive, rather than as belonging to a particular school among alternative equally valid schools. The neoclassical school is a broad church, offering a methodology and paradigm embracing many sects. The high priests of the church are well versed in mathematical technique, which they employ to trace out the consequences of individual behaviour on the assumption that economic agents constantly strive to maximize their economic well-being. These agents may not be, indeed typically are not, regarded as flesh and blood actors; they are mythical creations, designed so that their behaviour is perfectly predictable according to a hypothetico-deductive chain of reasoning. On the other hand, neoclassical economists would claim that: first, though the behaviour patterns assumed of these invented individuals, the economic *agents*, may not at all reflect the rich complexity of inconsistencies and uncertainties of human behaviour, yet the maximizing assumption recognizes one very important component of such behaviour, so that the conclusions reached are of practical relevance; second, only a rigorous methodological approach, as exemplified by mathematical techniques, can ensure that the conclusions reached are not logically erroneous.

The assumed one-dimensionality of the behaviour of economic agents, and the narrow selection of forces determining such behaviour, does not necessarily imply that neoclassical economists are theorists only, with the phenomena exhibited by the real world always regarded as an irrelevance. Historic events are used to check, where possible, theoretical models, and theory is employed in attempts to forecast the future.

The purpose of the few comments above is to give some idea both of the limited scope and the generality of neoclassical economics. Its

limited scope stems from its *a priori* deductive methodology; its generality stems from the lack of detail in the specification of its *a priori*
assumptions, which can often be appropriately modified in order to
analyse specific theoretical or empirical problems.

   The beautiful but sometimes very complex structures associated with
neoclassical economics are all derived, in one way or another, by
tracing out the logical consequences of individuals behaving so as to
maximize utility. This methodological procedure did not spring from
nowhere, and reflects both an implicit ethical stance and assumptions
about the correct method of scientific inquiry. To appreciate some of
the reasons why neoclassical economics takes its present-day form, it
is necessary to consider the history of the individualistic ethic and the
development of modes of scientific inquiry.

ORIGINS

The Ethos of Individualism

A necessary condition for the successful development of neoclassical
economics has been that the maximization of utility by individuals –
according to individuals' own assessment of their well-beings – has
become regarded as, at the least, ethically neutral or, more usually,
ethically desirable. This ethical stance is fundamental to the Western
democratic or liberal tradition.

   The validity of this ethic may seem almost self-evident, and indeed
some present-day neoclassicists would claim that their work has
nothing to do with ethics. Consider, however, whether it would have
been possible for a thinker of feudal Europe sensibly to propose a
research programme and paradigm for societal analysis based on the
egoistic principle. An important characteristic of feudal society was its
acceptance of the hierarchical order. The idea that a serf, say, should
have the freedom to order his affairs in a manner best suited to
himself, and perhaps rise through the societal ranks, would not only
have been regarded as odd, but also as blasphemous. In any case, the
teachings of the Roman Catholic Church tended to denigrate worldly
happiness, except in so far as leading a holy and ascetic life gives
spiritual contentment. Money making and wealth accumulation were
regarded with grave suspicion, as likely to corrupt and damn the soul.
The acceptance of the necessity for authority, order and hierarchy in
society was perfectly matched by the mode of philosophical and moral
inquiry. In determining such inquiry, the 'facts' appealed to were in

the writings of Aristotle, the Bible and the Divines. Complex chains of reasoning, which made much use of analogy and almost none whatsoever of recorded experience and empiricism, connected the writings of authority to provide definitive statements, the disputation of which could very well be heretical.

The foundations of the feudal order were slowly undermined by a synergy of economic, technological, political and philosophic factors. The Renaissance betokened a new approach to knowledge, one based on experimentation, observation and hypothesis, unrestricted by appeal to religious authority. The development of the longbow and gunpowder took away some of the *raison d'être* of the armoured knight. The increasing significance of trade and manumission of rents and personal services weakened the feudal links of direct obligation and custom. At the same time, the political influence and power of the merchant classes increased. The Reformation gave rise to different sects of Protestantism which stressed sobriety and prudence, and for which the accumulation of wealth indicated not only laudable individual traits but also God's favour. Many such sects saw the relationship between man and God as a personal matter enjoining self-discipline in the pursuit of salvation, rather than as a relationship that could only be defined and guided by a priest through the authority of the Church.

The enhanced status of individual conscience and greater freedom in economic life are not sufficient in themselves to explain the success of the neoclassical approach. Connections still need to be made between individual values and social values, and individual behaviour and social outcomes. These essential connections were predominantly made during the seventeenth and eighteenth centuries. On the moral and political philosophy side, we see a development from Hobbes, Mandeville, Locke, Hume and Smith, in which selfish 'passions' were not only seen to be morally neutral or laudable (especially prudence, which is concerned with future economic well-being) but socially desirable as well in the allocation of resources. Moreover, the growth of commerce was seen as a restraining factor in the arbitrary power of kings, as they came more and more to depend on the wealth generated by the natural working of the economy as determined by people behaving according to their self-interest.

The working of unfettered markets was seen to coordinate the attempts of divers individuals to maximize their economic well-being, given the objective opportunities open to them. The idea of equilibrium, in which supplies equalled demands to produce a social optimum, became paramount. There was a balanced harmony between individual and social welfare, which was very closely analogous to the harmony and predictability of the movement of the planets as explained by Newton's gravitational principle. So scientific inquiry in the natural sciences, moral and political philosophy, all marched together to demonstrate the beauty and beneficence of the workings of natural forces. Notice that the Divine Author is now manifest by the working of the natural universe He created, so there is nothing that cannot be reconciled with many versions of Christianity.

The Meaning of Utility

Many economists who regard themselves as neoclassicists would deny that their analyses of utility maximization by economic agents carry any normative implications, meaning a value judgement of what *ought* to be rather than what *is*. Such economists would regard themselves as *positivists*, restricted to analysing the actual behaviour of individuals and the economic outcomes of such behaviour. The desirability of alternative economic policies is seen as governed by moral considerations, as manifest by political decisions. The economist's role is simply to try to predict the economic outcomes of such decisions, not pronounce on the desirability of alternative policies.

Such a position cannot be entirely well founded. We are all conditioned to some degree by the ethos of the society in which we live. Consider the nature of the advice given by the neoclassicist when consulted as an expert by the policy maker. The economic expert will outline the likely results of alternative policies; but even if he regards himself as a positivist, these results are almost invariably predicated on the assumption that individuals maximize their utilities subject to the alternative policies, and so must be couched in terms of comparative utilities. Very often, he will compare likely outcomes according to net benefit as measured in money terms, where money is taken as a proxy for utility. Thus, even if the economist does not state overtly which policy he thinks should be undertaken, his analysis can carry a strong presumption as to which is *prima facie* the most desirable. And, of course, if economic analysis is totally devoid of normative implications, the economist will have very little persuasive power in the political decision-making process and suffer in social status accordingly. So, there is always an impulse to *advise*, which is normative, as well as to analyse. In so far as neoclassicists are intimately concerned with 'utility maximization', neoclassical economics must carry with it normative overtones. We need then to inquire what is meant by utility and to do so an historical perspective is useful.

The term 'utility', as used by neoclassical economists, denotes a subjective evaluation of: a thing; or a bundle of things; or a set of circumstances generally (a *social state*), by an individual who consumes such things or finds himself placed in a particular social state. There are two major emphases in the development of utility analysis by economists: the first is concerned with societal welfare and has overtly normative arguments; and the second with the relationship between subjective utility and exchange value. The first area of concern almost always employs the analysis of the second, but the analysis of the relationship between utility and exchange value sometimes has but tenuous connection with social welfare.

Utilitarianism is a moral philosophy based on individual utilities. Its social prescriptions are based on the assumption that the most desirable social objective is to maximize the 'sum total' of happiness. This sum total is arrived at by adding up all the pleasures experienced by all the individuals in society and deducting from them all the pains experienced. We stress here that not even the most naive and crude utilitarian would think for a moment that such a calculation could actually be made. As Jeremy Bentham, usually regarded as the founder of utilitarianism, put it, 'This addability of the happiness of different subjects,' however, when considered rigorously, it may appear fictitious, is a *postulatum* without the allowance of which all practical reasoning is at a stand . . .'.

Two important features of this social philosophy should be noted. The first is that what is important is each individual's own evaluation of utility, not idealistic notions imposed from without of what the individual's utility evaluation should be. The second is, that despite the reformist nature of utilitarianism, which supports institutional reforms that result in an increase in happiness, any reformist programme is initially based on the status quo. This tends to impart a gradualist rather than revolutionary impetus to reform. There is a contrast between this approach and that which may be suggested by the *social contract* approach to desirable social organization, which lends itself more readily to abrupt social change. As we shall see below, the utilitarian approach pervades much of contemporary neoclassical welfare economics.

As noted above, the other aspect of utility analysis emphasized by neoclassicists is the relationship between utility and exchange value. It was the development of this branch of analysis that initiated the neoclassical break with the classical school of economics. Critical attacks were made during the first half of the nineteenth century by some authors against what they took to be the underlying premise of orthodox British economic analysis, i.e. the Ricardian proposition that the value of any commodity depended on the labour expended in its production, and that labour was the *only* value measure, so that the relative values can only be arrived at by comparing the labour content of different commodities.

The earliest critic of the Ricardian approach was Jean-Baptiste Say, who quite clearly identified value with utility, of which price is the measure, and argued that commodity prices in turn give value to the factors of production and, hence, determine production costs. Samuel Bailey, perhaps the most influential of the early Ricardian critics, took the starting point that value, in any ultimate sense, is a purely psychological phenomenon, and denotes the 'esteem' placed by an individual upon any object. As individuals are different in tastes, the search for an absolute or intrinsic value measure is chimerical. This means that values can only be measured in *relative* not *absolute* terms. In equilibrium, relative exchange values merely reflect the relative evaluations of the goods held by the parties to exchange.

Those classical economists who may be regarded as Ricardian understood the elements of supply and demand theory, and appreciated that utility was a precondition for goods to have value. But their concern was with the long run, and if one takes the view that the vast bulk of commodities are produced under long-run constant costs, then relative prices will indeed be determined by costs of production, and the only role for utility and demand is to determine the quantities of goods produced.

To look at exchange values from the point of view of relative subjective utilities, and to seek for interdependencies between utilities in consumption and costs in production, is to take a very different standpoint from that which seeks to explain relative or absolute values in terms only of costs of production or labour content. The 'marginal revolution', which gave rise to the neoclassical school of economics, took utility as its starting point. Though it has been fashionable to claim that there was no 'revolution', that all the component parts of the neoclassical paradigm existed alongside classical economics, and that in any case classical economics was never truly monolithic, homogenous or dominant, yet there was at the very least a *gestalt* shift between the classical view and the pioneers of the neoclassical. Certainly, the early proponents of the new neoclassical view, Jevons (1871, 1970), Menger (1871, 1981) and Walras (1874, 1877) regarded themselves as revolutionary.

The plan of what follows is, first, to give an account of the neoclassical theory of pure exchange, which is entirely utility-driven; then to proceed to neoclassical general equilibrium theory; this will be followed by neoclassical welfare economics; then on to neoclassical market structure theory. Following this, some relations between neoclassical theory and current macroeconomics will be offered. We conclude with a brief summary.

THE NEOCLASSICAL THEORY OF PURE EXCHANGE

The contributions of Francis Edgeworth and Léon Walras underpin much of the modern-day neoclassical exchange analysis. Edgeworth's interest in economics stemmed largely from his utilitarian philosophy, and today he is widely regarded as the 'neoclassicist's neoclassicist'. We shall concentrate immediately below on that part of his analysis of exchange (as set forth in his *Mathematical Psychics*, 1881) in which he assumes 'every agent is actuated only by self interest'.

In his analysis, Edgeworth set out to generalize and improve on Jevons, his friend and fellow utilitarian, and Walras, whose device of the 'auctioneer' (which we shall further treat below) attracted his adverse criticism. In essence, Jevons's analysis of trading bodies described a barter exchange equilibrium, given an imposed rate of exchange. Jevons's analysis of the process by which a unique exchange rate would be reached was left very obscure. Edgeworth, on the other hand, demonstrated how a *range* of equilibrium trading positions may be identified. He initially assumed there to be two individuals, A and B, and started by considering the *total* utility of each derived from the consumption of two commodities. Also, whereas Jevons assumed that the consumer's utility derived from the consumption of good x was independent of the quantity consumed of good y, Edgeworth's formulation of the utility functions allowed the utilities to be *interdependent.* Hence, we may write:

$$U^A = U^A (x,y) \tag{1}$$
$$U^B = U^B (x,y) \tag{2}$$

Edgeworth, in the same spirit as Jevons, assumed that an increase in, say, x for A or B, holding the amount consumed of y constant, would increase total utility, but the increments of utility would fall with successive (equal) small increases in x, and similarly for y. (Formally, the assumption is that the total utility functions are *continuous and concave*.)

Given these assumptions, we can see that if, say, A consumes given

Figure 4.1   Indifference curves

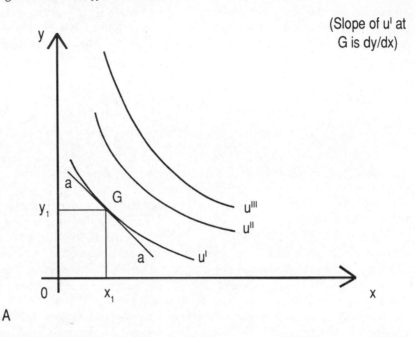

quantities of x and y, he will enjoy a particular level of utility. If some x is now taken away from him, and if his level of utility is to remain the same he must be compensated with extra y. Evidently, we can identify different combinations of x and y for A such that A attains a given utility level. These combinations give what is known as a contour of A's utility function, called an *indifference* curve. Indifference curves are shown in Figure 4.1, which is essentially the same as presented by Edgeworth.

Suppose, in the figure, A started off with x_1 of x and y_1 of y. This combination of x and y gave him a total utility of U'. The curve U' shows all the combinations of x and y which would yield the same utility for A. The curve is convex to the origin because of the assumptions made about the form of the total utility function. The other U curves show different utility levels, which are higher the further they are from the origin (again because of the assumptions made above about the form of the utility function). The *slope* of an indifference curve at any point is the 'marginal rate of substitution' of one good for the other. Thus, in Figure 4.1, dy/dx is the marginal rate of substitution of y for x at the consumption point G.

Now for the crucial bargaining assumptions made by Edgeworth. He assumed:

1 that no individual would be a party to exchange unless he ends up being at least as well off after the exchange as he was before the exchange;
2 two individuals would agree to exchange if it made at least one of them better off without making the other worse off.

To see how these assumptions allowed Edgeworth to define a *range* of possible exchange equilibria, suppose that the two individuals, A and B, start off with given quantities of x and y, x_e and y_e, distributed between them as follows:

$$x_e = x_e^A + x_e^B$$

and

$$y_e = y_e^A + y_e^B$$

These totals can be shown in the 'box' diagram, Figure 4.2, which combines the indifference curve maps of A and B, with the origin for B's map being at the top right-hand corner. The pre-trade division is shown at e in Figure 4.2, and the utilities of A and B are U_e^A and U_e^B respectively. Clearly, at any point in the box where the indifference curves of A and B cross each other the Edgeworthian trading assumptions above are not satisfied, because at such a point an exchange of x for y could make at least one individual better off without making the other worse off. Only for points at which the indifference curves of the individuals are tangential to each other is it true that further trade cannot make one individual better off *without* making the other worse off (remember that the curves represent higher levels of utility the further away they are from the individual's origins).

This implies that a post-trade distribution must: lie within the lens-shaped area enclosed by the pre-trade indifference curves, U_e^A and U_e^B (otherwise one of the parties would be worse off); and lie on that locus of points for which the indifference curves are tangential (otherwise the utility of at least one individual could be increased without a reduction in that of the other). Since the slope of an indifference curve at any point gives the marginal rate of commodity substitution (MRCS) of one good for the other, and since these slopes are common to the individuals for all equilibrium trade positions, it follows that in equilibrium A's and B's MRCSs of y for x must be equal.

Figure 4.2   Edgeworth Box showing core and contract curve

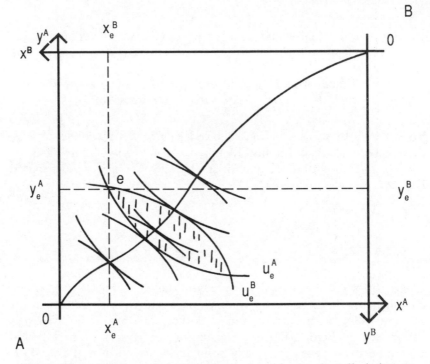

This locus of points within the lens-shaped area is called the *core*, and the locus of all the points of tangency is called the *contract curve*. It is impossible to exaggerate the significance of these two concepts for the neoclassical paradigm, and in fact it is only relatively recently that the importance of Edgeworth's work has come to be fully appreciated, especially for bargaining and game theory.

Walras was another of the principal architects of the marginal revolution and his chief claim to fame is as the pioneer of rigorous general equilibrium analysis. Though not strictly in the Walrasian spirit, we shall illustrate Walras's exchange analysis using Edgeworth's diagrammatic techniques.

In Figure 4.3, we show A's indifference map and assume that he has an initial endowment of x and y as indicated by point e in the figure. The slopes of the lines from e show hypothetical rates of exchange of y for x along which A could trade. Thus, if A starts with, say $100x$ and $50y$ at e, and the rate of exchange offered is $2y$ for $1x$, then A can exchange y for x (or x for y) as he pleases at that rate. The actual exchange chosen by A is assumed to be such as to maximize

Figure 4.3   A's indifference map and offer locus

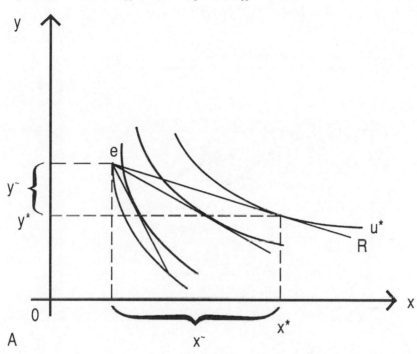

his utility. This will occur when he exchanges along the line until he reaches the highest attainable indifference curve. At that exchange point, the rate of exchange line must be tangential to this (unique) indifference curve, because of the assumptions made with respect to the form of the utility function. Hence, for the R exchange rate shown in the figure, A will exchange $\tilde{y}$ of y for $\tilde{x}$ of x to end up with y^* of y and x^* of x and so reach the highest possible attainable utility level U^*.

At A's original position e in the figure, given the exchange rate R, A is said to have a negative excess demand of $\tilde{y}$ for y (because he desires to reduce his stock of y at that exchange rate) and a positive excess demand of $\tilde{x}$ for x (because that is the quantity by which he would add to his stock of x). Notice that if we measure the *exchange value* of A's positive and negative excess demands, using either commodity as a *numeraire* (that is, unit or measure of value) the sum of these demands would be zero. Thus, A's exchange value, in terms of y, is

Figure 4.4   Indifference curve maps of A *and* B *showing excess demands given exchange rate* R

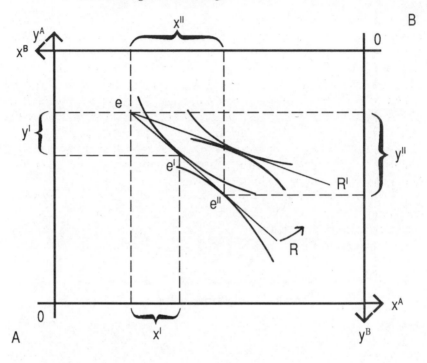

$$- \tilde{y} + \tilde{x}.\ dy/dx = 0.$$

The locus of desired trading points for different exchange rates from *e* is known as *A*'s offer curve, every point on which is an equilibrium exchange point for *A* at that rate of exchange.

In Figure 4.4 we follow the same procedure as for Figure 4.2, that is, we combine the two indifference maps of *A* and *B* and show the initial distribution of goods *x* and *y* between the two individuals at *e*. Take the rate of exchange *R* in the figure. At this rate of exchange *A* would be in exchange equilibrium at *e'* and *B* at *e''*. Thus, *A* would wish to exchange *y'* of *y* for *x'* of *x*, and *B*, *x''* of *x* for *y''* of *y*. Adding up the excess demands for *x* and *y* we see that there is a net negative excess demand for *x* (i.e. the market is over-supplied with *x* at that exchange rate) and a net positive excess demand for *y* (i.e. more is demanded of *y* by *B* than is supplied by *A*). To put the same thing slightly differently, the total amounts of *y* that *A* and *B* wish to hold after exchange is more than the initial endowment of *y*, and the total amount they wish to hold of x is less than the initial endowment. Clearly, the particular exchange rate shown is not a market equilibrium rate.

Walras then hypothesized that there was an 'auctioneer', whose role it is to adjust the relative prices of the goods, in this case to increase the relative price of those goods in net positive excess demand, and reduce the price of those goods in net negative excess demand. In the case shown in Figure 4.4, this would mean the exchange rate line would swivel more to the horizontal. In the diagram, when the exchange rate is R', then A's negative excess demand for y exactly equals B's positive excess demand for y, and B's negative excess demand for x exactly equals A's positive excess demand for x. The quantities of x and y offered or supplied exactly equals the quantities demanded. We are in exchange equilibrium.

We have spent some time on the origins and nature of neoclassical exchange theory because almost all later work in this field may be regarded as the development of Walrasian and Edgeworthian analysis.

GENERAL EQUILIBRIUM

For the neoclassicist, an individual is in economic equilibrium when, given the commodity prices he faces, given his ownership of factors of production and their prices, given his initial endowments in general, he cannot increase his utility through altering the mix of products bought or factor services supplied to others.

But the economy is made up of a large number of individuals and firms, and the general equilibrium theorist, therefore, asks two questions of the economy as a whole:

1. Is there a theoretical price configuration for all goods and services, from, say, bananas for final consumption, to steel used as an input (a factor of production) in the production process, such that *none* of the economic agents (individuals or firms) could increase their utilities through further trade, that is, supplies equal demands in all markets? Such a state is known as a general equilibrium.
2. If there is such a theoretical price configuration, can general equilibrium be attained, that is, are the price adjustments in the market likely to move towards it; and would the general equilibrium state be stable?

These concerns on the part of the neoclassicist cannot be regarded as slight. If it cannot be shown theoretically that a general equilibrium price configuration will always exist, and that a general equilibrium can be attained and maintained, *through free exchange between individuals* under reasonable assumptions, then it can hardly be shown that a spontaneous, harmonious, economic and social order is possible (let alone likely!). Recall the remarks made at the beginning of this chapter concerning the stress on individualism and the libertarian philosophical background to neoclassical economics.

The Existence of a General Equilibrium Price Configuration

Consider first the equilibrium positions of the individuals who make up society. They start off with given endowments of goods and factors of production. If the individual is to be in equilibrium, it must be the case that for any set of prices (for both goods and factors) his total market expenditures in the goods markets must equal his total receipts from his sales of goods and factors to the markets. (We have already established this proposition in the last section.) Total desired expenditures may be measured either in terms of x or y – that is, we can take any commodity to be the unit of account or, in Walras's terminology, the *numeraire*.

As the sum of the value of excess demands for any one individual must always be zero for individual equilibrium, the aggregate of the sums for *all* the individuals must also equal zero, *for any set of prices*.

Now consider the *firms* that transform factors into market goods. They buy the factors from individuals and then sell the outputs produced from the factor combinations in the product markets. It simplifies matters if we assume that firms just break even, that is their receipts equal their expenditures – the formal inclusion of 'normal' profit makes no real difference to the analysis. We may regard this state of affairs as being brought about by new entry of firms competing away positive profit, and if firms make a loss they will exit from the industry concerned.

As each firm's expenditures equal its receipts, it must follow that the sum of expenditures must equal the sum of receipts for all the firms taken together. That is, exactly analogous to individuals, the value of excess demands of the firms (positive for factors, negative for sales) equals zero if firms are to be in equilibrium.

Now, if we add up the values of the total excess demands for both individuals and firms taken together it must follow that this sum is also zero. Once again, we stress that this must be true for individuals' desired equilibria *for any set of prices*. This overall result, that the sum of the value of all excess demands equals zero is known as Walras's Law, in honour of its discoverer. Walras's Law is crucial to the proof of general equilibrium.

For general equilibrium, we require that the excess demand for *each and every* traded good and factor be equal to zero, that is, the market supply of, say, bananas must equal its market demand, so that its market excess demand is zero. Suppose that for a given price configuration some items are in overall positive excess demand (as we discussed earlier). Given that prices cannot be negative, by Walras's Law this must imply that other items are in negative excess demand. If we choose a different price configuration, then we would obtain a different configuration of positive and negative excess demands for the goods and factors. If we can change our price configurations *continuously*, and if this yields a continuously changing set of excess demands, then 'it can be shown that' there exists a *particular* price configuration that results in the excess demands for each and every good and factor to be equal to precisely zero. This is then the price configuration for which all individuals are in equilibrium, and their desired and actual sales and purchases are such that all the markets for goods and factors are in equilibrium – that is, market demand everywhere equals market supply.

The proof of the existence of a general equilibrium price configuration rests upon: the application of Brouwer's fixed point theorem, which requires a continuous 'mapping' from relative prices to excess demands (as if by a Walrasian auctioneer); and the operation of Walras's Law, which implies that relative prices can be 'normalized', so that the price of each good is expressed in terms of how much it can buy of each and every other good. This gives a set of relative prices which is 'closed', 'bounded' and 'convex', terms which describe its mathematical properties.

One can see that, from the general conceptual point of view, very little has been added to our earlier discussion of the neoclassical theory of pure exchange. The only difference is that individuals now also supply factors of production to firms who transform them into market commodities. So the number of markets that must be in equilibrium has increased.

The Attainment and Stability of General Equilibrium

Though 'it can be shown that' a general equilibrium price configuration exists, there remains the question as to whether general equilibrium can be attained. Suppose the economy starts off with a non-equilibrium set of relative prices. We have seen that in this situation Walras hypothesized an 'auctioneer' whose role was to increase the prices of goods in positive excess demand relative to those in excess supply. Walras considered that such price movements in fact mimicked the behaviour of real-world markets, in particular those in which no one individual had any influence on price because of the smallness of his own transactions as compared with the markets as a whole.

In the previous section we have seen that such price variation *could* result in exchange equilibrium. But the indifference maps there are specific in terms of their utility contours, and perhaps maps could be drawn for which an equilibrium cannot be attained or, if attained, is unstable. In general, a sufficient condition for commodity equilibrium to be stable in a Walrasian world is that goods are gross substitutes for each other, such that there will be an increase in the excess demand for some good when there is a decrease in its relative price. Let us see what can happen if this gross substitutability condition is not met.

Suppose there is a positive excess demand for margarine. In an attempt to regain market equilibrium, the 'auctioneer' raises the relative price of margarine. But this increases the wealth (the exchange value of the initial endowment) of the margarine holders, and the excess demand for margarine may *rise*. Here the positive effect that wealth or income has upon quantity demanded has outweighed the negative effect that the increase in price of a commodity has upon the amount demanded. In this case the behaviour of the 'auctioneer', and maybe that of real markets, is such as to cause the markets to move further away from equilibrium instead of returning them to it.

Thus, the possibility exists that the Walrasian 'auctioneer', starting from a non-equilibrium set of prices, may cause the market to move further away from equilibrium. Moreover, if an equilibrium set of prices happens to be achieved, any slight deviation from it may cause the 'auctioneer' to initiate price changes that move markets further and further away from equilibrium.

General equilibrium analysis has been much influenced by the Walrasian approach. In particular, his treatment of individuals as *price takers*, which implies perfectly competitive commodity markets, and the assumption that firms make no (or 'normal') profit, which implies competitive factor markets and freedom of entry into all industries, has largely dominated general equilibrium analysis. Notice that the Edgeworthian approach does not depend so much on price-taking assumptions, and on that ground may be considered more general; on the other hand, equilibrium analysis becomes correspondingly more difficult.

General equilibrium analysis is the cornerstone of neoclassical economics. We turn now to the neoclassical approach to welfare economics, which shows that Walrasian general equilibrium is *consistent* with societal economic welfare maximization.

NEOCLASSICAL WELFARE ECONOMICS

Neoclassical economics is arguably at its most elegant in welfare analysis, even though the practical import of its conclusions has proved disappointing. In previous sections, constant reference has been made to optimality in exchange and resource allocation and to individuals' optima being consistent with — indeed necessary for — the social optimum. As may be expected, the individualistic ethic is at the heart of neoclassical welfare economics, and the two typical basic assumptions made are that the individual is the best judge of his own welfare, and the individual is rational, in the sense that he has a consistent ranking of alternative economic states (environments) in order of preference to him (the *transitivity* assumption). The condition that must be met for social welfare to be maximized in a neoclassical world is that no one individual can be made better off without making another individual worse off. This condition for welfare maximizing is known as the Pareto welfare criterion, after Vilfredo Pareto (1906). Pareto's procedure was first to determine what consumption and production patterns would satisfy his criterion. He then went on to show that a particular institutional ideal, that of perfect competition, met his criterion – that is, in a perfectly competitive economy no one can be made better off without making someone else worse off.

The Pareto criterion is not only simple, but appears entirely reasonable if one accepts the status quo implication with respect to the distribution of resources. Clearly, unless it is satisfied, total welfare can be increased, and for this reason the criterion is closely related to the idea of *efficiency*. Hence the criterion is often referred to as the 'Pareto-efficient criterion'.

Pareto efficiency has long been a major concern in economic thought. For example, it is quite clear that Adam Smith believed a smoothly working freely competitive economy would be Pareto-efficient though, of course, he was not able to prove it in a formal mathematical sense. Edgeworth's contract curve is Pareto-efficient, and Edgeworth defined the mathematical properties of the curve.

Pareto extended this analysis to the general equilibrium system pioneered by Walras.

Earlier we explored the neoclassical theory of pure exchange, and defined an exchange equilibrium as a state where each agent was in individual equilibrium, and the quantities of x and y offered or supplied exactly equalled the quantities demanded. In equilibrium, the agents' marginal rate of commodity substitution of one good for another must be equal. Edgeworth's assumption, that two individuals would agree to exchange if it made at least one of them better off without making the other worse off, means that it is a Pareto-efficient exchange.

The conditions that must be met for Pareto-efficient production are very similar. Consider: if the output of one good can be increased through a transfer of factors of production between industries without reducing the output of some other good, then unambiguously more goods can be produced by society. But, if society can produce more goods at no greater sacrifice, this must mean that some individual could be made better off without making some other individual worse off.

We can utilize, by strict analogy, our analysis of Edgeworthian efficient exchange to derive the necessary conditions for efficient production. Instead of the utility of individuals A and B, we are now concerned with the output levels of goods x and y. Let us assume that two factors of production are employed in x and y production: capital (K) and labour (L). Then we can construct *isoquants* from the two production functions, $x = x(K,L)$ and $y = y(K,L)$, for x and y. These isoquants are analogous to indifference curves, except that each isoquant represents a specific output of x (or y) that can be achieved by various combinations of K and L in x (or y) production. The locus of points through the isoquants of a production function where their slopes are the same is called the efficiency locus. The slopes of the isoquants, (dL/dK), are termed the marginal rates of substitution of labour for capital in each industry, and must be common between industries for efficient production.

Given the efficiency loci for x and y, for common marginal rates of substitution of labour and capital, we know the various combinations of x and y that can be produced efficiently for fixed levels of the factors K and L. This same information can be expressed as a production possibility frontier, PPF, as shown in Figure 4.5.

The slope of the PPF gives the marginal rate of transformation of one good into another. It is convex from the origin because of convenient assumptions (from the point of view of mathematical tracta-

Figure 4.5 Production possibility frontier

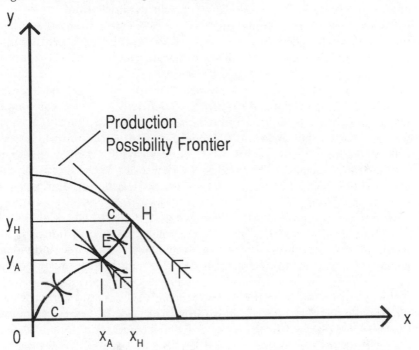

bility) usually made about the production functions, e.g. that there are diminishing returns to scale and diminishing marginal physical productivities of factors of production.

Suppose that society produces x_H and y_H at point H on the production possibility frontier. x_H and y_H may be regarded as society's *endowments* of the two goods. From these endowments and consumer preferences we can construct an Edgeworth contract curve, and this is shown as cc in Figure 4.5. Point E on the contract curve shows a particular distribution of x_H and y_H between individuals A and B, such that A gets x_A and y_A, and B gets $x_H - x_A$ and $y_H - y_A$. The line through E, tangential to A's and B's indifference curves, gives the common marginal rate of substitution of x for y for A and B, and this, as we know, gives the common relative marginal valuations of the goods by the consumers. *As drawn*, the marginal rate of substitution of the goods in consumption is equal to the marginal rate of transformation of the goods in production.

Suppose that this were *not* the case – suppose, say, that both individuals value $1x$ at $3y$ but only $1y$ need be sacrificed to produce $1x$.

Clearly, the consumers would increase their utilities if the production of x were increased, because each x produces more utility than each y. Hence one, or both, individuals could be made better off without the other being made worse off. Overall Pareto efficiency can only be met, and social welfare maximized, if the marginal rate of substitution equals the marginal rate of transformation.

This elegant analysis can readily be extended into a general equilibrium model. Pareto showed that free enterprise of a capitalistic mode, so long as there is *perfect competition*, meets his criterion. To show this, and for ease of exposition, let us assume the economy is monetized. We have already seen how free exchange between individuals can secure efficiency in exchange, so that price ratios between the commodities equal their marginal rates of substitution. Let us now turn to the production side.

In perfect competition, the factor markets are freely open to all firms and no one firm has any appreciable influence on the price of factors, because each firm's demand is negligible as compared to total demand for any factor. Hence, all firms will pay the same price for any like factor of production. Moreover, the rates of return for like factors must be the same for all the firms in the economy and between different industries, because any differences will be competed away through entry or exit of firms to or from industries. Also, in perfect competition no firm has any influence on the price of the product it produces and sells. It can be shown that, given these assumptions, the marginal rate of transformation between any pair of goods in production is equal to the marginal rate of substitution of those goods in consumption.

Suppose that such were not the case. Suppose that, to the contrary, x is rated more highly in consumption than it costs to produce in terms of y. If y production breaks even, the price of x must be such that abnormal profits are made in x production; hence, there will be a shift of factors to x production until equality between the marginal rates of substitution and transformation is achieved. In so far as individual factor rewards are concerned, so long as factors are perfectly mobile between industries, and so long as labour effort and saving are voluntary in the sense that the quantities supplied depend on the prices offered, then the perfectly competitive system will also ensure the optimal factor quantities supplied.

Once again, one cannot help but be impressed by this elegant analysis. But, at best, it can only reflect some possible tendencies in the real world. It may be that the economy does behave, in *broad* outline, according to the competitive model, and does reasonably well in harmonizing individual behaviour. But markets are by no means perfect: for example, there are rigidities in labour hours worked and pay received; there are monopolistic tendencies in industry; there is much less than perfect information. Even if these, and other, factors are not very important, the free enterprise market system does not take either public goods or production and consumption externalities into account.

It has long been recognized that the market cannot reflect all society's economic wants. Adam Smith, for example, recognized the administration of justice, national defence and even the provision of circuses to be public goods, in the sense that free market mechanisms would not ensure adequate supplies of such things. The modern analysis of public goods owes much to Samuelson (1954 and 1955), who may be regarded as the doyen of modern neoclassical economics.

All our analysis so far has been of private goods for which there is *rivalry in consumption*: that is, if individual *A* consumes a particular good, that same good cannot be consumed by any other individual. In the case of a public good, however, such as defence or street lighting, consumption by one individual does not deny the availability of the good for consumption by another.

Neoclassical economics tackles this problem by adding up the money measures of marginal utilities of all the individuals who consume the public good, and equating this sum with the public marginal utility. The policy proposal is that the marginal cost of providing the good (factor prices being determined in the free markets) should equal the marginal public utility of the good. So once again optimal marginal conditions are secured. The main problem here is to determine what in fact is the marginal public utility. If, for example, citizens are asked to give their money evaluations of different levels of public good provision, and think they will be taxed accordingly, there is an incentive to conceal their true preferences – especially if they reckon others will be more honest and so the good provided for at least in part. This is the so-called 'free rider' problem. Practical, but not theoretical, problems also arise when goods are hybrid, or when public good consumption also involves private good consumption.

An allied problem is that of *externalities*. Pigou (1920), Marshall's successor at Cambridge, offered the first extensive analysis, firmly in the Marshallian tradition. Externalities reflect market failure, in the sense that true costs and utilities are not reflected in competitive markets. The classical Pigovian example is that of a firm which pollutes. The firm does not pay for such pollution – these costs are borne by others. Because the firm's costs are lower than they would be had it to pay for pollution, its output will be higher than the Pareto-efficient output. Neoclassicists suggest two broad methods whereby the Pareto-efficient output could be reached. One is to tax the polluting firm so that marginal private costs are equated with marginal social cost which will in turn then be equal to the marginal social utility of the firm's product. The other is to set up a market for pollution rights. Suppose that the consumers own these rights: the producer would have to purchase from the consumers the right to pollute at alternative output levels. Suppose instead that the producer owns the rights: the consumers would have to pay the producer to restrict his output. Either way, the externality has become internalized, and the market mechanism will ensure Pareto optimality. But the initial holdings of the property rights will, of course, have distributional effects, that is, make one or other of the parties better off.

In all the above examples, neoclassical analysis successfully tackles the problem of defining the marginal conditions that must hold for Pareto optimality. Even if for some institutional reason achievement of all Pareto conditions is impossible, neoclassical analysis can still determine the 'second best' solution by imposing a further constraint on the economic welfare function to be maximized. But there is one area of welfare economics in which modern neoclassicists are powerless – that of determining the best *distribution* of welfare. One strong distributional theme stems from Adam Smith's belief that all men are innately the same, actual differences between them being the consequence of circumstance and specific upbringing. If one takes this view, together with the view that increasing wealth is subject to diminishing marginal utility (the idea that £1 to a rich man has a lower marginal utility to him than does £1 to a poor man), then social economic welfare would be maximized when income is perfectly equally distributed. Many of the early neoclassicists (including Pigou) tended to favour equal income distribution. On the other hand, if people are different, then welfare will still be maximized when marginal utility of income is equalized between individuals, but this will now entail some inequality of income. Edgeworth tended to this view. But, strictly speaking, such distributional proposals tend to imply cardinality of utility, so that different individuals' utilities can be added up to arrive at global totals. Interpersonal comparisons of this sort are by and large eschewed by modern neoclassicists.

Attempts have been made to extend the Pareto-efficient criterion to distributional questions. Thus, Kaldor (1939) suggested that a policy which affected distribution should be undertaken if the gainers could (hypothetically) compensate the losers and still be better off. Scitovsky

(1941), however, pointed to the possibility that a policy may pass Kaldor's test, yet in the new situation the losers could (hypothetically) compensate the gainers if a policy reversal were undertaken. But even for policies for which there is no such ambiguity, it is clear that such 'efficiency' arguments do not get at the heart of the problem, i.e. what should the distribution of income be? Attempts have been made to determine how a social welfare function, which includes 'right' distribution as one of its arguments, may be derived from individual preferences. Arrow (1951), following on the work by Bergson (1938), took an acceptable social welfare function to be one that (a) satisfied the Pareto criterion, (b) reflected individuals' preferences (assumed to be transitive, and hence rational), and (c) was not dictatorially imposed. He could find no rule whereby such a function could be constructed.

Thus, finally, neoclassical welfare economics has failed because of an understandable reluctance to make more than a minimal set of value judgements, that is to impose moral rules with respect to distribution other than to accept the status quo. Also, in view of the many instances of market failure, the practical relevance of imposing the Pareto criterion to specific market situations is called into doubt. Probably the best that can be done in practice is to undertake piecemeal reform in those parts of the economy which are relatively self-contained, i.e. have little interrelationship with the rest of the economy. High hopes have been dashed very low.

NEOCLASSICAL MARKET STRUCTURE THEORY

Mention has been made above of the 'firm', which is seen as an entity which transforms factors of production into commodities. The two basic and interrelated technological reasons that give rise to firms are 'indivisibilities' and economies of 'specialization'. Thus it is often the case that capital equipment such as, say, blast furnaces, must be of a certain size if metal ingots are to be produced at all. It may also be that the proportion between factor inputs and commodity output falls rapidly over some output range with the size, or 'scale' of the factor input mix. Thus, to take the blast furnace example again, heat loss and so the quantity of fuel decreases per unit of output up to some given plant scale; again, the carrying capacity of a ship increases more than in proportion to the quantity of steel for its hull or other materials required to increase the ship's size. With respect to specialization, we may recall Adam Smith's comments on the economies to be gained through the division of labour.

These technical factors however are by no means sufficient to call firms into being. Thus technical advantages could be secured if individuals struck bargains together according to the exchange analysis outlined previously, and came together in the production process. The economic reason for the existence of firms is that a supra-individual organization reduces the total of market transaction costs that would have to be met by the individuals in their coordination attempts. In other words, coordinating activities are more efficiently carried out if they are undertaken by a 'manager' or 'owner' or some similar institutional arrangement.

A key feature of the Walrasian approach to general equilibrium, as we have seen, is that individual market agents do not consider their strategic influence on price – prices are 'given' to the individuals by the 'auctioneer'. A problem with this is that, if economies of scale are significant, a large firm will be able to undercut the prices offered by a small firm, and there will be a tendency for the industrial output to be produced by one firm only. If the industry does end up with only one, or a few firms, then clearly the firm will be well aware that it has a strategic influence on the prices of factors of production and the product price. This is also true if unit costs are constant with respect to output. Even if all scale economies are exhausted at output levels for which each firm's output is a very small part of total industrial output, it still may be the case that a merger between the firms, or a buy-out of all the firms by an individual, would secure such bargaining strength in the factor markets as to violate the perfect competition assumption of zero or 'normal' profit.

These possibilities are important to the neoclassicist, for they could preclude optimal resource allocation even if there are no externalities. Though it was abundantly clear by the end of the nineteenth century that large firms had considerable market power which was used to exploit consumers and workers, neoclassical economists often wrote as though society followed the perfect competition pattern very closely, and lauded the economic performance of the capitalist system.

The long- and short-run cost structures and demand functions for a firm in equilibrium in perfect competition are shown in Figures 4.6a and 4.6b. In Figure 4.6a we see the total market supply and demand functions for the homogenous commodity X. Supply equals demand when industrial output is X_i and the market price is Pm. There are a great many firms in the industry, so no one has any influence on price. All firms just cover their total costs – if this were not so then there

Figure 4.6   Cost structures and demand functions for a firm in equilibrium in a perfect competition market

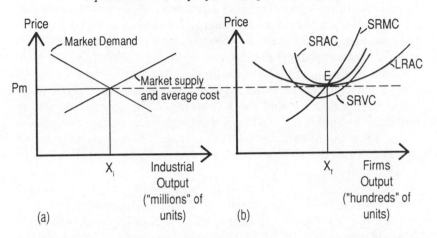

(a)   (b)

would be entry or exit of firms until just normal profits were made. Figure 4.6b represents the situation of one of the many firms in equilibrium in perfect competition markets. It faces the market price of *Pm*, and the LRAC cost curve represents lowest average costs of production at various *scales* of the firm. (Notice the 'U'-shaped assumption of the cost functions.) Clearly, the cheapest average cost at which it could produce occurs when output is X_f. For that scale, the SRVC and SRAC show the short-run average variable cost (labour and raw materials) and the short-run average costs respectively, which latter are SRVC plus necessary charges, fixed costs, for the firm's durable assets such as plant and machinery which cannot be altered in the short term. At output level X_f, the SRAC is tangential to the LRAC. At this output, short-run and long-run costs are just being covered by the price for which the commodity sells. At this output level, the firm's short-run marginal cost (SRMC) equals price equals SRAC equals LRAC. Marginal cost gives the addition to total cost that would be incurred in the short-run for a small increase in output. If this is below the price that can be obtained in the market for that output (*Pm*) then it would be in the firm's interest to increase output and sales, and thus profits, and *vice versa*. Hence the firm can only be in short-run equilibrium – which in the figure also corresponds to long-run equilibrium – if SRMC equals price.

This standard, simple neoclassical theory of the firm is supposed to be a formalization of Alfred Marshall's analysis. Marshall is recognized as being the dominant British neoclassicist of the late nineteenth and early twentieth centuries. In fact, it is so much of a caricature of Marshall's theory of the firm as to be almost unrecognizable.

Neoclassical economists have not, however, neglected the study of markets where interreactions between individual market agents have significant influence on market outcomes, whether or not the market agents are aware of their market power in this respect. As a rough guide, the distinguishing characteristics of the neoclassical theory of the firm and industry are that agents: maximize profits subject to constraints; are rational; and are well informed. Further, in the theory utility functions are exogenous; and there are many consumers of each product who are passive strategically. These characteristics may be contrasted with those mentioned in other chapters of this book, notably Chapters 3, 7, 8 and 9.

As an introduction to more modern market structure theory we will follow Cournot (1838) and suppose that firms in an industry produce a homogenous product. Each firm knows that market price will fall if it increases its supply to the market, but each firm assumes that the quantity supplied by other firms is not influenced by its own supply. This behavioural assumption, that firms do not consider the reactions of other firms in response to their own behaviour, is called *zero conjectural variation*. Thus, if there are only two firms, firm 1, say, will decide on its profit-maximizing supply given the amount supplied by firm 2, and similarly for firm 2. Each firm *reacts* in turn to the reaction of its rival, and it follows that the firms have *reaction functions*. Clearly, equilibrium occurs when it is in neither firm's interest to change own output, and the equilibrium is stable if chance departures from equilibrium cause reactions which return the market supply to equilibrium.

Figure 4.7 illustrates this model for the two-firm (duopoly) industry case. The horizontal axis gives output levels for firm 1 and the vertical for firm 2. I_{11} and I_{12} show firm 1's *isoprofit* curves, each isoprofit curve showing the different combinations of outputs of the two firms which yield a constant profit level for firm 1. Notice that the lower are Q_2 levels the greater is the maximum profit attainable by firm 1. At the extreme, if the output of firm 2 is zero, then firm 1 can earn monopoly profit of I_m.

Suppose, as in the figure, firm 2's output is Q_{21}. The highest profit that firm 1 can earn is I_{11}, achieved when it sets its output at Q_{11}. But, if firm 1's output is Q_{11}, firm 2 would maximize profits with an output of Q_{22}. In turn, firm 1 will now set output at Q_{12} and so on. E shows the position when neither firm can increase profit through a

Figure 4.7 Reaction functions for a two-firm industry case

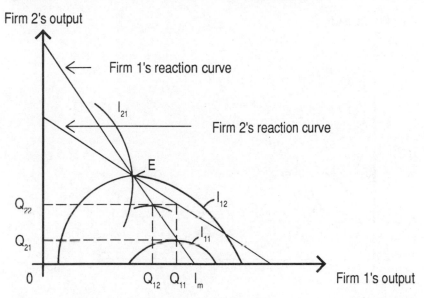

change in output, and a little thought shows that E is a stable equilibrium as the figure is drawn.

Our exposition has not formally derived the isoprofit and reaction curves from the underlying cost structures of the firms and market demand. But the model above is applicable to a wide range of cost and demand functions and can also be generalized to cover many firms. On the latter point, Cournot showed that when the number of firms becomes very large then the perfect competition solution is approached in which price equals marginal cost for all the firms. Also, we have considered quantities to be the firms' strategic variables, but other strategies may be employed instead. Price strategies, for example, especially for industries which produce heterogenous products, have received much attention in the literature. Similarly, advertising, or location, or product variation may be strategic variables for the firm. We shall stick with quantities for illustrative purposes.

The essential points to bear in mind about the zero conjectural variation class of models are: the agents do not consider the effects of own behaviour on that of others; and the firms do not *cooperate* to achieve higher profits. We shall employ the same basic framework to suggest alternative outcomes, and then proceed to cast further light on market structures by reference to neoclassical *game theory*.

In figure 4.8 we show two more possible strategies that might be

Figure 4.8   Leader/follower and cooperative strategies

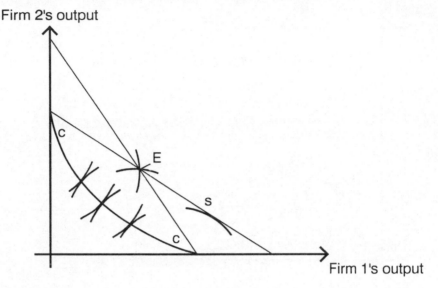

employed by the firms. First, look at point *S* in the figure. If firm 1
believes firm 2 has zero conjectural variation he will choose an output
such that, given firm 2's reaction output, his profits will be maximized.
So he chooses an output such that 2's reaction curve is tangential to
firm 1's highest isoprofit curve. We label this equilibrium position *S*
after Stackleberg (1952) who first analysed this leader/follower
strategy.

The second alternative we consider is that the firms *cooperate* in
order to maximize market profit opportunities jointly. Now we are
back in the Edgeworthian contract world, with the isoprofit contours
performing an analogous role to indifference curves in consumer
exchange theory. cc in the figure shows the range of possible cooperative outcomes. But, you may ask, what is the rule that determines the
particular point reached by cooperative firms on the contract curve?
There is an extensive and powerful literature on cooperative game
theory (important contributors include Zeuthen, (1930) and Nash,
(1953)), and for our purposes it suffices to say that the profit share-
out depends on the comparison between the *extra* profits the players
could gain through cooperation. Thus players on exactly equal footings
one with another would get equal shares.

We have now arrived at a position where each player has three
possible strategies, and we can construct an outcome or pay-off table

('matrix') that shows the pay-offs for all strategy combinations, as indicated in Table 4.1.

Table 4.1   Three-strategy matrix

		Firm 2's Strategy		
		C	S	NCV
Firm 1's	C	A,A	G,E	D,B
Strategy	S	E,G	H,H	C,F
	NCV	B,D	F,C	D,D

C, S and *NCV* are the three strategies: cooperative, Stackleberg, and non-conjectural variation respectively. The letter pairs show the pay-offs for each strategy combination for each player. Thus, if firm 1 employs strategy *S*, and firm 2 strategy *C*, then firm 1's pay-off is E and firm 2's pay-off is G, hence the E,G in column 1 row 2 of the pay-off matrix. The precise profits in pounds are not shown, but A is greater than B, B is greater than C and so on. This pay-off matrix is consistent with quantity being the strategic variable for two firms on precisely equal footing – hence the elements of symmetry in the matrix.

Now suppose that neither firm has any idea as to what strategy the other will follow, but each firm knows the outcomes for all strategy combinations – that is, just like us, each firm knows the pay-off matrix of Table 4.1. Suppose each firm wishes to maximize the minimum amount of profit he can earn. Thus, in the table, if firm 1 pursues strategy *C* he might get G at worst, if he follows *S* he might get H, but if he follows *NCV* the worst he could get is F. So his *maximin* strategy is *NCV*, which will secure him at least F. From the table, we see that if both firms are maximiners, then both will follow the *NCV* strategy and both earn D.

There are a number of insights that may be gleaned from our table. The first is that the firms could do a lot better by cooperating. Moreover, if they *do* cooperate then cooperation is likely to be stable for no firm could do better by pursuing a different strategy. But suppose, as will often be the case, especially if price is the strategic variable, that reneging on cooperation brings large (short-term) rewards. A+, to the non-cooperator. Now there is an incentive to 'cheat' and stability is weakened. Second, suppose firm 1 gets in first with the strategy *S*. Then firm 1 knows that *NCV* is now the most profitable strategy for firm 2 to follow, and it would seem that firm 1 has the advantage of firm 2. Can firm 2 do anything about this? Suppose firm 2 also threatens to follow the *S* strategy even though by so doing he would earn less than he does following NCV. In absolute terms, firm 2 can 'hurt' firm 1 by more than the self-inflicted loss borne by firm 2. So the threat may be believable and firm 1 now opts for *NCV*. All this may have been worked out by *both* firms *before* either makes the first move, so the first move may be *NCV*. Nevertheless, the important point is that the first move may be of crucial importance to final market outcome, especially when firms consider size and commitment upon entering an industry with a view to deterring further entry.

Another point to bear in mind is that the maximin assumption is very specific and open to criticism. More fundamental is that the firms are supposed to possess a remarkable degree of knowledge, and the models created both reflect this and follow very much the same fundamental neoclassical assumptions stressed above, i.e. rationality, maximization and so on.

Finally, we close this section by observing that stylized reality has been the driving force behind the construction of neoclassical market structure models that diverge from the neoclassical perfect competition paradigm. It is well to note in this context that 'contestable market structure theory', as pioneered by Baumol, Panzar and Willig (1982), reminds us that: though an industry may have but few firms, if entry and exit into the industry by other firms is costless, or nearly so, that is, if 'raids' can be made by 'fly-by-night' firms, then the firms already in the industry may be compelled to price their products at much the same levels as would perfectly competitive firms. So there being few firms need not necessarily imply a suboptimal allocation of resources.

NEOCLASSICAL ECONOMICS AND MACROECONOMICS

In perfect competition, the level of overall economic activity is determined by the preferences of rational individuals. Markets clear and there are no involuntarily unemployed factors of production. If there is imperfect competition, our section on market structure theory tells us that different behavioural strategies would have different output outcomes, so that there would be different levels of factor supply and utilization. This in turn implies that, though all markets may clear and there may be no involuntary unemployment, the degree of factor utilization may not be optimal in the Pareto sense. It would also imply that though there is no involuntary unemployment, voluntary unemployment may be high if the market wage rate is so low that many people prefer not to work. Imperfect competition, then, does not necessarily lead to involuntary unemployment. But imperfect information, especially about the future, coupled with price stickiness can, as we shall see below.

In recent years a 'new classical macroeconomic' programme has developed within the Chicago school, firmly based on neoclassical principles. It is developed more fully in Chapter 5. In its 'pure' form all markets clear and all economic agents are rational optimizers. There are, however, fluctuations in the level of economic activity because of imperfect information about present and future aggregate price levels. The basic assumptions and mechanism of this theory, based on the seminal work of Muth (1961) and Lucas (1973), are (very simply) as follows.

All owners or controllers of firms have 'rational expectations'. That is, they act *as if* they are in possession of models of the economy as good as those of professional economists. They know what the effects of their own and others' alternative plans for future output would be on the general price level, and formulate own plans so as to maximize profits. Individual profits are mainly determined by the structure of *relative* prices, and not by the absolute (general, nominal) price level. However, at any moment, they do not have complete information about the general price level; instead, they have rational-expectations-based estimates of it. These estimates depend on a model of the economy, plus information accrued in former time periods. They have full information of the prices of their own particular products, because all markets clear, so that each market is in temporary supply and demand equilibrium. But they do not have full information on other prices, which is why their estimates of the general price level may be wrong.

If there has been an unexpected shock to the general price level, which has not been picked up by the owners of the firms, then they will think that their *relative* prices have changed because of utility-driven changes in demands, for the primary information available to the owners is the level of price for their own particular products. Thus, if the general price level is higher than they believe it to be, owners will think there has been a favourable change in own relative price, and will increase output in the expectation of earning higher profits in the next time period – and *vice versa*.

In this way we can see why there are fluctuations in the demand for factors of production, even though all that might have happened was an increase in the money supply which had neutral impact, in that it did not change the relative price structure. The amplitude of the change in aggregate activity will depend on market structure detail and the degree to which ignorance prevails. Notice, though, that there is no involuntary unemployment because of the market-clearing assumption. Notice too, that if the government tries to instigate some economic policy, it should not base it on historical economic parameters (i.e. past observed strengths of response to economic variables), because our rational expectation agents will adapt their expectations, and hence responses, according to the interference in economic variables made by the government. This line can lead on to game-theoretic considerations.

Neoclassical assumptions also play an important role for the monetarists of the Chicago school (see Chapter 5). The monetarists' modelling of expectations is much simpler than that of the new classical macroeconomists' rational expectations. In general, monetarists assume that expected rates of inflation depend on adaptive expectations – that is, previous periods' rates and changes, and these are projected by extrapolation into the future. However, for the monetarists, markets do not necessarily clear quickly because of institutional rigidities, such as wage level agreements and long-term contracts. Hence there can be involuntary unemployment until the passage of time eliminates such rigidities, in particular, stickiness in prices. At its crudest, trade unions cause unemployment when they resist market clearing wage falls, and governments can engineer only short-term trade-offs between inflation and unemployment. In the longer term, expectations adjust to the new inflation rate, and employment fluctuates only if these expectations are wrong.

The feature of these macro programmes, especially those of the new classical macroeconomics, is their reliance on neoclassical market theory. However, some studies indicate that better informed market operators (whose rational-expectations models should presumably be better than those of less well informed market operators) do not seem to perform any better – that is, make larger profits – than the less well informed. Also, some studies tend to indicate that prices do not perform so vital a role as forecast by the new classical macroeconomic theory.

The new macroeconomics, however, has proved very fruitful as a research programme, not only in developing econometric techniques to test the hypotheses but, more important in our context, in forging links between neoclassical microeconomics, especially market structure theory, and the behaviour of macroeconomic variables. This, as the old history books used to say, is a good thing.

CONCLUDING REMARKS

The outlines above of some salient features of neoclassical economics have been brief in the extreme. Not only has the coverage of the topics selected perforce been very sketchy, but many topics have not been touched upon at all. In particular, capital theory, characteristics analysis, spatial economics, risk and uncertainty and other important neoclassical analyses have been ignored. Though no one definition can sum up the range of neoclassical economic inquiry, I consider the following to embrace much of it: 'A study of the market consequences of self-interested individuals maximizing utilities subject to constraints'. In one sense, successive neoclassical research programmes add little that is fundamentally new. In another sense, because new applications are constantly being formulated, the basic neoclassical research programme is broad-ranging and progressive.

FURTHER READING

The neoclassical economic literature is vast. The references below relate to the topics discussed in the chapter.

There are many undergraduate texts that offer a broad coverage. The two main honours texts used in Dundee are Koutsoyannis (1979) and Gravelle and Rees (1981). Blaug's (1985) extensive history of economic thought is written with a neoclassical stance. This may be contrasted with Canterbury (1980), whose alternative history of thought offers a critique of classical and neoclassical economics. A good reference source for topics and authors is *The New Palgrave: A Dictionary of Economics* (1987).

Seminal texts by 'founders' of the neoclassical school include: Cournot (1838, 1929); Edgeworth (1881); Edgeworth (1925); Jevons (1871, 1970); Marshall (1920); Menger (1871, 1981); Pareto (1906, 1971); Pigou (1920); and Walras (1874, 1877).

The texts above are the best sources for the section on utility. For exchange theory see Newman (1965), which is not only rigorous, but contains much history of thought. (See Creedy, 1986, for a guide to Edgeworth's contribution.) For general equilibrium see Hicks (1939) (a classic text); also, for a more modern treatment, Allingham (1975). One should also mention Samuelson (1947), which is another classic text, and which covers a very wide range.

For market structure one starts with Cournot and Edgeworth. Marshall is the great pioneer of the neoclassical theory of the competitive firm. (For a justification that his theory of the firm is misinterpreted see Gee, 1983. For more references to Marshall see J.K. Whitaker's entry in the *New Palgrave*.) Marshall's approach was continued by Chamberlin (1933).

For Stackleberg's analysis of leader/follower strategy see Stackleberg (1952).

The references for game theory in chronological order are: Zeuthen (1930); Nash (1951); Nash (1953); Luce and Raiffa (1957); and Shubik (1983).

The new contestability theory is by Baumol, Panzer and Willig (1982).

There are many excellent modern tests on market structure theory. I hope I will not be pilloried if, after some heart searching, I plump for Friedman (1977).

See Pareto and Pigou for classic welfare texts. The debate on public goods was launched by two articles by Samuelson (1954, 1955).

Seminal articles on policy approval criteria are: Kaldor (1939) and Scitovsky (1941).

For the social welfare function and the elusiveness of a rule whereby an acceptable one may be formulated, see Bergson (Burk) (1938) and Arrow (1951), respectively. A good general text on welfare economics is Sen (1970).

I restrict myself to three references for macroeconomics: Lucas (1973); Lucas and Sargent (1981); and an influential statement of the monetarist view by Friedman (1968).

SUMMARY OF THE NEOCLASSICAL SCHOOL

World View

Individualistic, atomistic society.
Equilibrium and markets are 'natural'.
The working of unfettered markets coordinates the attempts of divers individuals to maximize their economic well-being, given their preferences and resources.

Values (Claims to be value-free)

The satisfaction of wants is a good thing.
A rational individual is best judge of own welfare; consumer sovereignty.
Individuals' optima are necessary for social optimum.
Utilitarian maximization of 'sum total' of happiness (utility) – given status quo; leads to a gradualist approach to reform.
Pareto efficiency, given the status quo, takes priority.
Libertarian. Anti government intervention in markets.

Goals

To show that a complete unfettered market system coordinating the exchange activities of rational utility-maximizing individual economic agents, *given* their resource constraints, *could* lead to market clearing in all commodities (i.e. there is a set of prices which could fulfil this condition), (and thus non-government intervention leads to spontaneous economic and social harmony).
Prediction (association of regular observed events), rather than explanation. (No prediction of novel phenomena).
Practical relevance of conclusions.
Predict likely results of alternative policies – often in terms of comparative utilities.

Methodological Practice

Deductive reasoning, rigorous logic, abstract, mathematical.
Historic events (data) are used to check theoretical models.
Empirical analysis employed to test the rationality hypothesis, and to predict future outcomes upon parameter change.

Application of theoretical models to a variety of situations, and to estimate elasticities.

Hard Core

Rational (consistent, i.e. transitive, ranking of preferences), well-informed economic agents, strive to maximize their economic well-being (ordinal utility).
Deals with lowest rank of feelings only.
Altruism can form part of individual preferences, but altruistic goals will be striven for at least cost by the rational agents (in the sense that alternative behaviour cannot increase agents' utilities).
Distribution of tastes and endowments are given (determined exogenously).
Static analysis (mainly), marginal decisions.
Subjective theory of value.
Exchange relationships.

Concepts

Rationality (agents behave so as best to satisfy their wants).
Indifference curves.
Consumer's equilibrium; general equilibrium (market clearing).
Contract curve, core, offer curves.
Walrasian auctioneer.
Pareto efficiency.
Perfect competition.
Externalities.

Positive Heuristic (Agenda)

Explore the market consequences of utility-maximizing behaviour by self-interested individual economic agents subject to constraints.
Define the marginal conditions.

1. Can one identify a unique price configuration for all goods and services such that all markets clear and thus none of the economic agents could increase their utilities through further trade, given their preferences and endowments?
2. If such a configuration of prices can be identified, what are its marginal conditions, and is it stable?
3. Show that some such outcomes can be Pareto-efficient.

4. Find policies to secure best social outcomes if there are externalities preventing the achievement of social optima.

Protective Belt Assumptions

(The following are examples of assumptions made only for the sake of analytical tractability in the initial simple models, to be relaxed in the analysis of more complex, theoretical and real, problems)
Prices cannot be negative.
Consumers are price takers.
Diminishing marginal physical products.
Specialization, and division of labour.
Mobility, and substitutability between the services, of factors.
U-shaped short-run average cost curves.

Themes

Consumer choice.
Exchange.
Production.
Market structures.
General equilibrium and welfare (efficiency).
Capital theory.
Characteristics analysis.
Spatial economics.
Risk and uncertainty.

Evidence

Intuitive (appeal to common experience).
Testing of basic hypotheses is sometimes regarded as unnecessary.
The indirect testing of the rationality hypothesis, by affirming the consequent, is mainly 'successful', but often only by careful specification and manipulation of assumed underlying preference structures. Some indirect testing in laboratory conditions of the maximizing hypothesis, and also of the sub-hypothesis that social norms form part of the preference structure, is rather inconclusive.

Conclusions (Simple Theoretical Examples)

Consumer's equilibrium: MU/price is a constant for all commodities.
Producer's equilibrium: Marginal physical product/factor price is a constant for all factors.

General equilibrium: there is a closed, bounded, convex set of prices.
If all markets were to clear, then marginal rate of commodity substi-
tution would be equal to marginal rate of factor substitution.
With general equilibrium, there would be no involuntarily unemployed
factors of production.
Impossibility theorem.

5. The Macroeconomics of the Chicago School

Frank Harrigan and Peter G. McGregor

Inevitably, attempts to define the central features of particular 'schools' are prone to be simplistic and Procrustean. However, a measure of agreement can, we think, be discerned in the literature directed at the delineation of the 'Chicago school' of economic thought. First, the school is characterized by its treatment of the economy as approximating to the competitive ideal. Of course, the existence of at least some market failures is acknowledged, but the case for public sector intervention, in particular, is generally rejected, often on the grounds that policy activism would be likely to make things even worse. This policy conservatism of the Chicago school in part reflects what is judged to be the typically transitory nature of many instances of market failure. Accordingly, the period of time over which economic issues are analysed is important for members of the Chicago school, and is the source of some differences among them.

Advocates of the Chicago school consequently view the economy as behaving 'as if' it were populated by households and other agents who pursue their own interests independently of the behaviour or well-being of others. The 'as if' qualification serves to highlight the second critical distinguishing feature of the school, namely its methodological stance. For members of the Chicago school the validity of theory is to be assessed not by the 'realism' of its assumptions, but rather by the accuracy of its predictions. On this view, the fact that economic agents are unfamiliar with the way in which their economic behaviour is represented by the members of the school is entirely beside the point.

In this chapter, we explore only a part of the Chicago school's collective contributions, namely that part which has been concerned with macroeconomic behaviour. This selectivity reflects the constraints of space, the background of the intended readership and last, but by no means least, our own limitations. For most first-year students, the 'Chicago school' is probably synonymous with various 'monetarist'

perspectives on the macroeconomy. Those who wish to pursue the
school's developments in other areas, notably in industrial economics
(particularly associated with Stigler), the economics of the family
(Becker), and in law and economics (Posner) are referred to Reder
(1982) for a starting point and references.

The organization of our chapter reflects the historical development
of the school's thought from early versions of monetarism to contemporary business cycle theories. Initially, monetarism provided a theory
of the determination of aggregate demand which dissented from the
then orthodox Keynesian position. We discuss the Keynesian – monetarist debate about aggregate demand in the next section. Professor
Milton Friedman's 1967 Presidential address to the American Economic Association then marked a shift in emphasis to the supply side
of the economy – a change in emphasis which has been sustained.
This development is discussed in the first part of the section which is
concerned with two extensions of early monetarism. Our account of
the 'natural rate hypothesis' (NRH) is followed by a discussion of the
extension of the debate to an open-economy context. The 'new classical macroeconomics' (NCM), the initiator of which, Lucas (1977), was,
and remains, a leading member of the Chicago school, is discussed in
a later section. NCM marks a departure from monetarism in a number
of respects, not the least of which is a de-emphasis of the role of
money. Finally, we present some concluding remarks.

EARLY MONETARISM

Undoubtedly an important stimulus to Friedman's initial development
of monetarism in the 1950s was the judgement of the then prevalent
Keynesian orthodoxy that money 'did not matter', and that maintenance of full employment required fiscal activism (see Chapter 6). To
Friedman, steeped in what he, at least, perceived to be the University
of Chicago's 'oral tradition' of maintaining the 'quantity theory of
money', which emphasized both the uniqueness of money and the
stability of the real economy, the message of Keynesianism was an
anathema. For advocates of the quantity theory of money, the aggregate demand for money is basically a stable function of aggregate
nominal income. Money is demanded essentially for transactions' purposes. The role of money is to bring buyers and sellers together with
a minimum of fuss: it is the glue which links demand and supply.

The Keynesian orthodoxy's theoretical progenitor was Keynes's
General Theory. This seminal work was interpreted as implying the

unimportance of money. Keynes regarded money and bonds as close substitutes and, in the extreme case of the 'liquidity trap', as perfect substitutes. In the Keynesian view, money is demanded not only for the services it renders as a medium of exchange, as in the quantity theory, but is also seen as an asset which may be substituted for other assets. Hence, in addition to income, the demand for money is sensitive to the relative returns on different assets and, in particular, to the interest rate. This view of money, together with the Keynesian belief that the demand for goods is generally interest-inelastic, was taken to imply the unimportance of money for the real economy. The significance of this was that monetary policy was typically regarded by Keynesians as being effected through an open-market operation involving a substitution of one form of government debt for another in the private sector portfolio – money for bonds or *vice versa*. The greater the interest elasticity of the demand for money, the lower the interest rate fall in response to any given open-market purchase of bonds. Similarly, the lower the interest elasticity of expenditures, and in the simple Keynesian models investment was regarded as the most likely source of sensitivity, the lower the stimulus to commodity demand associated with any given interest rate fall. Naturally, if the 'monetary transmission mechanism' is confined to occur only through substitutability with bonds, then either their high degree of substitutability or completely interest-inelastic expenditures would ensure that monetary disturbances could have no effect at all on aggregate demand, and money would indeed become irrelevant.

The Keynesian view of money–bonds–commodities substitution, however, equally implied that any stimulus to autonomous consumption, investment or government demands would be likely to be very effective in terms of expanding aggregate demand. An expansionary fiscal policy might, for example, involve a bond-financed increase in government expenditure. The efficacy of such a policy is directly related to the interest elasticity of money demand because the greater is this value, the smaller the interest rate rise required to induce the private sector to hold voluntarily more bonds, thus containing any interest rate-induced reductions in expenditure. The effectiveness of fiscal policy also varies inversely with the interest rate elasticity of expenditure because ultimately this determines the negative feedback, crowding out effects of any given induced increase in interest rates. Clearly, in either of the extreme Keynesian cases in which money is completely ineffective, in terms of its impact on aggregate demand, changes in fiscal policy are subject to the full commodity market multiplier as observed in the standard 'Keynesian cross' diagram. In the liquidity trap case this is because interest rates do not have to rise and in the interest-inelastic expenditure case it is because the induced change in interest rates simply has no adverse feedback effect on demands for commodities.

Of course, in principle, the Keynesian version of the money–bonds–commodity model did not preclude monetary effects on aggregate demand, except in the extreme cases. However, the Keynesian orthodoxy certainly did not regard monetary policy as likely to be very effective in practice. This perspective is reflected in the UK, for example in the Radcliffe Report (1959) which emphasized that the focus of any such policy should be stabilization of interest rates, rather than control of the money stock. A pure policy of interest-rate setting implies that the supply of money becomes infinitely elastic at the going rate. The supply of money thus becomes entirely demand-determined in such circumstances, and the multiplier for exogenous expenditures is again maximized.

It was against this hostile background that Friedman developed the modern quantity theory of money. The two key elements in this theory are an exogenous nominal money stock, and a representation of the quantity theory as a demand for real money balances. The assumed exogeneity of the supply of nominal money balances is, as we shall see, a critical issue in the interpretation of available empirical evidence. In fact although Friedman adheres to a bank credit multiplier account of the determinants of the supply of money in his most recent exposition of the quantity theory, he acknowledges the possible endogeneity of the 'proximate determinants' – the high-powered money base, the deposit to currency and deposit to reserve ratios. Whilst this arguably opens the door to critics, only in the extreme case would the money supply become entirely passive.

There is, in general, no unique way of tying down the precise definition of money and this has given rise to an obvious strand of criticism of monetarism. Friedman's line on this has tended to be rather pragmatic, involving an assertion that there is 'wide agreement' as to its appropriate definition over a particular period in a given location. In practice there does remain, however, the problem of different monetary aggregates telling different stories. More fundamentally, it has been suggested that whichever definition the authorities seek to employ for control purposes, private agents in a sophisticated financial system can substitute alternatives. This paradox of control is known, in the UK at least, as Goodhart's Law.

Friedman's reformulated theory of the demand for money was, in common with Keynes's, a theory of asset demand. Recall that in the classical version of the quantity theory, the only motive for holding money is for transaction purposes. However, in contrast at least to certain aspects of Keynes's account, the demand for money was judged to be a stable function of key variables. The critical scale variable for an asset demand was, Friedman emphasized, wealth, which is the sum of assets and the present value of labour income. Wealth can alternatively be expressed in terms of a constant income stream, namely permanent income. This emphasis on permanent rather than on simply current income, as in the Keynesian account, proves important in interpreting the empirical evidence discussed below. Given their relative tradabilities, the ratio of human to non-human wealth was assumed to exert a negative influence on money demand for a given level of aggregate wealth. Given its perceived uniqueness in all 'quantity theories', money was judged to have no especially close substitutes. Rather than depending on just the interest rate on bonds, as in simple Keynesian theory, the demand for money was rather held to depend on its own expected rate of return, namely the inverse of the expected commodity inflation rate and on expected returns on a wide range of alternative assets including physical as well as financial assets.

The emphasis on a wide range of alternative assets, and an assertion of some direct transmission mechanism from money to commodities, together with replacement of current by permanent income, is the basis of monetarists' reluctance to accept the simple money–bonds–commodities model, characteristic of the IS/LM system, as an appropriate framework for analysis. It is also the source of the criticism that the monetarist transmission mechanism is simply a 'black box'. Nonetheless, monetarists have on occasion been tempted to present their arguments in this context (Friedman, 1970). Here monetarists' emphasis on the uniqueness of money and the absence of a close substitute among financial assets suggests a low interest elasticity of money demand. Indeed, although Friedman's modern quantity theory allows a role for interest rates in principle, he asserts that this is unlikely to be important in practice, suggesting, in the limit, a completely interest-inelastic demand for money schedule. Together with the assumed exogenous nominal money stock, this implied a strict 'classical' quantity theory of money perspective on the money market. Friedman judged the interest elasticity of expenditures to be high, and he raised the extreme case of infinitely elastic expenditures on one occasion.

The monetarist perspective on the money–bonds–commodities system effectively stood the then Keynesian orthodoxy on its head. The demand for money is interest-inelastic and the supply of money is exogenous, so that a given increase in the money supply, for example, will generate a significant reduction in interest rates. Furthermore, since expenditures are very sensitive to interest rates, any given fall in these rates will exert a greater impact on aggregate commodity demand. In the extreme cases of interest-inelastic money demand or infinitely elastic investment demand, the full money multiplier applies, and monetary policy is at its most effective in terms of its ability to influence aggregate demand.

Monetarist views of interest elasticities also imply that real disturbances are considerably less effective than the Keynesian orthodoxy implies and, in the extreme monetarist cases, have no effect whatsoever on aggregate demand. Thus, for example, if the demand for and the supply of money are completely interest-inelastic, a bond-financed fiscal expansion pushes up interest rates by just enough to choke off an equal amount of investment demand. There is, in this case, complete financial crowding out, and fiscal policy merely results in a reallocation of a given level of aggregate demand between, say, public sector and private investment demand. Again, this case can be associated with traditional accounts of the quantity theory.

It is this particular case which gives rise to monetarists being associated with the view that 'only money matters'. There are two important points to note about this caricature. First, in all but the extreme cases, both money and autonomous expenditures 'matter', although their relative importance in monetarist and Keynesian perspectives is, of course, as the caricature indicates. It should be noted that these extreme cases did not lack advocates. Second, it is important to appreciate that disturbances here 'matter' only in terms of their impact on aggregate demand. We have not yet considered how any changes in demand are reflected in price and output responses, a point to which we now turn.

The theoretical core of the Keynesian orthodoxy was essentially a 'fix-price', money–bond–commodities system, at least in what were then presumed to be the generally prevailing conditions of under-employment equilibria. In these conditions, commodities were typically represented as being in perfectly elastic supply, although in the very special conditions of full employment the aggregate supply curve becomes vertical (see Figure 5.1). Except at full employment, shifts in aggregate demand influence real output and employment. Whilst many advocates of the orthodoxy had accepted that price and wage flexibility could, in principle, restore full employment through the operation of wealth effects on expenditures, this was held to be of little practical importance. First, such 'Pigou effects' were thought to

Figure 5.1   The Keynesian aggregate supply curve

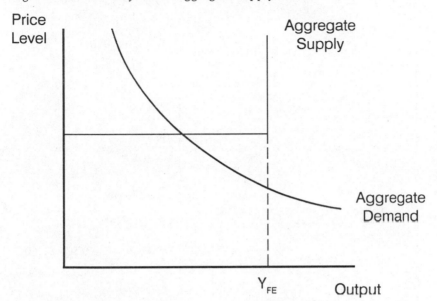

be quantitively small with only 'outside money' to bite on. Second, for usually institutional reasons, prices and wages were inflexible, at least in a downwards direction. It should be remembered that the significance of 'fix-price' models is not that prices are literally fixed but rather that they are determined independently of excess demands, so that 'cost-push' accounts of inflation at less than full employment can be accommodated.

In traditional formulations of the quantity theory (QT), full employment is regarded as the norm in contrast to the Keynesian vision of a persistently depressed economy. Indeed QT is often interpreted as implying that output is tied to its full employment level. The market failures which were perceived to be at the core of the Keynesian orthodoxy were not a part of QT tradition which, at least implicitly, assumed competitive markets and instantaneous wage and price adjustments to the relevant excess demand. The Chicago school's vision of the efficacy of markets led Friedman to the judgement that ultimately, at least, economies would tend automatically to the 'full employment' level of output. Admittedly, this would not happen immediately. Indeed, the primary impact of demand disturbances in the 'short run' might well be on output and other quantities.

However, in the long-run the economy would return to full employ-

Figure 5.2   The conventional monetarist view of aggregate supply and aggregate demand

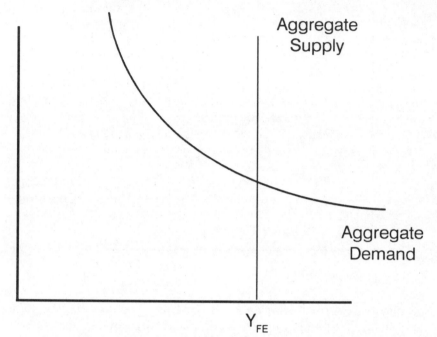

ment, so that stimuli to aggregate demand could only ultimately increase prices starting from an initial long-run equilibrium (see Figure 5.2). In the long-run the aggregate supply is tied to the full employment level of output (Y^{FE}). The long-run aggregate supply curve, LRAS, is vertical at Y^{FE}. Aggregate demand, which is primarily dependent on the level of money supply, therefore only influences the price level in the long run. Thus 'money is all that matters for changes in *nominal* income and for short-run changes in *real* income' (Friedman, 1970). This was subsequently regarded as an 'exaggeration' by Friedman, on the grounds that this constant velocity case requires a completely interest-inelastic money demand, or an infinitely interest-elastic expenditure schedule. Monetarist views on the supply side were more fully developed, in a dynamic context, at a later stage, and so we leave further discussion of this topic until the next section.

The early theoretical monetarist model generated few clear-cut recommendations for policy. True, the extreme monetarist position implied that 'only money matters' for aggregate demand. However, since in the short-run aggregate changes may impact significantly on the real economy, there is no *a priori* case for rejecting monetary policy activism. Except in the extreme position, fiscal policy activism could also be effective in influencing aggregate demand and, therefore, output in the short-run. Furthermore, there might be thought to be considerable motivation for intervention given that there was no presumption that, over the short-run, wages would necessarily clear labour markets. In particular, therefore, the possibility of involuntary unemployment, where labour is forced off its supply curve, is not precluded.

Given the presumed stability of the money demand function, without which pursuit of a coherent monetary policy based on control of the money stock would not be possible, does the powerful impact of money on the real economy not suggest a potentially important counter-cyclical role for monetary policy? Traditional monetarism would respond in the affirmative, but would emphasize that this potential is not, in practice, realizable. The critical point here is the flexibility of counter-cyclical policies relative to that of markets. The monetarist judgement is that difficulties in short-term forecasting, exacerbated by long and variable lags in the effects of monetary policy, imply that use of monetary policy for fine-tuning, for this is all that is required given monetarists' longer-term 'market optimism', is ill advised and could as easily reinforce cyclical behaviour as counteract it.

Thus early monetarism rejected activism primarily on pragmatic, not on theoretical grounds. However, this position also reflected monetarist fears of the inflationary consequences of pursuing expansionary monetary policies. Ultimately, such policies would simply impact on prices, so that 'monetary neutrality' is eventually established. 'Excessive' monetary expansion is, of course, ultimately reflected in the inflation rate. Inflation is 'always and everywhere' a monetary phenomenon. Thus, wage-push pressures can cause unemployment, but if the authorities hold the line on the money stock, they cannot cause persistent inflation. Misguided attempts to tie the economy to some 'full-employment' target would allow cost-push measures to be reflected in inflation, but the real cause of the inflationary process is viewed as the monetary accommodation of such pressures. The early version of monetarism raised three main issues which are, at least in principle, amenable to resolution by appeal to available empirical evidence. First, how do the interest elasticities of money demand and of expenditure compare, and in particular, do they offer any support for the extreme or moderate versions of the Chicago school? Second, is the demand for money a stable function of a few key variables? Third,

does the evidence support the emphasis given to money–output linkages in the short-run and money–inflation linkages in the longer term?

Whilst these issues may appear straightforward enough, their proper
resolution is plagued in practice by a plethora of difficulties including,
for example, identification problems, the inherent unobservability of
some variables, e.g. expectations, and limitations in the quantity and
quality of relevant data. (For an accessible discussion in the context
of the demand for money see Laidler, 1985, Chapters 7 and 8.)
Consequently any conclusions are, of necessity, tentative and subject
to revision in the light of new or improved data or statistical techniques.

Although Friedman's (1959) early work on the demand for money
found no evidence of interest rate influences, virtually all other studies
have found evidence of a significant negative interest elasticity, of less
than unity in absolute value, and considerably less in many circumstances depending on the precise definitions of variables. The extreme
monetarist (i.e. quantity theory) case can, therefore, be fairly emphatically rejected on both US and UK data.

However, these findings also suggest that there is not much evidence
either of the interest elasticity of money demand varying inversely
with the level of interest rates as the liquidity trap requires. Indeed,
there is little evidence of a liquidity trap *per se* ever having existed
(although see Laidler, 1985, Chapter 10). Thus the extreme Keynesian
perspective on this interest elasticity can be rejected almost as emphatically.

Early studies of expenditure functions – consumption and investment
functions – both of an econometric and of a survey kind, found little
evidence of interest rate effects, in contrast to credit availability
effects. But with the availability of more and arguably better data,
the increasing sophistication of statistical methods and improvements
in theoretical formulations focusing on the role of financial variables,
there has been some evidence of apparently well determined interest
rate effects, but again typically with elasticities of less than unity. (See
the review of UK macro-model investment functions by Wallis *et
al.*, 1988.) It seems likely that the extreme Keynesian perspective of
completely interest-inelastic expenditures can be rejected, and no
doubt at all that the QT view of aggregate demand cannot be validated
by this particular route. Therefore the issue of the relative sizes of
the elasticities remains an open question as does, on the orthodoxy's
narrow focus of the transmission mechanism, the issue of the efficacy
of monetary as opposed to fiscal policy in determining aggregate

demand. (See Goodhart, 1975, Chapter 9 for a review of the earlier evidence.)

The question of the stability of the money demand function and, in particular, the stability of the interest rate link has also proved to be a recurring source of controversy at various points in time. Keynes's emphasis on the 'speculative motive' had implied an instability in the money demand function which was at variance with monetarist perspectives. The evidence is, perhaps not surprisingly, very mixed. As already noted, little support for the liquidity trap has been found and apparently robust and stable estimates of interest elasticities have been established for a range of time periods and countries. However, the early 1970s and 1980s saw evidence of parameter instability in what had previously been regarded as stable demand functions for money in both the US and UK. A number of possible explanations have been advanced, including the idea that money may perform a buffer role, resulting in an initial voluntary acceptance of money supply shocks with no corresponding change in any of the usual demand influences. The gradual reallocation of buffered stocks is suggestive of one possible direct mechanism by which money impinges on commodity demand (see Laidler, 1984). Nonetheless, this example emphasizes our warning on the tentative nature of empirical judgements.

Friedman cites an impressive array of evidence for the impact of money on nominal income. This consists partly of historical case studies of which the archetypal example is his and Schwartz's classic *A Monetary History of the United States* (1963). Evidence from specie (metallic standards) and hyperinflations has also been carefully marshalled. However, one of the main objections which continues to be raised is the possibility of a reversal of the causal sequence. On this view, money income changes, perhaps driven by Keynesian-type forces, cause money supply changes. Kaldor (1970) was one of the best known advocates of this position. In his opinion, the lender of last resort function of the central bank in many sophisticated banking systems necessarily implies the complete passivity of the money stock, which is therefore necessarily entirely demand-determined. Monetarists acknowledge the possibility of partial feedback and endogeneity of the money stock, but continue to maintain that by far the predominant causal sequence is from money to nominal income and not *vice versa*. One supporting argument invoked here asserted that money leads nominal income. However, as Tobin (1970) demonstrated, the timing evidence appears to be as compatible with an ultra-Keynesian – infinitely interest-elastic money supply – model as with the monetarist model. Another form of evidence involved reduced form estimates of monetarist and Keynesian models (Friedman and Meiselman, 1959). These studies apparently offered evidence of a stable money–nominal income link and a weak and unstable government expenditure–money income link. However, many Keynesians objected to the model employed to represent their views and, of course, the causality issue remains.

MODIFICATIONS AND EXTENSIONS TO EARLY MONETARISM

The Natural Rate Hypothesis (NRH)

By his 1967 Presidential address to the American Economic Association, Friedman (1968) felt that crude Keynesianism of the 'money does not matter at all' form had been rejected almost uniformly. However, the notion that 'money matters' in terms of its impact on aggregate demand had led many to advocate roles for monetary policy that it was incapable of fulfilling. Specifically, some had advocated that monetary policy be employed to peg the rate of unemployment. Friedman argued that just as the 'cheap money' policies associated with the aftermath of the Keynesian revolution had proved impossible to sustain, so too would any attempt to peg the rate of unemployment.

The attempted pegging of interest rates to low levels, which was the essence of 'cheap money', involved an incomplete understanding of the relationship between money and interest. Interest rates are kept low by open-market purchases of bonds which increase the money stock. However, the inverse relation between monetary expansion and interest rates, apparent in the money–bonds–commodities model discussed previously, reflects only an impact effect. Any increased spending raised incomes and, perhaps, prices, both of which increase the demand for nominal money balances, thus tending to reverse the initial reduction in interest rates. Eventually, interest rates would be restored to their initial level. Although Friedman does not explicitly say so, the initial downward movement in interest rates would only be completely offset if the economy were operating at the 'natural' level of output and the initial interest rate was at its 'natural level' (see below). Indeed, if a higher rate of monetary expansion was sustained and led to expectations of inflation, borrowers would become willing to pay, and lenders would require, a higher rate of interest. Thus, sustained monetary expansion must ultimately lead to higher, not lower, nominal interest rates and the latter are clearly seen as a misleading indicator of the stance of monetary policy.

Advocates of 'cheap money' policies could possibly object that these policies were intended to apply in the presence of excess capacity, thereby precluding inappropriate 'crowding out' in the face of fiscal expansion, and that continual demand stimuli once at full employment were, of course, inappropriate. Monetarists' judgement, however, was certainly that this was not the way the policy had in fact operated. This response failed to acknowledge the stock–flow linkages which tie monetary and fiscal policy and overlapped with the inappropriateness of using monetary or fiscal policy to achieve a target output level.

Attempts to peg the unemployment rate using monetary, or indeed any aggregate demand, policy were ultimately doomed to failure. At any point in time there exists an equilibrium *real* wage which clears the labour market and is associated with unique 'natural' levels of employment, of output and of unemployment.

Friedman (1968) defines the natural rate as follows:

> The 'natural rate of unemployment', in other words, is the level that would be ground out by the Walrasian system of general equilibrium equations, provided there is embedded in them the actual structural characteristics of the labour and commodity markets, including market imperfections, stochastic variability in demands and supplies, the cost of gathering information about job vacancies and labour availabilities, the cost of mobility and so on.

The 'natural rate' is 'natural' only in the sense that actual unemployment tends to move automatically towards that rate. If unemployment lies below its natural rate this implies the presence of an excess demand for labour, since the natural rate is defined by reference to labour market equilibrium. This excess labour demand puts upward pressure on real wages, thereby reducing employment and increasing unemployment. If unemployment lies above its natural rate, the implied excess supply of labour induces a gradual fall in real wages which stimulates employment and reduces unemployment. The market pressure for changing real wages is only eliminated when the actual rate of unemployment is equal to the 'natural rate' of unemployment.

Here is the 'market optimism' of the Chicago school once more. What is, in effect, being asserted is that, at least over some longer time interval, the real economy exhibits a unique and stable equilibrium. Essentially, the classical notion of automatic full employment is being reasserted, although the definition is modified to reflect a variety of frictions, including imperfect information, and is being attained only

Figure 5.3   The Phillips Curve

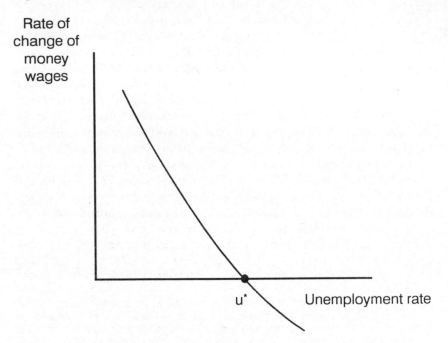

gradually. The notion of a unique and stable equilibrium for the real economy is, of course, anathema to Keynesians used to thinking in terms of the existence of an infinity of real equilibria sensitive to the level of real aggregate demand. The notion of an infinity of real equilibria was, of course, apparent in early Keynesian notions of entirely passive aggregate supply, up to full employment, whereby real output simply adjusted to equal aggregate demand at the prevailing price level. It was also apparent in what had come to be the standard Keynesian representation of the supply side, namely the Phillips Curve.

The Phillips Curve (Phillips, 1958) was born of painstaking empirical observation. It showed an inverse, non-linear relation between the rate of change of *money* wages and the unemployment rate of the form depicted in Figure 5.3. The supposed rationale of the curve came later. Lipsey (1960) suggested that what it showed was that the price of labour changed at a rate and in a direction determined by the level of excess demand in the labour market. Since measured unemployment might reasonably be considered a good proxy for the state of excess supply in the labour market, the rate of change of the price of labour, which was taken to be the *money* wage rate, would vary inversely with the unemployment rate. The non-linearity of the function was taken to reflect the non-linear relationship between unemployment and excess labour demand, given that unemployment is necessarily positive. The Phillips Curve was interpreted by Keynesians as implying a potential trade-off between the wage rate and, via a mark-up pricing hypothesis and productivity growth assumption, price inflation and unemployment. Every point on the Phillips Curve was viewed as representing a sustainable real equilibrium, albeit associated with different inflation rates. Policy makers were thus free to select from the menu of inflation rate – unemployment combinations.

The Phillips Curve had become a fairly standard framework for analysing macroeconomic policy choices by the time Friedman delivered his 1967 Presidential address to the American Economic Association. The NRH, by insisting on the existence of a unique and stable real equilibrium implied a complete rejection of the Phillips Curve framework. There was only one sustainable unemployment rate, and that was the natural rate, u^* in Figures 5.3 and 5.4. The error in the Phillips Curve was in relating the rate of change of the *nominal* wage to unemployment. It is not *nominal* prices, but *relative* prices which would be expected to adjust to own-market excess demands. The relative price of labour is the *real* wage. Accordingly, instead of the conventional Phillips Curve.

$$\dot{W} = f(u) \tag{1}$$

where $\dot{W}$ is the rate of change of money wages,

$$\frac{1}{W} \cdot \frac{dW}{dt},$$

the relation should have been written:

$$\left(\frac{\dot{W}}{P}\right) = \dot{W} - \dot{p} = f(u), \text{ or } \dot{W} = f(u) + \dot{p} \tag{2}$$

Comparison of Equations (1) and (2) suggests that the problem with the former specification is that money wage changes are determined entirely independently of the rate of price inflation, that is, the simple Phillips Curve implies that workers suffer from complete 'money illusion', so that they value their money wage independently of what is happening to price and hence its purchasing power. Such a perspective implies ultimately that workers are irrational.

In fact, as already noted, Friedman did allow for imperfect information flows and the possibility of limited 'money illusion'. In particular, he recognized that current money wage contracts may be struck prior to the current period's inflation rate being known. By making the conventional substitution of the rate of change of prices for wages in (2) we obtain:

$$\dot{p} = f(u) + \dot{p}^e \tag{3}$$

where $\dot{p}^e$ is workers' expectation of the rate of price inflation. This is the expectations-augmented Phillips Curve. The first term on the right-hand side reflects the labour market pressure on nominal wages (and, therefore, on prices given a 'mark-up' and constant productivity).

However, additionally, $\dot{w}$ and $\dot{p}$ fully reflect the expected inflation rate. With $\dot{p}^e = 0$ in (3), the conventional Phillips Curve results, but there exists a different curve for each value of $\dot{p}^e$, with the vertical distance between curves reflecting this, as in Figure 5.4. In full equilibrium, the expectations-augmented Phillips Curve implies not only that unemployment will be at its natural rates ($f(u) = 0$, $u = u^*$ in Figure 5.4) but also that expectations are correct so that $\dot{p}^e = \dot{p}$. It is possible to show that violation of one of these requirements generally implies violation of the other. At the natural rate, $f(u) = 0$ since there is, by definition, no excess supply or excess demand for labour. Clearly this implies that $\dot{p} = \dot{p}^e$, i.e. inflation is fully anticipated. Of course, fulfilment of expectations is itself a requirement of long-run equilibrium, from which $f(u) = 0$ can be inferred.

Suppose the economy is initially in long-run equilibrium with a zero expected inflation rate at A in Figure 5.4. Now imagine the authorities endeavour to reduce unemployment to u_1, by means of a monetary expansion. In the standard account, the stimulus to the money supply impacts more rapidly on commodity prices than on wages, but the latter too begin to move up. Since workers initially expect no inflation they misinterpret their *nominal* wage increases as *real* wage increases and offer more labour. However, *real* wages are actually falling. Firms, therefore, demand more labour as the marginal product of labour now rises above the real wage. Thus output and employment initially rise and unemployment falls to point B at which the target unemployment level, u_1, is achieved with $\dot{p}_e$ still being zero.

In the conventional Phillips Curve analysis this is the end of the matter: point B is a sustainable equilibrium and an unemployment reduction of u^*-u, has been bought at the price of $\dot{p}_1$ inflation. However, in the NRH view, point B is not a sustainable equilibrium, since it is implausible that workers will continue to expect zero inflation in the face of actual inflation of $\dot{p}_1$. But as expectations gradually adapt

Figure 5.4   The natural rate hypothesis

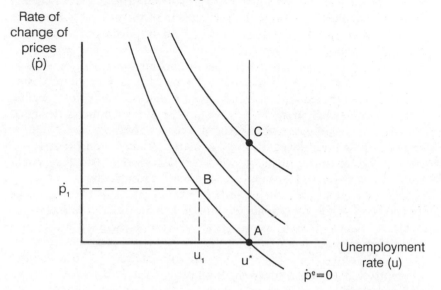

to experience, Friedman postulated that if expectations are formed autoregressively, i.e. solely on the basis of past observations of inflation, the Phillips Curve shifts upwards, workers begin to make good their loss of real wages and unemployment begins to rise again. Those workers who were fooled into believing their real wages had increased realize their mistake and press for increased wages. As real wages rise, firms lay off workers as the marginal product of labour falls below real wage settlements. This process ceases only when unemployment is re-equated to its natural rate (at point C, say) where real wages are restored to their original equilibrium level, albeit with equiproportionally higher rates of growth in *nominal* wages and prices. Therefore in the long run there is no trade-off between inflation and unemployment: the expectations-augmented Phillips Curve is vertical. A monetary expansion, or indeed any expansion of aggregate demand, is, therefore, ultimately incapable of influencing the real economy and 'monetary neutrality' is thereby assured. The notion that the authorities have the ability to select from an infinity of sustainable real equilibria is destroyed. In the long run there can be no involuntary unemployment since the labour market clears. Consequently, demand management policies can exert at best purely transitionary effects on output, employment and unemployment.

However, this prognosis does not imply that the natural rate is policy-invariant. What it does imply is that only those policies which exert their impact effects on the supply side of the economy can have lasting real effects. Whilst demand management policies are ultimately ineffective, supply management policies, which focus directly on shifting the long-run aggregate supply and demand functions for labour, do exert lasting effects on the real economy. Curtailing union power, reducing the real value of unemployment and social security benefits, inducements to labour mobility are all examples of policies designed to shift the aggregate labour supply curve outwards and thereby increase the natural levels of employment and output and reduce the natural rate of unemployment. Reductions in income tax rates might similarly be perceived as supply-side stimuli, through the work/leisure substitution effect, although there is a countervailing income effect and, of course, an accompanying simultaneous stimulus to aggregate demand, except in the extreme monetarist cases discussed in the previous section.

Notwithstanding the fact that they are ultimately doomed to failure, attempts to maintain a target unemployment rate which differs from the natural rate by misguided monetary policies will be associated with accelerating inflation or deflation. For example, the level of unemployment which is below the assumed 'natural rate', u_1, can only be sustained by continuous increases in demand to generate the unanticipated inflation necessary to induce workers to supply more labour at a reduced real wage. Ultimately, given Friedman's adaptive expectations mechanism, 'fooling the public' would require ever-accelerating inflation.

Monetary policy could, however, be used to choose the desired long-run rate of inflation from the points along the vertical Phillips Curve. Given that inflation is fully anticipated at each of these points, however, the conventional costs of inflation, for example, adverse distributional effects, are simply irrelevant. However, since the demand for money is inversely related to the expected inflation rate, the higher the latter, the greater the 'shoe leather' costs associated with economizing on the use of money balances.

Another role for monetary policy was its ability to govern the path of adjustment to any point on the long-run Phillips Curve. In the UK context, a debate developed over the speed at which the rate of growth of the money stock should be reduced to achieve lower inflation. Laidler advocated gradualism in the light of his judgement that the short-run output effects of a monetary contraction could be severe. A gradualist approach, it was felt, would accommodate a gradual moderation in inflationary expectations and so minimize transitory output losses. Others, including Hayek, were advocates of a 'short sharp shock' which would compel rapid adjustment of expectations if workers were to retain their jobs. A slow, smooth adjustment rather than a quick sharp one would involve less loss of welfare under the usual concavity assumptions about agents' utility functions. Fellner (1979), among others, emphasized the importance of credibility in determining the short-run adjustment path. If the authorities could persuade the population of its commitment to contractionary monetary policies, this would operate directly on expectations causing them to adapt more rapidly and thereby reduce the costs associated with the adjustment process.

Friedman's arguments are more about the potential power of monetary policy to stabilize unemployment at its natural rate. Friedman is emphatically negative, but on pragmatic rather than on theoretical grounds. It is worth noting that Friedman believes that there is likely to be a long lag until the NRH is re-established. Essentially, the problem is the chronic uncertainty faced by the authorities. To begin, they may not even be able to identify correctly the natural rate, and the potentially dire consequences of aiming at the wrong target have already been made clear. This difficulty is compounded by the fact that the natural rate may itself be changing through time. The authorities would have extreme difficulty determining whether disturbances are temporary or not, even given timely information about the size and direction of disturbances. For Friedman, monetary policy should be directed at the magnitudes under the control of the money-issuing authorities, notably the rate of growth of monetary aggregates. Real variables, such as output and real interest rates, ultimately cannot be controlled through nominal variables. Furthermore, monetary policy should be conducted in such a way as to avoid the unnecessary swings which Friedman saw as reflecting the authorities' inability to allow fully for the long and variable lags in the effects of policy. Again, he advocated steady growth in a monetary aggregate.

The NRH has been criticized on a number of grounds. One issue is the 'voluntariness' of unemployment in the presence of stable inflation. To the extent that this macroeconomic equilibrium is associated with significant disequilibrium in micro-markets across space and industries, unemployment may be undesirable. This type of consideration has led some to adopt the more neutral NAIRU (non-accelerating inflation rate of unemployment) label and provides a justification why governments may wish to pursue policies which reduce unemployment even when inflation is stable. Others have expressed scepticism about the notion that all markets inevitably clear eventually. If they do not, the NRH is rejected, and the multiple equilibria associated with the literature on non-market clearing and quantity rationing remain relevant even over the longer term. It is perhaps worth emphasizing that there is nothing in conventional monetarism which precludes the existence of involuntary unemployment, although few have emphasized it. What is precluded is the persistence of such unemployment. Accounts of the NRH have often been presented on the basis of markets behaving 'as if' they are competitive, characterized by price-taking agents. Although the mere existence of imperfect competition in commodity and labour markets need not do damage to the basic NRH, it may do especially where markets are incomplete in the sense that some prices have more than one job to do (Layard and Nickell, 1986; Harrigan and McGregor, 1989).

It has also been argued that the 'natural rate' itself depends on the actual unemployment rate. One way in which this may arise is through the loss of human capital of those who lose their jobs. Lack of work experience may cause some people to become unemployable, so that the higher the actual rate of unemployment, *ceteris paribus*, the higher the natural rate becomes (Hargreaves-Heap, 1980). Another mechanism which has been suggested for such persistence or 'hysteresis' effects is the predominance of 'insiders' (employed) in the wage-determining process. Where employment of 'outsiders' (unemployed) is not of concern to 'insiders', expansions to demand, for example, may be reflected primarily in wage increases rather than employment growth, and unemployment may persist (see Lindbeck and Snower, 1988; Blanchard and Summers, 1986). In its extreme form, hysteresis implies complete rejection of the NRH.

One piece of evidence that has been widely cited against NRH was the experience of the Great Depression. Surely unemployment was then above its natural level so that accelerating deflation should have been implied given the NRH? However, it has been argued that, in fact, the natural rate of unemployment itself increased over this period, due to supply-side shifts, such as the unemployment benefit system (Benjamin and Cochin, 1979). There have been numerous empirical investigations of the expectations-augmented Phillips Curve based on an equation such as:

$$\dot{W} = f(u) + A\dot{p}^e \qquad (4)$$

Estimates of equations such as (4) appear capable of discriminating among simple Phillips Curve models (in which $A = 0$) and NRH models (in which $A = 1$). Intermediate values of A imply a negatively sloped long-run Phillips Curve, so that the trade-off persists, but is much steeper than in the short run:

$$\dot{p} = \frac{f(u)}{1-A} \qquad (5)$$

Early studies of the expectations – augmented Phillips Curve found A to be significantly less than unity, but greater than zero, so that naive Phillips Curve and NRH models were both rejected in favour of a model which did, however, imply that the traditional Keynesian view that there exists an infinity of real equilibria from which the authorities may choose was vindicated, although the scope for choice was less than had originally been thought. However, most later studies generated estimates of A which were insignificantly different from unity, and thus lent some credence to the natural rate hypothesis.

Of course, it has been recognized that the expectations-augmented Phillips Curve represents a rather restrictive context in which to attempt to discriminate among competing visions of the macroeconomy, since it simply represents a relation between two of a number of endogenous variables of the entire macroeconomic system. Much recent work has explored labour market structural models, characterized by the estimation of labour demand, supply and/or wage functions. One of the most thorough and influential studies of this type is that by Layard and Nickell (1986), which is based on an imperfectly competitive model of the UK labour market. Some of their findings are reported in Table 5.1. Whilst union activity was found to be a main explanation of the changes in unemployment as between the 1956–66 and 1967–74 periods, demand factors were held largely responsible for the sharp rises in unemployment between 1975–79 and 1980–83. Neither unemployment benefits, as measured by the replacement ratio, nor structural change, as measured by the 'mismatch' proxy, proved terribly important, especially in accounting for comparatively recent experience.

Tests for hysteresis effects are, as yet, in their infancy. Certainly there is evidence of a degree of segmentation in the labour market by duration of unemployment. In particular, the long-term unemployed appear to matter less in terms of their impact on wage determination. However, given a long-term equilibrium relationship between long and short duration of unemployment, the NRH is not threatened by these results (Layard and Nickell, 1986). Others have also found evidence of hysteresis effects in the context of 'insider–outsider' models (see Blanchard and Summers, 1986) which, if accepted, would imply

Table 5.1 Breakdown of the change in male unemployment rates in the UK 1956–83

	(Percentage points)		
	1956–66 to 1967–74	1967–74 to 1975–79	1975–79 to 1980–83
Employers' labour taxes	0.25	0.38	0.44
Benefit replacement ratio	0.54	−0.09	−0.10
Union	1.18	1.17	0.80
Real import prices	−0.58	1.47	−0.93
Mismatch	0.16	0.20	0.49
Demand factors	0.12	0.54	6.56
Incomes policy	–	−0.36	0.49
Total	1.67	3.31	7.75
Actual change	1.82	3.01	7.00

	1955–56	1967–74	1975–79	1980–83
'Natural' unemployment rate (conditional on zero trade balance)	1.96	4.19	7.63	9.07
Actual unemployment rate	1.96	3.78	6.79	13.79

Source: Layard and Nickell (1986), table 1.

outright rejection of the NRH. As yet, the evidence permits no emphatic conclusions. However, at least until the recent work on hysteresis effects, the NRH was widely accepted by mainstream macroeconomists, especially in the US.

The Open Economy

Much of early monetarism was developed, at least implicitly, in a closed-economy context. Whilst this once appeared a reasonable approximation for the US economy, where much of monetarist theory was developed, it is clearly a hopelessly unrealistic characterization of most other economies, including the UK. From a Chicago perspective, however, the critical question is whether this matters in terms of the predictions of the theory. In fact, the source of international monetarists' dissatisfaction with the then standard open-economy model associated with the Keynesian orthodoxy was such as to suggest that openness may matter a great deal. First, the standard Keynesian open-economy model, associated with Fleming (1962) and Mundell (1962), implied that, in the then prevailing Bretton-Woods system of pegged but adjustable exchange rates, there was no automatic adjustment mechanism operating to equilibrate the balance of payments. This was at odds with monetarist beliefs in the self-regulating properties of a market system. The Fleming–Mundell model also shared key features of its closed-economy Keynesian counterpart, including a passive supply side, but this has already been dealt with and we focus here on the specifically open-economy features of interest. Second, monetarists' 'market optimism' led them naturally to question the Keynesian model's typical assumption of insular markets. Markets work not only within countries, but also between them. In extreme cases, small open economies can be regarded as little more than perfectly competitive firms operating in a world of completely integrated commodity and financial markets. In such circumstances the 'law of one price' would be established partly through arbitrage in commodity and financial markets. The implications of this differ radically across fixed and flexible exchange rate regimes.

It is perhaps worth noting that international monetarist models exhibit rather more variety than their closed-economy counterparts, especially in their judgement as to the degree of integration of particular markets over the short and long runs. Thus Friedman (1980) appeared to assume insularity of financial markets, which gave rise to the label 'current-account' monetarism in recognition of the importance which his views attributed to adjustment in the account of the balance of payments. Many international monetarist models in contrast assume perfect financial capital mobility. The 'law of one price' is taken to apply to international bond markets. Space precludes anything other than a very brief account of key perspectives.

In practice the developed world was largely characterized by pegged, but adjustable, exchange rates until 1972, and thereafter by 'dirtily' floating exchange rates. To simplify the discussion, however, we focus on the two simpler worlds of rigidly fixed and entirely flexible exchange rates. Openness is reflected in the Fleming–Mundell model in a number of respects. First, commodity markets incorporate international trade. Thus import demands, related to current income and relative prices, and export demands, related to exogenous world income and relative prices, are accommodated. Second, international trade in bonds is allowed for. At one extreme, financial capital mobility is assumed to be zero, and at the other, perfect. The latter case implies, given a fixed exchange rate, that the interest rate is dictated to the domestic economy by the world bond market. Except in this latter case, explained below, however, the domestic money market is assumed to be entirely unaffected by the balance of payments. Since an overall balance of payments deficit necessitates a running down of foreign exchange flows which, *ceteris paribus*, will reduce the high-powered money base, the assumed insularity of the money market requires some explanation. In effect, the Keynesian model assumes that the monetary authorities will offset the impact of foreign exchange flows on the domestic money stock – an operation known as 'sterilization'.

In general, a monetary expansion in this framework increases demand and output, given the passive supply side, and reduces interest rates, just as in a closed-economy context and its efficacy depends on similar elasticities. However, the expansion in demand leads to a deterioration in the current account and the reduction in interest to a deterioration in the capital account of the balance of payments. The fall in domestic interest rates makes foreign residents less willing to lend to the domestic economy, i.e. buy its bonds, and *vice versa* for domestic residents. Under perfect capital mobility, however, any tendency for domestic interest rates to fall is immediately countered by a potentially massive outflow of capital on a scale which cannot be sterilized. Interest rates are, therefore, tied to world levels and the domestic money stock has to adjust to ensure this. An independent monetary policy, whether defined in terms of a target money stock or a target interest rate, is simply not feasible in this case.

Except in what was regarded, at least from most Keynesians' perspective, as the extreme case of perfect capital mobility, overall balance of payments disequilibria were viewed as sustainable over a considerable interval, subject, in the case of a deficit, to availability of reserves and official borrowing. An outstanding feature of the 'monetary approach to the balance of payments' which, in its modern manifestation is traceable to Mundell, but developed most fully by Johnson (1972), both of whom were associated with Chicago, was its denial of the feasibility, and certainly the desirability, of sustaining balance of payments disequilibria. 'Sterilization' was simply not feasible over the longer term. In the case of a monetary expansion, for example, the induced overall deficit would lead to a decline in foreign exchange reserves, and in turn, in the high-powered money base. The contractionary impact on the money stock would continue until the deficit was eliminated, at which point the original monetary stimulus would be completely reversed. The balance of payments is self-correcting, a result of some comfort to monetarists. However, the counterpart to this further dimension of 'natural adjustment' is the result that the authorities ultimately have no control over the monetary base. The domestic component of this base is assumed to remain under policy control, and this becomes the focal point of Keynesian criticisms of the exogeneity assumption, but changes in this will ultimately be exactly offset by induced changes in the foreign component of the monetary base. 'Openness' clearly does matter, for international monetarists assert the inability of the monetary authorities of open economies to control their money stock if they wish to maintain a fixed exchange rate. Under zero capital mobility this money stock endogeneity implies that fiscal expansion is ineffective in influencing aggregate demand because the current account deficit is only eliminated when output returns to its original level. Under high capital mobility, however, where a fiscal expansion generates an overall balance of payments surplus, the efficacy of fiscal policy is enhanced, due to the induced increase in the money stock, provided neither of the extreme monetarist perspectives on interest elasticities discussed above hold.

Clearly, the greater the degree of integration of bond markets, the less scope there is for independent monetary policy under fixed exchange rates even in the short run. As already noted, international monetarists tended to adopt an 'integrated' view of markets including the commodity as well as bond markets. In the former context, the 'law of one price' implies a purchasing power parity relationship which asserts equality of the common currency prices of domestic and overseas commodities. If the nominal exchange rate is fixed, this ties domestic prices to world prices. It is 'as if' the domestic economy is a perfectly competitive firm. Accordingly, in the extreme case, the authorities cannot influence interest rates or commodity price levels – they become 'price takers' in world markets. Many monetarists view this as a reasonable account of the small open economy in the long run, but opinions differ on adjustment speeds. Thus, in international monetarist models neither monetary nor fiscal policies can ultimately exert any impact at all on interest rates, prices or output, given the NRH. The complete redundancy of demand-management policy instruments is not a matter of concern, however, since policy instruments are both ineffective and redundant. There are no macroeconomic problems to be solved, since output is at its natural level, the balance of payments is in equilibrium and inflation is determined exogenously.

The crucial point to recognize here is that the flexibility of exchange rates restores control of the money stock to the domestic monetary authorities, since the foreign component of the monetary base is fixed in the absence of exchange market intervention. Thus flexible exchange rate regimes are the natural habitat of policies associated with conventional monetarism. For example, here purchasing power parity simply reflects the fact that a monetary expansion ultimately generates an equiproportionate increase in the domestic price level and depreciation of the nominal exchange rate.

In a flexible exchange rate regime, monetary expansions are normally regarded as generating depreciations of domestic currency which, under stability conditions, impart further stimuli to aggregate demand. This much is known, even from the conventional Fleming–Mundell model. Accordingly, the thrust of international monetarism's contributions in this context have largely reflected incorporation of the lessons from their closed-economy counterparts in terms of the nature of aggregate supply and the importance of expectations. The contributions which are specific to open economies have primarily focused on a shift from an insular to an integrated perspective on world markets, mirroring the developments in the closed economy, and accommodating expectations more fully into models of exchange rate determination. One feature of this work has been the development of monetary or, more generally, asset market theories of exchange rate determination which have found their way into many macro-models.

NEW CLASSICAL MACROECONOMICS

In new classical macroeconomics (NCM), the Chicago tradition of 'market optimism' receives its most vigorous and elegant expression. All markets are assumed to clear continuously, for failure to do so would imply that not all mutually advantageous opportunities for trade would be exploited (Barro, 1977). Individuals and firms are regarded as continuously optimizing, subject only to technological and endowment constraints. In particular, the quantity constraints which arise in the presence of non-market clearing do not appear in the optimization calculus. 'Macroeconomics' is increasingly seen as redundant. Macroeconomic outcomes merely reflect the aggregation over individuals in Walrasian general equilibrium models augmented to reflect risk. NCM can be regarded as having been founded by Lucas (1972, 1973), a prominent member of the Chicago school who is best known for his advocacy of the rational expectations hypothesis (REH) in a macroeconomic context. However, whilst the REH is undoubtedly an important feature of NCM, it is the combination of REH and 'market optimism' which is responsible for the more radical NCM results. We turn first, however, to a brief consideration of REH.

The Rational Expectations Hypothesis

Under Muth's (1961) REH, transactors are assumed to form their expectations on the basis of the implicit predictions of the relevant and correct economic theory. REH assumes that transactors' subjective expectations are equated with those determined objectively from a knowledge of the 'true' economic structure of the economy. Prior to Lucas's (1972) application of REH to macroeconomics, it had typically been assumed in the macroeconomic literature that transactors formed their expectations autoregressively, that is solely on the basis of the past behaviour of the variable for which expectations were being formed. This is, for example, implicit in Friedman's (1968) account of the NRH in which transactors are assumed to adapt their expectations of inflation only very gradually to their past experience of it.

The attraction of the REH is that it is the only expectations-formation hypothesis which does not generate *systematic* prediction errors, that is, errors do not cancel out on average. Intuitively, this is clear from the structure of the hypothesis. If expectations do not conform to REH, they are not tied to the economic model which actually generates the data and so they must be systematically in error. By contrast, transactors' expectations are, on average, validated under REH. Expectational errors are made under REH, but these only reflect the random error terms associated with the behavioural functions of the underlying macroeconomic model. The expectational errors must, therefore, be random and, in particular, unrelated to expectational errors in previous periods. In the absence of random errors associated with the underlying behavioural functions, the 'true' model would become deterministic rather than stochastic, and REH would simply imply perfect foresight. The Chicago school's emphasis on the 'rationality' of transactors and the efficacy of markets provides a receptive context for the REH. It is unreasonable to assume that rational transactors will continue to employ expectations-formation schemes which are associated with expectational errors. However, note that the REH implies much more than this: transactors simply do not make systematic prediction errors. Perhaps not surprisingly the REH was regarded, at least initially, as rather extreme and the response of traditional monetarists, including Brunner and Friedman, was rather lukewarm (Klamer, 1984).

One source of criticism of REH has focused on its informational requirements. The question of how transactors acquire sufficient knowledge to avoid systematic prediction errors is simply not addressed. Furthermore, information should be exploited only to the point where its marginal benefit equals its marginal cost. Under REH, the information set on which transactors form their expectations is apparently assumed to be costlessly acquired. Muth-type rational expectations may not, in general, be fully 'economically rational', in the sense of implying optimal use of information. Lucas and Sargent (1978), would appeal to a Chicago methodological stance, emphasizing the 'as if' assumption and the econometric testing of model predictions, to which we return below. It is also worth noting that REH is now rather less controversial and has become widely employed outwith NCM in the new Keynesian macroeconomics. However, this anticipates the finding of the next section that the key distinguishing feature of NCM is its extreme 'market optimism', and not its advocacy of REH.

The market-clearing interpretation of the Phillips Curve

The Phillips Curve has traditionally been interpreted, as we have seen, as reflecting the impact of actual excess supply in the labour market on wage changes. Friedman's NRH emphasized that it was the expected *real* wage which responds to excess supplies in a properly formulated model, rather than the *nominal* wage as in his original formulation. Although Friedman (1968) was not explicit on the issue, certainly he and other monetarists continued to be content to adhere to the conventional disequilibrium interpretation of the Phillips Curve as reflecting a price reaction function (Laidler, 1981). Lucas and Rapping (1969), in contrast, developed an explicitly continuous market-clearing account of the labour market. In this model, since the wage is assumed to equate continuously the demand and supply of labour, there could never be any actual excess supply of labour. Thus, the 'involuntary unemployment' emphasized by Keynesians as a persistent phenomenon and accepted by most, if not all, conventional monetarists as a transitory phenomenon, is simply not admitted as a possibility. Naturally, in such a context, the notion that the Phillips Curve reflects the reaction of wages and prices to labour market disequilibrium is not sustainable.

In effect, the NCM market-clearing perspective suggests a reversal of the causal sequence in the expectations-augmented Phillips Curve. To clarify this, consider simple functional form for Equation 6:

$$\dot{p} = a\,(u^* - u) + \dot{p}^e \tag{6}$$

Equation 6 simply asserts that $\dot{p}$ is linearly, and positively since $a > 0$, related to the excess of the natural rate of unemployment over its actual level. Rearranging Equation 6 yields:

$$u = u^* + \frac{1}{a} (\dot{p}^e - \dot{p}) \tag{7}$$

Equation 6 suggests reinterpretation of the expectations-augmented Phillips Curve as a surprise supply function (SSF), where it should be noted that output moves inversely with unemployment. If inflation is greater than expected $(p > p^e)$, unemployment will be below its 'natural' rate and *vice versa*. Note that 'only surprises matter' in the sense that, in the absence of price surprises, unemployment is tied to its natural level. A market-clearing interpretation of the NRH under autoregressive expectations would imply that, following a monetary expansion, transactors would systematically underpredict inflation over a prolonged period. Thus expectational errors would be persistently negative over a sustained period until expectations eventually fully adapt to experience. This was the implication of the Lucas–Rapping model.

Lucas (1972, 1973) investigated the impact of adopting the REH in this context. First, note the consequences of perfect foresight. Here, expectations are always exactly correct and expectational errors are identically zero. The surprise supply function implies that 'only surprises matter' and perfect foresight implies that there can be no surprises. The combination of the two hypotheses implies that unemployment would be equal to its natural rate in each and every period. The Phillips Curve is *always* vertical if the surprise supply function is combined with perfect foresight. The implications of REH combined with the SSF are only slightly less dramatic. Expectational errors do exist so that unemployment and output can deviate from their natural levels (see Equation 6). However, these expectational errors are purely random, exhibiting none of the serial correlation apparent under autoregressive expectations-formation schemes. Accordingly, the combination of REH and SSF implies that unemployment fluctuates randomly around its 'natural rate'.

The policy implications of this result are startling, for u fluctuates randomly around u^* irrespective of what is happening to aggregate demand. Under REH, the systematic component of monetary policy, for example, that is the non-stochastic component of the policy rule, becomes part of the information set of the private sector. It consequently becomes fully anticipated and therefore incapable of generating expectational errors. This is so whether the monetary rule is of a Friedman type or notionally 'activist', in the sense of being directed at a target unemployment level. Accordingly, the systematic component of monetary policy becomes useless in terms of its ability to influence the real economy. This is so even in the short-run, which is not characterized by monetary neutrality under conventional monetarism. An anticipated x per cent increase in the money stock immediately causes an x per cent increase in prices and all nominal values with all real variables unaffected. The economy jumps immediately to a higher point on the vertical Phillips Curve. True, the random or stochastic component of policy does matter. By its nature, it cannot be foreseen by the private sector and it creates expectational errors. However, the greater the random component of monetary policy, the greater the variability of unemployment. Thus policy in this sense is worse than useless, since it actually contributes to instability.

These results suggest why NCM was initially regarded as an extreme form of monetarism. The original models focused on money as the source of disturbances, and monetary neutrality was prevalent. However, monetarists had traditionally regarded neutrality as a long-run proposition, with the implication that money could exert significant impacts on the real economy over the short-run. Furthermore, it is precisely this non-neutrality of the short-run that reconciled monetarist theory with 'observed' Phillips Curves. Our account of NCM so far appears to render it incapable of accommodating anything other than a vertical Phillips Curve.

In fact, Lucas's (1972) model assumed that individuals have expectations of the general level of prices and the prices of the goods they sell, for example, labour services. Whilst they observe the current prices of their own goods, the general price level only becomes known with a one-period lag. When the price of their own good rises, individuals have to decide on the extent to which this reflects an increase in their own relative price as against a general increase in prices. From past experience they will, in general, attribute a part of the total price increase to a relative price increase and a part to general price increases. Accordingly, unanticipated inflation (deflation) leads to an increase (decrease) in output and labour supply. There is a non-vertical Phillips Curve, but of one-period duration.

A rational individual will, of course, attempt to minimize the scale of any confusion of absolute and relative price changes. There is a 'signal extraction' problem. The individual attempts to 'extract the signal' – the relative price change – from the surrounding 'noise' – the variability of inflation – as efficiently as possible. The greater the noise, the more difficult it is to extract an accurate signal and the smaller, therefore, will be the response to any given change in prices. Thus the transitory Phillips Curve will be steeper the more variable the rate of inflation.

A further tension with conventional monetarists concerned the nature of the monetary transmission mechanism within NCM. As we have seen, this was viewed as involving substitution with a wide range of financial and non-financial assets and, over a considerable interval, relative price adjustments would be involved. In contrast, early NCM models incorporated rudimentary views of money and, for anticipated disturbances, the monetary transmission mechanism is instantaneously short-circuited with no change in relative prices. Immediate and equip-roportional changes in all nominal prices are implied. In the labour market, for example, workers claim immediate and full compensation for the correctly anticipated inflation rate. Finally, conventional mone-tarism had emphasized a monetary theory of business cycles. The point is not simply that money can in principle have some effect on output. Rather, it was asserted that money did in fact have a sustained impact on output. The combination of the SSF and REH, however, implies the complete absence of any systematic fluctuations such as those which characterize a stylized 'cycle' in unemployment or output: these simply fluctuate randomly around their natural rates. NCM has developed equilibrium theories of the business cycle in which, accord-ing to some accounts, money has persistent effects, while other models downplay the role of money altogether.

Equilibrium models of the business cycle

The problem that faced NCM was to explain the business cycle in the real economy in a manner compatible with that economy being continuously in a competitive equilibrium, in which all markets clear. In NCM, the proximate cause of any deviation from the natural rate is expectational errors. However, under REH these expectational errors are, of necessity, purely transitory. Yet the apparent cycle in many aggregates implies that changes in these aggregates are sustained over a number of periods. NCM models of the business cycle are distinguished primarily in terms of the sources of impulses they empha-size and, in particular, whether the original source of disturbances is monetary or real, notably productivity and technology stocks. The models also differ to some degree, however, in the propagation mech-anisms through which disturbances as transmitted. These propagation mechanisms have included the presence of long-lived capital, of lags in the labour demand function and the use of stocks of finished goods as a buffer. Consider, for example, the impact of a surprise monetary expansion in an NCM model with stocks. Firms may choose to meet the unexpected increase in demand by running down their stocks and to replace these only gradually. The real impact of the shock, which lasts only one period, may consequently be spread over several periods.

Whilst Lucas's work has tended to emphasize money as the source of fluctuations in activity, it is clear that this is not a distinguishing feature of NCM as a whole. Thus Sargent in Klamer (1984) suggests that the neutrality properties of his earlier NCM models, which he developed with Wallace, received undue emphasis. *Real* business cycle theorists have, as their title suggests, tended to de-emphasize the role of money. For some, this is a theoretical convenience, but for others it reflects a judgement from the time series properties of macroeconomic aggregates that money is not of great importance empirically. Furthermore, at least one NCM model treats money in traditional extreme Keynesian style, i.e. as entirely demand-determined. None of this finds ready acceptance from traditional monetarists, who would respond that at best the evidence referred to runs contrary to continuous equilibrium REH models of the business cycle which, as we have already noted, differ in significant respects from the traditional monetarists' own position. What the new classicists share with traditional monetarism is an emphasis on rationality, individual optimization, market optimism and a similar stance on methodology. This emphasis is apparent throughout the development of the Chicago school's perspective on macroeconomics and through time has found more formal and elegant expression. The 'importance of money', however, is certainly not as central to the new classicists as it is to monetarists.

CONCLUSIONS

This chapter has traced the development of the Chicago school's macroeconomic thought from the early states of monetarism of the 1950s and early 1960s, through extensions in the form of the natural rate hypothesis and applications to the open economy, to the formulation of new classical macroeconomics. The critical common feature is a vision of transactors as rational optimizing agents operating 'as if' in a world of competitive markets. Through time, 'market optimism' has tended to increase significantly, which is in part responsible for a declining emphasis on the 'importance of money' which is central to conventional monetarism. The existence of a coherent Chicago school is, however, in no sense challenged by the absence of unanimity within its ranks on the appropriate degree of market optimism.

Whatever the judgement on specific contributions of the Chicago school to macroeconomics, there can be little doubt concerning its immeasurable stimulus to both the theoretical and econometric investigation of the behaviour of macroeconomies. This is so, even though the thrust of the argument is increasingly to encourage the demise of macroeconomics, in favour of explicit individual transactor-based stochastic general equilibrium models.

FURTHER READING

Friedman, M. and A.J. Schwartz (1963) *A Monetary History of the United States, 1867–1960*, Princeton University Press for the NBER: Princeton.
Klamer, A. (1984) *The New Classical Macroeconomics: Conversations with the New Classical Economists and their Opponents*, Harvester: Sussex.
Laidler, D. (1985) *The Demand for Money: Theories, Evidence and Problems*, 3rd edn, Harper and Row: New York.

SUMMARY OF THE CHICAGO SCHOOL

World View

Individual, atomistic society.
Rational economic agents, with utility-maximizing motivation.
Only money matters.
Market optimism.

Values

Individual is best judge of own welfare.
Consumer sovereignty.
Libertarian.
Anti-government intervention in markets.

Goals

To show that complete unfettered market system, coordinating the exchange activities of utility-maximizing economic agents given their resource constraints, will lead in the long run to market clearing in all commodities and factors (i.e. there is a set of prices which could fulfil this function).

Methodological Practice

Instrumental; pragmatic.
Theory accepted/rejected on basis of adequacy of prediction.

Hard Core

Altruism not a behaviour variable.
Deals with lowest rank of feelings only.
Distribution of tastes and endowments determined exogenously.
Exchange relationships.
Market clearing.
Importance of money.

Concepts

Equilibrium: general equilibrium.
Pareto efficiency.

Walrasian auctioneer.
Perfect competition.
Quantity theory of money.
Natural rate of unemployment.
Rational expectations.

Positive Heuristic

Explore market consequences of utility-maximizing behaviour by self-interested economic agents, subject to constraints.
Explore impact of money on nominal income.
Identify natural rate of unemployment.
Explore conditions for zero rate of inflation.

Protective Belt Assumptions

Prices cannot be negative.
Consumers are price takers.
Diminishing marginal physical products of factors of production.
Specialization and division of labour.
Mobility of factors of production.
Nominal money stock is exogenous.
Quantity theory of money is demand for real money balances.
Economic agents behave 'as if' they understand relevant and correct economic theory.

Themes

Inflation.
Money supply.
Market clearing.
Expectations.
Rationality.
Law of one price.
Monetary theory of business cycle.

Evidence:

Friedman and Schwartz: 'Monetary History of the United States'.
Controversial and inconclusive evidence on:
– interest elasticities of money demand,

– stability of demand for money,
– money–output and money–inflation linkages.

6.   The Orthodox Keynesian School

James Love*

J.M. KEYNES

Textbook exposition of the macroeconomic framework developed by Keynes has changed quite dramatically over the past three decades, particularly in North America. The extensive, geometric representation of the *General Theory*, as contained in Samuelson's text which largely dominated students' reading in classes during the latter parts of the 1950s and the 1960s, has given way to a generation of texts in the 1980s which contain substantially less comprehensive, and certainly less detailed treatment of Keynes's ideas and the Keynesian framework developed from those ideas. This shift in emphasis is part of an evolutionary process of economic thought in which new ideas emerge as refinements of, or as reactions to, what has gone before. Contemporary textbooks tend to restrict their discussion of Keynes to those 'Keynesian' ideas which are regarded as essential to an understanding of the Keynesian–monetarist debate of the 1970s and which serve as a counterpoint to the new classical views so much in vogue during the 1980s (see Chapter 5).

Just as the views expressed in the *General Theory*,[1] although continuing to provide the source from which the post-Keynesians (see Chapter 7) and new Keynesians draw intellectual inspiration, have been largely displaced in debate about the macroeconomic circumstances of industrial economies of the 1980s, so Keynes's work represented an important new phase of economic thought replacing the set of ideas which had held sway until the 1920s. As with contemporary treatment of the *General Theory*, the introductory textbooks of the 'Keynesian era' tended to provide limited treatment of earlier theory as applied to macroeconomic problems. Yet to appreciate the impact of Keynes it is necessary to set his views in the context of the economic circumstances and the previously dominant theoretical framework which formed the backdrop to his thinking. Only then is it possible to

* The author is indebted to Roy Grieve and Roger Sandilands for constructive comments and suggestions. Errors remaining are entirely the responsibility of the author.

145

appreciate the substantial and radical intellectual contributions which Keynes made to thinking about macroeconomics. Of all Keynes's writing on economics the *General Theory*, published in 1936, is his most significant contribution and this chapter concentrates on that work.

Against the background of persistent unemployment during the Depression of the 1920s and 1930s, Keynes pursued two objectives in the *General Theory*: first, to identify and explain the failings of the prevailing, classical orthodoxy; and second, to set out an alternative explanation of the determination of output and employment levels. He explicitly stated in the preface to the *General Theory* that his primary concern was with theoretical questions and that only second-ary consideration was given to matters of practical application.

The economists Keynes described as comprising the 'classical school'[2] had been concerned primarily with theories of value and distribution. They sought to explain how a market system character-ized by atomistic competition could account for the operation of a capitalist economy. Their economic thinking focused mainly on issues of a basically microeconomic nature. The central economic problems of determining the composition of output of goods and services, the allocation of factor inputs and the distribution of factor rewards were resolved in terms of a market structure dominated by competitive pressures. The competitive pressures were taken to be such that no individual agents, on either the supply or demand side of a particular market, could exercise effective control over prices. Economic agents were also taken to be of the variety *homo economicus*. Rational economic man sought to maximize the gain and minimize the disutility involved in economic activity. Driven by self-interest, producers, con-sumers and resource owners strove to maximize profits, utility and income respectively.

While Keynes made the point that it would be absurd to suggest that earlier analysis had ignored discussion of the actual level of employment of available resources, he argued that discussion of 'the size of the employable population, the extent of natural wealth and the accumulated capital equipment' (G.T. p. 4) had tended to be descriptive and that the underlying theory had 'been deemed so simple and obvious that it has received, at the most, a bare mention' (G.T. p. 3). In essence, as illustrated by the treatment of the labour market in Pigou's *Theory of Unemployment*, and to the extent it took place, classical thinking on macroeconomic problems involved extension of the analysis of markets, characterized by atomistic competition and economic rationality.

PRE-KEYNESIAN MACROECONOMICS

Contained within classical analysis is a set of ideas which comprise, given the initial assumptions, an internally consistent, deductive framework for analysing macroeconomic issues.[3] Keynes's comments on the classical theory and the reaction to the *General Theory* by proponents of classical thought helped concentrate attention on the nature of, and interrelationships among, the important elements of traditional theory as applied to macroeconomics. Put baldly, the main elements of classical macroeconomics are:

1. An analysis of the labour market and of the determinants of output which suggests that there will be an automatic tendency towards full employment and an associated level of full-employment output.
2. Say's Law of Markets which is required to avoid the danger of 'overproduction'.
3. A theory of interest which serves as a necessary complement to Say's Law.
4. A theory of the price level.

With respect to the labour market the classical perception was of the supply of, and the demand for, labour being related to the real wage, with competitive pressures causing any departure from the market-clearing real wage to be temporary rather than persistent. Excess supplies of labour would tend to be eliminated by competition among workers for scarce jobs driving down disequilibrium real wage rates, while excess demand for labour would tend to disappear as competition for scarce labour resulted in employers bidding up real wages. The outcome was an apparently automatic tendency for market-driven elimination of labour market disequilibria. Moreover, the level of employment which obtained at the market-clearing real wage was regarded as the 'full employment' level for two reasons. First, leaving aside frictional unemployment which Keynes attributed to 'various inexactnesses of adjustment', (G.T. p. 6) the market-clearing condition meant that the volume of labour sought by employers matched the volume of labour offered by workers. Second, workers were thought to be able to influence the real wage through the money wage bargains they agree with employers. Under these conditions, any unemployment, other than frictional unemployment, remaining at the prevailing market-determined real wage rate is taken to be voluntary.

With the employment level arrived at in this fashion, output could be determined by reference to the notion of a generalized production function. Just as the aggregate demand for labour was held to embody the same properties as the individual firm's labour demand curve, so the aggregate production function was taken to reflect the production conditions for the firm. In the short run, output varies with labour inputs and is subject to diminishing returns where the other determinants of output, namely, the capital stock, land and technology, are taken to be relatively constant. With labour market equilibrium defined as tending to full employment, application of the market-clearing labour input to the production function produces a level of output which correspondingly tends to the full employment level.

Say's Law is invoked to avert the possibility of unemployment arising from a deficiency of aggregate demand. Production of goods and services creates an equal-value set of incomes which comprises the basis of the community's demand. There is then no threat to employment levels from 'overproduction' when, according to Say's Law, acts of production generate an equal amount of demand. There is, however, the possibility that aggregate demand may fall short of the total value of incomes in production by an amount equal to that which the community wishes to save. This possibility is averted, in turn, by recourse to the classical theory of interest. With both the supply of saving and the demand for loanable funds taken to be dependent on the rate of interest, market adjustment ensures that saving is transformed into another form of expenditure, i.e. investment. There is then no 'leakage' from aggregate demand resulting from decisions to save. Thus the classical theory of interest maintains the validity of Say's Law.

The final element in the classical framework involves the role of money in the determination of the price level. Money serves in the classical system to facilitate the process of exchange. The end purpose of economic activity is to acquire control over goods and services and the function of money is that of permitting the exercise of such control. Changes in the money supply thus affect aggregate demand. With output tending to full employment and the velocity of circulation taken to be relatively constant, being determined by spending habits and the institutional framework, increases (decreases) in the money supply must then lead to a higher (lower) price level. Since the money supply influences the price level through the quantity theory of money, monetary policy is regarded as exerting an influence somewhat separate from the forces affecting the real economy.

KEYNES'S REFUTATION OF THE CLASSICAL SYSTEM

In attempting to refute classical macroeconomic thinking, Keynes, himself well-versed in the Marshallian tradition, did not seek to deny long-established views on the operation of markets. Rather he accepted substantial parts on conventional thought and his adherence to classical price and distribution theory is evident in the *General Theory*. Keynes argued, for example, that if the level of output, explained by some body of analysis other than the classical system, is taken as given, then

> there is no objection to be raised against the classical analysis of the manner in which private self-interest will determine . . . what is produced, in what proportions the factors of production will be combined to produce it, and how the value of the final product will be distributed between them. (G.T. pp. 378–9)

Keynes suggested, however, that certain, although by no means all, of the relationships in what constituted classical thinking on the determination of output and employment were based on incorrect premises. The resulting misspecifications led, in his view, to a flawed analysis of the theory of employment. Keynes's reservations about classical theory encompassed each of the main elements in their analysis.

With respect to the labour market the classical labour demand function represented an extension to the aggregate level of the analysis employed at the level of the individual firm. Driven by the profit-maximizing objective, the firm was held to employ labour up to the point at which the value of the marginal product (marginal revenue), determined by a production function characterized by diminishing returns and by the prevailing market price for the particular product, was equal to the cost of hiring additional labour (marginal cost), determined by the money wage and by the increase in numbers employed. Given the firm in an initial profit-maximizing position, a fall (rise) in the real wage due to either a rise (fall) in the product price or a fall (rise) in the money wage generates increased (decreased) demand for labour. The principle of diminishing returns to labour is central to this analysis of labour demand and Keynes did not become involved in the *General Theory* in discussing the technical attributes of the production function, an omission which led to fairly immediate debate with his critics. He acknowledged an 'important point of agreement', arguing that:

with a given organisation, equipment and technique, real wages and the volume of output (and hence of employment) are uniquely correlated so that, in general, an increase in employment can only occur to the accompaniment of a decline in real wages . . . I am not disputing this vital fact which the classical economists have (rightly) asserted as indefeasible. (G.T. p. 17).

However, Keynes's perception of the inverse relationship between the real wage and the level of employment differed from that contained in the classical demand for labour function. He suggested in the *General Theory* that, when aggregate demand was rising, prices would rise relative to money wages and workers, with job opportunities increasing, would not resist the associated fall in real wages. Keynes also took issue with arguments which in the classical view were thought to underpin the supply side of the labour market. The classical school saw the ultimate objective of involvement in economic activity as that of acquiring access to goods and services and, consequently, with labour not subject to money illusion, labour supply was held to vary directly with the real wage. Keynes was sceptical about this formulation on two counts. First, he felt that the 'normal case' as revealed by 'ordinary experience' is a situation where labour negotiates for a money rather than a real wage (G.T. p. 9). He contends, in support in his position, that 'whilst workers will usually resist a reduction of money wages, it is not their practice to withdraw their labour whenever there is a rise in the price of wage-goods' (G.T. p. 9). Second, he contests the basis of the classical position that workers are able to determine the real wage through the bargains they strike with employers. Keynes felt that the classical preoccupation with the view that the price level was dependent on the money supply caused the relationship between prices and wage costs, an important component of the classical school's own analysis of the theory of the firm, to be overlooked. The firm's marginal costs are largely governed by money wages and marginal costs themselves determine prices. Thus any negotiated increases in money wages result in corresponding prices. It follows that workers are not in a position to establish real wages through their money wage agreements. For these two reasons, Keynes disputed the classical view of the labour supply curve and argued that 'if the supply of labour is not a function of real wages as its sole variable, their argument breaks down entirely and leaves the question of what the actual employment will be quite indeterminate' (G.T. p. 8).

Keynes then turned to the role played by Say's Law and argued that the classical economists confused two 'similar-looking' but analytically different propositions, namely 'that the *costs* of output are always covered in the aggregate by the sale-proceeds resulting from demand' and 'that the income derived in the aggregate by all the elements in the community concerned in a productive capacity necessarily has a value exactly equal to the *value* of the output' (G.T. p. 20). Keynes describes the second of these propositions as 'indubitable' but argues that the first is based on the incorrect view that the incomes generated in the process of production will necessarily be spent at a rate which ensures market clearing.

The criticism of Say's Law crystallizes one of the central themes of the *General Theory*, that decisions taken by different groups of agents within the economy and based on quite different sets of considerations are not necessarily neatly compatible. The classical theory of interest provides an important second illustration of the application of this theme in Keynes's refutation of traditional thinking.

As with Say's Law, Keynes points to the confusion of two quite different propositions in the classical formulation of the theory of interest. It is, he stresses again, 'indubitable' that 'the sum of the net increments of the wealth of individuals must be exactly equal to the aggregate net increment of the wealth of the community' (G.T. p. 21) but this is quite distinct from the view that planned saving by the community automatically generates a parallel and equal act of planned investment. Keynes's position is that the differences in motives for savers and investors mean that there is no simple connection between decisions by these groups operating through the rate of interest. Moreover, in developing his own theoretical framework Keynes provides a very different account of the determination and role of the interest rate. The importance of Keynes's comments on the classical theory is that once the nexus between saving and investment is broken, Say's Law no longer serves to avoid the possibilities of 'overproduction' and the possibility is admitted of having unemployment due to a deficiency of effective aggregate demand.

The questions of what factors determine the rate of interest and what role the rate of interest plays in the economic system also enter into Keynes's respecification of an important part of the final main element of classical thought, the quantity theory of money. In his analysis of the importance of money Keynes departs substantially from the classical tradition and indeed, from his own earlier thinking on the matter. He acknowledges that before the *General Theory*, when writing his *Treatise on Money*, he was 'still moving along the traditional lines of regarding the influence of money as something so to speak separate from the general theory of supply and demand'. In the *Gen-*

eral Theory, however, the 'classical dichotomy' is squarely rejected and Keynes develops the argument that through its impact on the rate of interest and, hence, on the level of aggregate demand the money supply can affect the real economy.

The classical view that money is neutral with respect to the real variables in the economy hinged on the perception of money being important only because of its function as a medium of exchange. Money was regarded as having no other inherent properties which made the holding of money *per se* attractive. Since the demand for goods and services depends on income, the classical demand for money is a function of income. Moreover, since any price rises will necessitate the holding of larger money balances to pay for more expensive goods and services, the determinant of the demand for nominal money balances is nominal income. Whenever money balances exceed the demand for money, spending rises.

From Ricardo onwards, this transactions-based demand for money served to deliver the stable velocity of circulation against which changes in the money supply exerted an impact on the price level. Only with the development of the Cambridge version of the quantity theory did the demand for money attract more attention. This version maintained that the community holds cash balances as a stable fraction of national income, although changes in the community's 'confidence' (G.T. preface, p. xxii) might cause the fraction held to exhibit short-run variations. The community's propensity to hold cash balances remained explained in this way until Keynes examined the demand for money in greater detail in the *General Theory*.

Building on earlier work in his *Treatise on Money*, Keynes shifted attention much further towards the demand for money as part of the development of a quite radical alternative theory of the money market and the rate of interest.[4] The propensity to hold money, or liquidity preference, was accounted for in terms of not one, but three motives: the transactions, precautionary and speculative motives.

Of the three, the transactions motive is the most direct inheritance from the classical tradition. Individuals require cash balances to 'bridge the interval between the receipt of income and its disbursement', while businesses hold cash 'to bridge the interval between the time of incurring business costs and that of the receipt of the sale proceeds' (G.T. p. 195). In each case, the transactions demand is a function of income and the time interval involved. The precautionary motive relates to provision, for example, 'for contingencies requiring sudden expenditure and for unforeseen opportunities of advantageous purchases' (G.T. p. 196). This motive is also taken to be primarily related to income and as such is frequently subsumed within the more substantial transactions motive.

Keynes's main innovation with respect to the demand for money lay in the speculative motive. Economic agents are thought to hold some part of their assets in the form of money balances with 'the objective of securing profit from knowing better than the market what the future will bring forth' (G.T. p. 171). The important function of money here is not along the classical lines of medium of exchange but rather as a store of wealth. Money is held in preference to other forms of asset holding as individuals and businesses look for opportunities to make capital gains and avoid capital losses by judicious purchase and sale of market instruments such as bonds. The main determinant of the amounts of money held for Keynes's speculative motive is the rate of interest. His introduction of the rate of interest as a determinant of events in the money market is predicated on the importance he attaches to the existence of uncertainty about future movements in interest rates and to the intimately related role of the expectations formed by the community about future movements in interest rates and bond prices, which move in inverse relation to one another.

The existence of uncertainty as to future interest rates is identified by Keynes as a necessary condition for wealth to be held in the form of money, a non-interest bearing asset (G.T. p. 168). If future rates of interest could be forecast with certainty from present rates for debt of different maturities, then 'it must always be more advantageous to purchase a debt than to hold cash as a store of wealth' (G.T. p. 169). Given uncertainty, however, the purchase of a debt carries the risk of a capital loss, as compared to holding money balances. Thus whereas the classical economists saw the interest rate as a reward for choosing to save rather than consume, Keynes treats the interest rate as the 'price' that is necessary to induce those holding money balances for speculative purposes to surrender liquidity for a specified period.

Expectations, which Keynes describes as being 'fixed by mass psychology', account for decisions about movements between money and other forms of assets. The relevant barometer of expectations is not the absolute level of interest rates but the extent to which rates diverge from those regarded by market participants as 'fairly safe' (G.T. p. 201). When interest rates are low relative to the 'safe' rate, then not only is the opportunity cost of holding money low but the balance of market opinion is likely to expect the next movement in bond prices to be downwards rather than upwards. In this 'bearish' climate the speculative demand for money will be relatively strong. In contrast, when rates are high in relation to the 'safe' level a 'bullish' market will generate a relatively weak demand for money to hold as an asset.

With the demand for money specified as a function of income (through the transactions and precautionary motives) and of interest rates (through the speculative motive), there are fundamental implications for two of the principal elements of classical theory. First, the classical theory of interest is rejected by Keynes. The interest rate is no longer the price which brings the demand for investment resources into line with the willingness to save rather than consume. Rather its role as a price is that of bringing the community's demand for money balances into line with the available quantity of money. Second, the impact of monetary policy is substantially revised. Whereas classical theory emphasized the impact of money supply changes in the price level, Keynes's analysis introduced the possibility that monetary policy might exert an influence on the rate of interest. This possibility, taken in conjunction with other concepts developed in the *General Theory*, particularly the marginal efficiency of capital, leads to the proposition that the real variables in the economy may be affected by monetary policy changes. In other words, the classical dichotomy between the real and monetary spheres of the economy breaks down.

In identifying deficiences in principal elements of earlier thinking on macroeconomics, Keynes was, in effect, dismantling the internal logic of the classical system. Certain of Keynes's criticisms were themselves later to become the subject of much debate but were consistent with the experience of the Depression which suggested that there was no inherent, automatic tendency for competitive markets to deliver solutions to the problem of persistent, high levels of unemployment. To address this problem, Keynes constructed an alternative explanation of the operation of the economic system which was quite radically different from that of the classical school. He went very much further than simply respecifying those aspects of classical macroeconomics he had criticized as flawed. His alternative framework introduced new concepts and married them together in a fashion that effectively provided the basis for discussion of macroeconomic issues as extensive as that afforded to microeconomics and for the development of 'modern' macroeconomics.

KEYNES'S ALTERNATIVE FRAMEWORK

Keynes begins construction of his alternative framework by considering the nature of the decisions taken by entrepreneurs. In the short term, businesses form expectations concerning costs and sale proceeds and those expectations determine the amount of employment they offer. Although he stressed that short-run expectations are not adjusted violently or rapidly in response to the actually realized results of production and sale (G.T. pp. 47–8), Keynes argued that 'the most recent results usually play a predominant part in determining what these expectations are' and that 'producers' forecasts are more often gradually modified in the light of results than in anticipation of prospective changes' (G.T. p. 51). While long-term expectations with their influence on the scale of productive capacity and their relationship to constantly changing short-term expectations are discussed by Keynes, the primary concern of the *General Theory* is with the impact of expectations on employment levels in the short term. Keynes argues that 'past expectations, which have not yet worked themselves out, are embodied in the to-day's capital equipment with reference to which the entrepreneur has to make to-day's decisions' (G.T. p. 50).

The central issue is the extent to which business will hire labour to operate the existing stock of capital equipment. Through his definition of the 'aggregate supply price', Keynes makes it clear that what underpins firms' decisions to offer a certain level of employment 'is the expectations of proceeds which will just make it worth the while of the entrepreneurs to give that employment' (G.T. p. 24). This provides the basis for his aggregate supply function which relates expected receipts to employment levels. Subsequent, Samuelson-type textbook presentations formulate the aggregate supply function by relating expected proceeds not to employment levels but to level of output (income). The familiar 45° line relates proceeds and output in constant price terms. Alternatively, aggregate proceeds and output may be related in terms of current prices to reflect the influence of diminishing returns and increases in costs, including money wage rates, as production expands with rising labour inputs. The constant price version has the merit for discussion of the real economy that employment levels are related to changes in the volume rather than the nominal value of output.

Whether in its original or subsequent forms, Keynes's aggregate supply function demonstrates the derived nature of the demand for labour. Firms offer employment because of their expectations that they can sell at a profit the goods and services which labour is capable of producing. There remains, however, the issue of how the level of aggregate output and its associated level of employment are determined. Again expected proceeds are of critical importance. Firms' expected proceeds are, of course, the amounts that economic agents are expected to spend. Keynes's aggregate demand function, like his supply function, is expressed as a function of employment, since employment generates incomes which form the basis for expenditure. Subsequent formulations of the aggregate demand function, again like their treatment of the supply function, relate expenditure (firms' expected proceeds) to income (output).

While through Say's Law the classical school held that output and expenditure are equal for all levels of output and employment, the essential message of the *General Theory* is that in the short run the extent to which firms employ labour to operate existing productive capacity depends on the level of aggregate demand. Thus, the Ricardian view that the aggregate demand function can be safely neglected and which, Keynes points out (G.T. p. 32), had triumphed over Malthus's concern with the importance of demand, was replaced by Keynes's view that the level of employment and hence output depends on the level of effective aggregate demand.

Moreover, since decisions on spending and on employment and production level are taken by different groups with different motivations, the level of employment resulting from the interaction of the aggregate demand and supply functions is not automatically a position of full employment. Decisions to spend may in the aggregate determine a level of effective demand which is insufficient to justify an output level that provides employment for all those individuals seeking employment. Nevertheless, the volume of employment may be at a stable level in the sense that the aggregate supply of goods and services has been adjusted to the prevailing level of aggregate demand. The possibility that market clearing may occur at less than full employment of labour, which represents the basis for Keynes's claim to provide a generalized theory, adds a third category, namely 'involuntary' unemployment, to the frictional and voluntary unemployment discussed by the classical economists.

The role of aggregate demand in Keynes's analysis leads to a reversal of the direction of causation contained in classical thinking. In the classical framework discussion of the real economy begins with their analysis of the labour market and then, having determined the level of (full) employment, establishes the associated level of output by reference to the production function. Say's Law is then used to account for aggregate demand. Keynes, in contrast, accepting the production function as a determinant of the aggregate supply function, employs the concepts of aggregate demand and aggregate supply to determine output and associated derived employment levels.

This elevation of aggregate demand to centre stage in explaining output and employment levels and Keynes's refutation of Say's Law required an analysis of the forces determining demand. Only then could the functioning of the macroeconomic system be properly understood. Keynes argued that:

> The amounts of aggregate income and of aggregate saving are the results of the free choices of individuals whether or not to consume and whether or not to invest; but they are neither of them capable of assuming an independent value resulting from a separate set of decisions taken irrespective of the decisions concerning consumption and investment. (G.T. p. 31).

Consequently, much of the *General Theory* (from chapters 8 to 18) is taken up with discussion of the factors influencing consumption and investment spending. Specifically, Keynes identified the propensity to consume, the marginal efficiency of capital and the theory of the rate of interest as 'the three main gaps in our existing knowledge which it will be necessary to fill' (G.T. pp. 91–5).

Within Keynes's framework, the propensity to consume, or consumption function, is one of the two determinants of the proceeds which firms in a private enterprise economy expect to receive, the other being investment expenditure. Keynes regarded the propensity to consume as a 'portmanteau function' which might be influenced by a number of objective factors, namely: a change in the wage unit; a change in the difference between income and net income; windfall changes in capital values not allowed for in calculating net income; changes in the rate of time discounting; changes in fiscal policy; and changes in expectations of the relation between the present and the future level of income. In addition, a series of subjective factors were identified as affecting consumption behaviour. These are assumed, however, to change only slowly in the short-run and serve to form the background against which consumption decisions are made (G.T. pp. 107–10). This background role is assigned also to most of the objective influences. Of the objective factors, aggregate income, as measured by the wage unit, is take to exert the principal influence on aggregate consumption. Thus, as is familiar from textbook representation, the Keynesian short-term consumption schedule is a stable, increasing function of real income, and the saving schedule is similarly a stable, increasing function of real income, a relationship quite different from that thought to obtain in the classical analysis.

The manner in which consumption expenditure varies with income arises from Keynes's famous 'fundamental psychological law', according to which 'men are disposed, as a rule and on the average, to increase their consumption as their income increases, but not by as much as the increase in their income' (G.T. p. 96). As incomes rise, some part of the increase is spent and some part is saved. The marginal propensities to consume and to save are necessary to understanding Keynes's consumption and saving functions and also because, by accounting for the behaviour induced by a change in income, they provide the basis for Keynes's elaboration of Kahn's concept of the multiplier. Kahn's concern was that of explaining how an initial increase in employment in investment activities leads to an expansion of total employment greater than the initial change. Keynes's multiplier is different from this employment multiplier in that, in line with his emphasis on the importance of demand, attention is focused on the ultimate impact on total income of an initial change in investment spending.

In contrast to the mechanistic, technical exposition of the multiplier customarily found in introductory textbooks, Keynes was at pains to follow Kahn in identifying a number of potential offsets to the expansion of output and employment. In line with classical fears about 'crowding out', the method of funding increased government investment spending and the increased transactions demand for money resulting from higher incomes and possibly higher prices, may raise the rate of interest and so deter other forms of investment spending. Furthermore, the 'confused psychology' associated with increased government spending may damage confidence and further retard investment spending; some part of the increased demand may 'leak' into higher employment levels abroad in an open economy; the marginal propensity to consume, which centrally affects the value of the multiplier, may diminish at higher income levels; the share of income accruing to entrepreneurs will tend to rise as income expands; and employment expansion will tend to reduce negative saving and, thereby, reduce the marginal propensity to consume (G.T. pp. 119–21). After allowing for these qualifications, the multiplier provides a general principle capable of explaining how changes in investment demand or, more widely, changes in any component of aggregate demand can result in much more extensive changes in output and employment.

The second of the three gaps identified by Keynes was filled by the development of the concept of the marginal efficiency of capital. This Keynes defined as 'equal to that rate of discount which would make the present value of the series of annuities given by the returns expected from the capital asset during its life just equal to its supply price' (G.T. p. 135). Keynes stresses a number of points about the marginal efficiency of capital, which he acknowledges as identical to

Fisher's concept of the rate of return over cost developed six years before the publication of the *General Theory* (G.T. p. 140). First, the marginal efficiency of capital is the factor through which expectations about the future influence the present. It depends not simply on current yield but on prospective yield over the lifetime of the asset and on the asset's current supply price. Second, investment will take place up to the point at which the marginal efficiency of capital in general equals the market rate of interest. Third, information on prospective yields and the marginal efficiency of assets is quite separate from, and does not enter into, the determination of rates of interest in money markets.

Keynes felt that the then prevailing orthodoxy embodies 'a large element of unreality' (G.T. p. 146) since 'even the rate of interest is, virtually, a current phenomenon' (G.T. pp. 145-6). He saw the marginal efficiency of capital as the means through which discussion of investment decisions could be shifted away from a static state by incorporating expectations about the future. Inevitably, long-term expectations are formed on the basis of uncertain knowledge and, consequently, the state of business confidence about the future assumes great significance. Business confidence, Keynes points out, is not separate from, but rather helps determine the marginal efficiency of capital.

The discussion of how the state of confidence is formed is seen by Keynes as a 'digression . . . on a different level of abstraction' (G.T. p. 149) from most of the *General Theory*. Keynes distinguishes between speculation, the attempt to forecast market psychology, and enterprise, the attempt to forecast the prospective yield of assets over their whole life (G.T. p. 158). Moreover, he introduces the idea of 'animal spirits' as a force on investment decisions by arguing that:

> a large proportion of our positive activities depend on spontaneous optimism rather than on mathematical expectation, whether moral or hedonistic or economic. Most, probably, of our decisions to do something positive, the full consequences of which will be drawn out over many days to come, can only be taken as a result of animal spirits – of a spontaneous urge to action rather than inaction, and not as the outcome of a weighted average of quantitative benefits multiplied by quantitative probabilities. (G.T. pp. 161-2)

However the state of business confidence is arrived at, it is taken to have a significant part in the *General Theory*'s focus on aggregate demand. The more or less confident the business community is about the future, the greater or lower will be the inclination to invest in new plant, machinery and equipment, i.e. the stability of investment spending is largely a function of business confidence. Nevertheless, Keynes was of the view that interest rates still have a great, though not necessarily decisive, influence on the rate of investment.

Given Keynes's specification of the demand for money and his view of the function of interest rates, the third gap he identified, i.e. the determination of the rate of interest, was readily filled. The rate of interest depends on the interaction of the liquidity preference schedule and the available amount of cash. It follows that the rate of interest may be raised (lowered) when the monetary authorities decide to contract (expand) the money supply.

The introduction of money as a causal influence on output and employment, in contrast to the classical view of the neutrality of money, also follows readily. Changes in the money supply may bring about changes in interest rates which alter the relationship between interest rates and the marginal efficiency of capital. A relative rise (fall) in interest rate will tend to decrease (increase) investment spending which will, in turn, affect aggregate demand and then output and employment.

This possibility that monetary changes can affect the real economy does itself, however, complicate the determination of interest rates. Through the transactions and precautionary motives, the demand for money is partly a function of the income level which may be affected by changes in investment spending resulting from changes in interest rates. Thus 'whilst an increase in the quantity of money may be expected, *cet par*, to reduce the rate of interest, this will not happen if the liquidity preferences of the public are increasing more than the quantity of money' (G.T. p. 173). These interrelationships, requiring the simultaneous determination of the rate of interest, investment and income, led subsequently to Hicks's development of the IS/LM framework, widely used as an expository device (Hicks, 1937).

As Moggridge points out, Keynes's development of his analytical framework was largely Marshallian in nature, because, as well as using a variant of comparative static analysis, he followed 'the master's habit of taking the argument one step at a time in a manner that looks like undirectional causation but is not' (Moggridge, 1976). In effect, Keynes constructed a series of building blocks, the principal of which are set out above. To these he added discussions of money, wages and prices and notes on the trade cycle and mercantilism. Notably missing from the *General Theory*, other than in occasional references, is consideration of the impact of the foreign-trade sector on aggregate demand. Moreover, although the impression created by the textbook presentation of Keynes's argument within the neoclassical synthesis emphasizes the role of government in influencing aggregate demand, the *General Theory* does not contain a discussion of the public sector *per se*. Nevertheless, it is the case that Keynes ascribes a much greater role to government than his predecessors.

The *General Theory*'s conclusion that the economic system could be in a stable, short-run position at an output level below that required to deliver full employment contains important implications for public policy. Through deliberate policy initiatives, government, in a period of depression, might stimulate the level of aggregate demand and thus raise levels of output and employment. This was in marked contrast to classical thinking which suggested that there was no case for government intervention to resolve problems of involuntary unemployment since such problems were only temporary and full employment, as it was defined, would be automatically restored through labour market adjustment. Keynes repudiated the idea of non-intervention by government, advocating the need for public policy measures to shift the system from one stable equilibrium to another, i.e. to eliminate a deflationary gap.

It is evident that Keynes's shift away from classical *laissez faire* reflects his concern over the impact of long-term expectations on investment spending. He argues that 'individual initiative will only be adequate when reasonable calculation is supplemented and supported by animal spirits' and that the fear of ultimate loss means 'not only that slumps and depressions are exaggerated in degree, but that economic prosperity is excessively dependent on a political and social atmosphere which is congenial to the average business man' (G.T. p. 162). That there is a case for moving away from reliance on private calculation is explicit in his discussion of the multiplier. With his much cited example of the Treasury burying old bottles filled with banknotes in disused coalmines and leaving their extraction to private enterprise, he argues, in a heavily sarcastic passage of the *General Theory*, that this is preferable to inaction if political and practical difficulties stand in the way of more 'sensible' activities, such as house building, since it will raise the community's real income and employment levels (G.T. p. 129). Concern with social rather than just private returns underlines the case for government assuming greater responsibility for direct intervention to raise the level of investment expenditure.

Keynes's advocacy of public investment spending rather than relying on influencing private investment through monetary policy largely follows from his reservations about certain parts of the chain of causation linking the money supply and investment. In contemporary textbooks,

Keynes's views about the impact of money supply changes on interest rates and about the sensitivity of investment spending to changes in interest rates are frequently compared with the quite different views on these relationships of the modern monetarists[5] (see Chapter 5). Keynes appeared to regard the liquidity preference schedule as interest-elastic since a large increase in the quantity of money may exert a comparatively small influence on the rate of interest (G.T. p. 172) and, in extreme circumstances, where the rate of interest has fallen to very low levels, 'liquidity preference may become virtually absolute in the sense that almost everyone prefers cash to holding a debt' (G.T. p. 207). Although Keynes recognized that this latter possibility had not previously arisen, it is represented in most textbooks as 'the liquidity trap' with little indication of its position in the *General Theory* as something of passing, but not central, importance. With regard to the rate of investment, Keynes stressed that investment spending might well be relatively insensitive to interest rate changes since the state of business confidence is a chief determinant of the marginal efficiency of capital. Thus even though interest rates are being reduced, businessmen pessimistic about the future may have little inclination to invest.

Keynes did not believe that a flexible wage policy could deliver a tendency towards full employment. Classical theory suggested that money wage cuts would permit employers to offer their output at lower prices and, thereby, to stimulate demand. Keynes shifted the emphasis from this preoccupation with supply-side cost analysis by pointing out that money wages were also a significant source of demand. Contraction of aggregate demand induced by money wage cuts would tend to lead, he suggested, to lower employment levels as entrepreneurs revised downwards their expectations of sales proceeds.

Thus, while the balance of outcome of the supply and demand effects working in opposite directions is unclear, Keynes felt that money wage cuts would have no lasting tendency to increase employment levels. Interestingly, however, given the closed-economy framework of the *General Theory* and in the light of exhortations during the 1980s by government ministers for workers to 'price themselves into jobs', one of Keynes's several qualifications about the repercussions of money wage cuts had an international dimension. He argued that if domestic money wages are reduced relative to money wages abroad, 'it is evident that the change will be favourable to investment, since it will tend to increase the balance of trade' (G.T. p. 262)

Keynes's preference for direct public investment rather than monetary policy or wage cuts came to be synonymous, following the Samuel-son-type neoclassical distillation, with advocacy of deficit financing to resolve problems of depression. His fiscal prescriptions were quite specific, however, and certainly more limited in scope than the impression which might be gleaned from subsequent textbook treat-ment. Against the background of the high levels of unemployment experienced during the Depression, the government spending favoured by Keynes in the *General Theory* was of a particular form, namely investment spending. A policy of social investment was required not to compete with or to displace private investment but to undertake projects such as road or house building in order to raise the level of aggregate demand.

The other component of fiscal policy, tax changes, attracted little explicit discussion in the *General Theory*. It is possible, however, to establish the basis of arguments about the impact of the reductions in a period of depression. When discussing the objective factors affecting the propensity to consume, Keynes points out that 'a change-over from a policy of government borrowing to the opposite policy of providing sinking funds (or vice versa) is capable of causing a severe contraction (or marked expansion) of effective demand' (G.T. p. 95). Moreover, he argued that redistributive tax measures aimed at achiev-ing a more equal distribution of incomes will increase the propensity to consume.

Reliance on fiscal rather than monetary measures during the postwar period up to the 1970s manifested itself in attempts at 'fine tuning', with chancellors frequently adjusting government expenditure and tax rates. The fine tuning approach was reinforced in the late 1950s follow-ing the publication of Phillips's empirical work on the relationship between money wage rates and unemployment (see Chapter 5). Keynes had argued that even in periods of substantial unemployment money wages would be inflexible in a downward direction as those employed sought to protect their relative real wages and that expan-sion of aggregate demand would exert little upward pressure on money wages in the presence of high unemployment. Money wages would begin to rise, however, as demand expansion moved the economy towards full capacity utilization. The Phillips Curve appeared to pro-vide empirical support for these views. Moreover, the Phillips relation-ship was attractive to policy makers since it suggested that through fiscal changes the economy could be shifted to stable positions along the Phillips trade-off between wage (or price) inflation and unemploy-ment. The stability of the Phillips Curve and the 'stop–go' pattern associated with fine-tuning policies represented the basis for the Keynesian–monetarist debate of the 1970s. Whether the approach to macroeconomic management adopted during the 1950s and 1960s is something of which Keynes would have approved is a debatable matter. It has been argued frequently, as, for example, by Leijonhufvud (1968) that Keynesian economics and its associated policy prescriptions are not the economics of Keynes.

AFTER THE GENERAL THEORY

Controversy over the *General Theory* began immediately after its publication. In the concluding paragraph of his preface Keynes observed:

> The composition of this book has been for the author a long struggle of escape, and so must the reading of it be for most readers if the author's assault upon them is to be successful, – a struggle of escape from habitual modes of thought and expression. The ideas which are here expressed so laboriously are extremely simple and should be obvious. The difficulty lies, not in the new ideas, but in escaping from the old ones, which ramify, for those brought up as most us have been, into every corner of our minds. (G.T. p. xxiii)

Earlier in the preface he commented

> Those who are strongly wedded to what I shall call 'the classical theory' will fluctuate, I expect, between a belief that I am quite wrong and a belief that I am saying nothing new. (G.T. p. xxi)

Throughout the *General Theory*, Keynes stressed the novelty of his approach and undoubtedly a great deal of the complexity and repetition of text, as for example with his discussion of liquidity preference, owes much to his efforts to emphasize what he saw as his break with previous thinking. As Keynes forecast, much of the initial reaction was hostile as seen, perhaps most forcefully, in reviews and comments by Pigou (1936), Schumpeter (1936), Knight (1937) and Hansen (1947), although the last of these authors subsequently became a leading American advocate of Keynes (Hansen, 1953). Lerner (1936), Reddaway (1936) and Austin Robinson (1947) were, however, much more favourably disposed.

An interchange with Harrod before the publication of the *General Theory*, cited by Moggridge, illustrates the difficulty of challenging orthodox views. With respect to Keynes's view that the rate of interest should not be regarded as the price which equates the supply of and demand for saving, Harrod argued that the effectiveness of Keynes's work would be diminished if he tried to eradicate 'very deep-rooted habits of thought unnecessarily. One of these is the supply and demand analysis' (Keynes 1973, XIII, p. 533). Harrod's warning proved accurate and the ensuing Keynes versus the classics debate concentrated on the extent to which there were important differences in theoretical analysis.

Moggridge points out that 'by the time of Keynes' death the view had emerged that his contribution to pure theory was relatively minimal' and Leijonhufvud observed that 'Keynes is no longer universally acclaimed as a major theoretical innovator' (Leijonhufvud, 1968, p. 12). The debate continued long after the publication of the *General Theory* and two of the relatively more recent contributions provide some indication of the manner in which the debate unfolded. In an attempt to assess the critical, i.e. necessary and sufficient, assumptions accounting for differences between Keynes and the classics, Leijonhufvud (1969) compared, *inter alia*, the classical assumption of flexible money wages and the Keynesian assumption of 'sticky' wages. He suggests that adding Keynes's restriction on money wages to the classical system means that the demand for labour determines the employment level and that 'the only use left for the labour supply function is that it then enables us to find out the amount of unemployment' (Leijonhufvud, 1969, p. 14).

On a different tack, Kaldor argued that Keynes's claims to novelty 'merely disguised the extent to which his theory suffered from an almost slavish adherence to prevailing (Marshallian) doctrine – to which his own ideas were "fitted" more in the manner of erecting an extra floor or balcony here or there, while preserving the pre-existing building' (Kaldor, 1983, p. 6). Kaldor's view is that Keynes's macro-economics amounts to very little since, as long as it is rooted in neoclassical microeconomics, the question of why markets do not generate the full utilization of resources cannot be resolved. What was required, he contends, was incorporation of the assumption of imperfect competition. Despite contemporaneous development by Chamberlin and Robinson, there was no such integration. Rather, following Keynes's predisposition to Marshallian theory, analysis proceeded along a general equilibrium framework with Hicks (1937) and Modigliani (1944).

The examples from Leijonhufvud and Kaldor illustrate two contrasting approaches to assessing Keynes's theoretical contribution. The former attempts to build an assumption derived from Keynes's analysis into the classical framework in an attempt to judge whether it makes any difference, while the other argues that Keynes failed to move sufficiently far from orthodox assumptions. But Keynes's work was not without support. Although subject to the criticism, as made by Yeager, that 'ample excuses for not having done or said something are not, after all, the same as actually having done or said it' (Yeager, 1986 p. 30), Leijonhufvud (1968) himself and Clower (1965) might be seen as attempting to interpret and, thereby, resuscitate elements of the theoretical import of the *General Theory*. They suggest that, although Keynes did not actually write of factors such as sluggish price and quantity adjustments, interdependence between individuals' transactions in different markets and imperfect information, these might account for a price system's inability to maintain equilibrium by furnishing a microeconomic analysis of disequilibrium processes.

Moggridge (1976) argued that Hicks's IS/LM representation of the *General Theory*, 'which has entered the textbook literature of modern economics so completely' is doubtful as an accurate representation of Keynes's work. Citing the argument in a letter from Keynes, Moggridge argues that every IS/LM diagram assumes a given state of expectations and, therefore, by not reflecting the nexus between expectations and uncertainty 'does not pick up the full Keynesian challenge to classical theory' (Moggridge, 1976, pp. 173–5). More recently, Tobin (1983) has argued that the main basis on which neoclassical theorists reject Keynes, namely stickiness in nominal wages and workers' irrational money illusion, is perhaps misplaced. Keynes's assumptions about decentralized money wage bargaining and workers' concerns with relative wages, along with some help from Kaldor's arguments on non-competitive markets, are, Tobin suggests, capable of explaining why it is easier to lower real wages by raising economy-wide prices (as a consequence of demand expansion) rather than by lowering money wages without recourse to money illusion. Tobin protests that the 'argument is perfectly clear in the *General Theory*. I don't know why it is so widely ignored' (Tobin, 1983, p. 33). Arguments on matters such as the above were subject to much debate and the issue of Keynes versus the classics generated a substantial literature involving many of the most eminent economists since the 1930s. There was also, following the *General Theory*, a very extensive expansion of aggregative analysis and empirical testing. In part, this was a consequence of attempts to expand the simple model of Keynes. In order to fill some of the model's gaps, Klein (1966) points out that several extensions were required: government and foreign trade sectors had to be added; and Keynes's static model had to be made dynamic

(Klein, 1966, pp. 194–6). Dissatisfaction with the static nature of Keynes's analysis, for example, led Harrod (1939) and Domar (1946) to consider the relationship between the capital stock and investment as income expands and in the light of Keynes's equilibrium condition of an equality between *ex post* saving and *ex post* investment.

In part also, growth in the literature followed from attempts to measure comprehensive aggregates and to model and test Keynes's macroeconomic concepts, particularly the consumption function. Patinkin (1976 p. 1092) commented that:

> the desire to quantify the *General Theory* provided the major impetus for the exponentially-growing econometric work that began to be carried out in the late 1930s on the consumption, investment, and liquidity-preference functions individually and, even more notably on econometric models of the Keynesian system as a whole.

The proliferation of macro-modelling based on his theoretical framework sits uneasily with views expressed by Keynes about the translation of economic theory into mathematical forms. In the following passage from the *General Theory* a strong antipathy to mathematical expression of economic ideas is readily apparent:

> It is a great fault of symbolic pseudo-mathematical methods of formalising a system of economic analysis . . . that they expressly assume strict independence between the factors involved and lose all their cogency and authority if this hypothesis is disallowed; whereas, in ordinary discourse, where we are not blindly manipulating but know all the time what we are doing and what the words means, we can keep 'at the back of our heads' the necessary reserves and qualifications and the adjustments which we shall have to make later on, in a way in which we cannot keep complicated partial differentials 'at the back' of several pages of algebra which assume that they all vanish. Too large a proportion of recent 'mathematical' economics are merely concoctions, as imprecise as the initial assumptions they rest on, which allow the author to lose sight of the complexities and interdependence of the real world in a maze of pretentious and unhelpful symbols. (G.T. pp. 297–8)

This antipathy also found vent in Keynes's (1939) well known comments on Tinbergen's (1937) attempts to test theories of the business cycle. Keynes's scepticism over Tinbergen's mathematical approach is fully set out by Moggridge (1976, p. 285–306). Keynes was much criticized for his views on Tinbergen[6] and Patinkin (1976) attributes these views largely to econometric inadequacies on Keynes's part.[7] The matter is not, however, simply one of technical competence but embraces the wider issue of methodological approach. There is a substantial body of literature attesting to Keynes having formed the view long before the *General Theory* that predictions of economic phenomena could not be based on statistical probability and that Keynes regarded economics as organic rather than mechanistic.[8]

This, and the contention in the lengthy quotation above that mathematical formulations obscure complexities and interdependencies, may be linked to Shackle's view (1949 and 1972) that the message of the *General Theory* is substantially different from the outcome generated by the rigid neoclassical synthesis. Shackle stresses the discussion of long-term expectations where Keynes elaborates on the incompatibility of uncertainty about the future and 'calculated mathematical expectation'.[9] On Shackle's interpretation, the central message of the *General Theory* is that with an unknown and unknowable future, the logic of equilibrium analysis is effectively rendered redundant – economic events are really much less certain than predicted by neoclassical orthodoxy. In the nature of debates about Keynes, Shackle's views on methodology and meaning have attracted opposition, as from Meltzer (1981) and Coddington (1983), and support, as from Earl and Kay (1985).

The third area in which Keynes has provoked extensive discussion is in public policy. While much of the economics profession was initially resistant to acceptance of Keynes's theoretical framework, his policy prescriptions attracted almost immediate adherence in the UK. Kaldor suggests that the outbreak of war lowered resistance to new ideas in the UK (Kaldor, 1983, p. 2). There was less ready acceptance of Keynes's policy prescriptions, however, in the US. Friedman suggests a possible reason for the difference in reaction by reference to a comparison between himself and Lerner. Friedman attributes Lerner's enthusiastic conversion to Keynes to his training at the London School of Economics where it was held that the Depression was the inevitable result of earlier boom; that it was deepened by resistance to lower prices and wages; that the monetary authorities were responsible for inducing and prolonging the Depression; and that the only sound policy was to let the Depression exhaust itself, reduce money costs and weed out weak firms. Seen against these views, Keynes 'offered a more immediate, less painful and more effective cure in the form of budget deficits' (Friedman, 1986, p. 49). In contrast, Friedman studied at Chicago where the Depression was seen as a consequence of misguided government policies which had allowed banks to fail and the quantity of deposits to decline. The Chicago case was for government action to stem the deflation and 'so far as policy was concerned,

Keynes had nothing to offer those of us who had sat at the feet of Simons, Mints, Knight and Viner' (Friedman, 1986, p. 49).

The widespread postwar adoption of fiscal policies as a primary instrument of macroeconomic management engineered two types of reaction. First, it was contended that there was nothing novel in Keynes's advocacy of direct government intervention. Attention has been directed to the fact that in the UK Keynes and Pigou jointly advocated countercyclical fiscal policies in the early 1930s and that further 'Pigou and Robertson were more consistently in favour of such policies than Keynes, whose interwar support for them waxed and waned with his evolving theoretical position' (Moggridge, 1988, p. 55). Salant points out that in the US Currie 'had independently developed ideas that were not greatly different from those of Keynes before the *General Theory* was published . . . and had become discouraged about the possibility of obtaining economic recovery through expansionary monetary policy alone and had become convinced that an expansionary fiscal policy involving a government deficit was needed' (Salant, 1988, p. 67). Moreover, Moggridge argues that with their predilection for the work of Kalecki, Joan Robinson and her followers frequently suggested that Keynes was 'little more' than a rather important pre-Keynesian or post-Kaleckian when they held that Kalecki in the early 1930s developed the theory of employment and appropriate policy responses before Keynes (Moggridge, 1988, p. 53).

It may be argued, however, in defence of Keynes that the importance of the *General Theory* lay in its presentation of both a consolidated critique of the then orthodox view and an alternative set of relationships which provided a rationale for a policy of government intervention. The experience of high and prolonged unemployment during the Depression sat at odds with pre-Keynesian theory and the *General Theory* 'made respectable what seemed obvious to common-sense observation of the lay observer but was rejected by sophisticated theorists as fallacy indulged in by amateurs' (Salant, 1988, p. 67).

The second main reaction evolved through the 'monetarist revival' begun in the 1950s by Friedman and which came to full fruition in policy terms in the late 1970s. This revival began when, during the first 25 years or so of the postwar period, the industrial economies enjoyed unprecedented growth accompanied by low inflation and unemployment rates. Whether these conditions resulted from the implementation of 'Keynesian' policies during that period or would have happened anyway is a matter of conjecture and debate. Monetarists felt, however, that the *General Theory* with its stress on the real economy had distracted attention away from the importance of analysing the significance of monetary disequilibrium. The marriage between fiscal prescriptions and the Phillips Curve was challenged by the Fried-man–Phelps adaptive expectations school with its emphasis on the micro-foundations of macroeconomics. Simultaneously, there was a shift toward general equilibrium models as devised by Barro and Grossman (1976) which incorporated the 'Keynesian' assumption of fixed money wages. Rejection of that assumption was subsequently instrumental in Barro's conversion to the new classical school with its adherence to rational expectations influencing both long- and short-run wage flexibility (see Chapter 5).

Whether or not the pre-1973 developments were attributable to Keynesian policies, Dow (1988) suggests that the economic environment of that period was markedly different from the circumstances of the 1930s and that it would not have been surprising if 'Keynes' way of thinking . . . had slipped out of use' (Dow, 1988, p. 106). The specific problems Keynes sought to address did not assert themselves, Dow argues, since 'stable financial markets and stable, and optimistic, long-run expectations minimise the power of uncertainty to reduce effective demand and thus raise unemployment' (Dow, 1988, p. 106). Even if the circumstances of the 1980s are characterized by greater uncertainty than earlier postwar decades, a number of important features are much different from the 1930s. The first concerns the substantial expansion of the public sector. Although by political inclination Keynes was a Liberal, he advocated the socialization of investment. It is self-evident that the role of government, perhaps encouraged by Keynes's advocacy of intervention, now extends far beyond his suggestion of contracyclical public works. Government transfers and taxes serve as automatic stabilizers moderating cyclical changes in the economy. Second, the economies of individual countries have become much more interdependent. The negotiation of reductions in tariffs and non-tariff barriers to trade through GATT, the formation of the European Community and trading blocs elsewhere, and the shift to more freely fluctuating exchange rates since the early 1970s have increased the importance of the international dimension in national policy formulation. This stands in marked contrast to the closed-economy framework of the *General Theory*.

What Keynes himself would have said about postwar developments in theory and policy and about the implication of changes in economic structure is, of course, unknowable. In 1983 Leijonhufvud argued that the Keynesian tradition had fallen into disarray and confusion. He declared that 'quite generally, Keynesian economics has adapted badly to opposition' and that 'to the younger generation of economists,

Keynesian economics – all of it, not just Keynes himself – belongs to the history of economic thought' (Leijonhufvud, 1983, p. 180). There has emerged, however, a group of new Keynesians, including Stiglitz, Taylor and Howitt, as a response to the new classical school of the 1970s and 1980s (see Chapter 5).

The new Keynesians employ the same general equilibrium framework, incorporating rational expectations, as the new classical school. They do not, however, take on board the assumption of market clearing. Matters such as implicit contracts and problems of price signalling are invoked to justify the assumptions of non-market clearing.[10] Thus, for example, they have attempted to demonstrate that involuntary unemployment can arise where wages are predetermined for certain periods, even if individuals have rational expectations. The link between non-market clearing and involuntary unemployment embodies echoes of the *General Theory*. There is, moreover, a role for government since the new Keynesians 'see individual decisions leading to macroexternalities, so that individual decisions do not necessarily lead to socially optimal results'. (Colander, 1988, p. 93).

This emergence of a group described as new Keynesians so long after the publication of the *General Theory* is the latest testament to the continuing association of economists with ideas which can be traced to Keynes. The influence which Keynes has exerted on the economics profession and on policy makers is rapidly borne out by contents of the numerous volumes published around the fiftieth anniversary of the *General Theory*'s publication. At a theoretical level, contributions to such volumes include topics such as Keynes's influence on subsequent debates about a wide range of particular macroeconomic variables and instruments. With regard to public policy, contributions embrace discussion of Keynes's views in historical perspective, the acceptance and repudiation of 'Keynesian' policies, and Keynes's political legacy. Although his policy recommendations in the *General Theory* were directed to government investment spending as a response to his concern over the impact of uncertainty on private sector investment, Keynes is seemingly inevitably invoked in debates over the relative merits of fiscal and monetary policies. Much is also written about Keynes the man. Moreover, the fascination with Keynes extends beyond debate about what is actually contained within, or what Keynes meant to say in, or what is directly descended from the *General Theory* to topics such as what Keynes would have thought about rational expectations.[11]

The number, range and variety of the writings about Keynes reflect the length, complexity and scope of the *General Theory*. Evidence suggests that Keynes himself had begun almost immediately to refine and perhaps rethink arguments. Moggridge points out that Keynes had drawn up by the spring of 1937 a draft of contents for a book entitled 'Footnotes to the General Theory of Employment, Interest and Money' although 'what would have evolved from this rethinking if it had continued, one cannot tell: many of his previous books had started from just such a set of footnotes to the last book he had published' (Moggridge, 1976, p. 115). But whatever direction Keynes's thinking might have taken had he been able to complete a successor book, the *General Theory* stands as a significant milestone in the development of macroeconomic thought.

NOTES

1. All references throughout this chapter to the *General Theory* (G.T. p.) are to *The General Theory of Unemployment, Interest and Money*, Volume VII of *The Collected Writings of John Maynard Keynes*, Macmillan for the Royal Economic Society, 1973.
2. Keynes included in the 'classical school' not only Ricardo, James Mill and their predecessors but also followers of Ricardo such as J.S. Mill, Marshall, Edgeworth and Pigou (G.T. p.1, footnote 1).
3. A brief exposition of economics before Keynes can be found in Stewart (1967).
4. In the *General Theory* Keynes presents his views on the money market at a relatively late stage in the analysis (Ch. 17) and not as part of the refutation of the classical system which comes mainly in Chapters 2 and 3.
5. See, for example, Wonnacott and Wonnacott, 1986, pp. 274–85.
6. See, for example, Klein (1954).
7. Keynes's views on econometric analysis and the debate and developments which his views stimulated are succinctly presented in the three chapters by Bodkin, Klein and Marwah; Rina; and Ramsay; in Hamouda and Smithin (1988).
8. See note 7.
9. This phrase is used by Keynes in the *General Theory*, p. 152. Shackle's views are set out in (1949) and (1972).
10. For a useful brief discussion of the evolution and assumptions of different schools of thought see Colander (1988).
11. See, for example, the two volumes edited by Hamouda and Smithin (1988) and that edited by Worswick and Trevithick (1983).

FURTHER READING

Institute of Economic Affairs (1986), *Keynes's General Theory: Fifty years On*, Hobart Paperback No. 24, London: IEA.

Moggridge, D.E. (1976), *Keynes*, London: Macmillan.

Worswick, D. and Trevithick, J. (eds) (1983), *Keynes and the Modern World*, Cambridge: Cambridge University Press.

SUMMARY OF THE ORTHODOX KEYNESIAN SCHOOL

World View

Aggregative macroeconomic society.
Rational economic agents with utility-maximizing motivation.
Decisions taken by different groups of economic agents not necessarily compatible.
Full employment equilibrium not necessarily attained.
Price/wage stickiness: markets may not clear.

Values

Individual is best judge of own welfare; consumer sovereignty.
Liberal.
Role of government to influence aggregate demand to achieve full employment equilibrium.

Goals

To show that a complete unfettered market system of utility-maximizing economic agents will not necessarily achieve full employment equilibrium.
To struggle to escape from habitual modes of thought and expression.

Methodological Practice

Inductive; abstract.
Emphasis on psychology and rejection of mathematical formalism.
Partial equilibrium; comparative static.

Hard Core

Distribution of tastes and endowments determined exogenously.
Exchange relationships.
Expectations; animal spirits.

Concepts

Marginal propensity to consume/save.
Marginal efficiency of capital.

SBC Responsien
- Butler
- Harris
- Thompson
- Currie
- Sabado
- Izban (billing)

Consumption function.
Multiplier.
Speculative demand for money.
Liquidity trap.
Aggregate demand.

Positive Heuristic

Explore macroeconomic consequences of consumption, savings and investment decisions of different categories of economic agents.
Analyse the determinants of aggregate demand and supply.
Explore the implications of expectations on the decisions of economic agents.

Protective Belt Assumptions

Prices cannot be negative.
Consumers are price takers.
Diminishing marginal physical products of factors of production.
Specialization and division of labour.
Mobility of factors of production.

Themes

Full Employment.
Aggregate demand.
Involuntary unemployment.
Socialization of investment.

7. The Post-Keynesian School*

Sheila C. Dow

The ideas now classified as post-Keynesian have a long history. But the notion of a post-Keynesian school as such is a relatively recent one. As a result its boundaries are not yet settled, in so far as boundaries can ever be defined. Indeed, the post-Keynesian school benefits from constructive interchange of ideas with most of the other schools of thought dealt with in this volume. Some have argued that what unites post-Keynesians is a negative factor: the rejection of neoclassical economics. But in fact the post-Keynesian school of thought represents a positive statement in terms of methodology, ideology and content. It is inevitable, given the dominance of neoclassical economics within the discipline, that much post-Keynesian writing includes analysis of differences from the mainstream, to clean the slate as it were for post-Keynesian analysis. But the trend now, as post-Keynesian economics matures, is for the emphasis to be progressively on developments within the school, with less reference to the mainstream. The work of the school is thus becoming more accessible to those not already fully conversant with all the intricacies of the mainstream, at the same time as solidifying its own identity.

Before embarking on a discussion of the main preoccupations of post-Keynesian economics in a later section, we shall set out in turn the post-Keynesian view of methodological issues and ideology respectively. All three aspects of the school of thought are interdependent. But the distinctive post-Keynesian attitude to methodology and ideology are profoundly important to the way in which the contents of post-Keynesian theory are understood. It is no accident that much (particularly of the early) post-Keynesian writing includes statements of methodological and ideological difference from neoclassical economics, within which methodological and ideological concerns are commonly left implicit. Having said that, the methodology and ideology of post-Keynesian economics result in turn from a preoccupation

*This chapter has benefited from helpful comments and suggestions from Philip Arestis, Victoria Chick, Geoff Harcourt, Avi Cohen and the editors.

with the laws of motion of capitalism, economic growth, income distribution, and unemployment, and the attendant role of the state.

In what follows, Begg, Fischer and Dornbusch's introductory textbook will constitute a reference point for the discussion of post-Keynesian economics. The question of what an introductory post-Keynesian text should look like, and whether the notion of a text is methodologically compatible with post-Keynesian economics, will serve to highlight the main features of the school of thought. But in the first section we discuss the main cast of characters and their role in the development of the school.

FOUNDERS AND CURRENT REPRESENTATIVES

As the name 'post-Keynesian' suggests, the work of John Maynard Keynes is a significant influence. But Keynes is not the sole influence on the school, and indeed the earlier writers who influenced Keynes himself are often identified by post-Keynesians as having influenced them directly. We therefore precede an account of the founders and representatives of post-Keynesianism with a chronological discussion of early influences.

Post-Keynesianism has its roots in classical economics. Other schools of thought also refer back to the classical period; post-Keynesians draw on particular classical writers, a particular interpretation of their work, and a particular view of the relevance of the history of economic thought to the development of economics.

Adam Smith is regarded as the first key figure, in common with many schools. His *Wealth of Nations* provided the basis for the development of classical economics, with its primary focus on policy issues, growth and distribution, and the working of specialist capitalist economies. More significant for post-Keynesian economists now is the methodological groundwork laid by Smith, which has lain virtually dormant until renewed attention was paid to it in recent years. In particular, Smith's *Theory of Moral Sentiments* and *History of Astronomy* set out a view of scientific activity which was only developed in the philosophy of science in the 1960s, but can be identified in Keynes's work in the 1920s and 1930s. The relevant ideas will be explored in the next section.

As far as the content of post-Keynesian economics is concerned, the key classical figures are Malthus, Ricardo and Marx, each influencing different groups within post-Keynesian economics. Malthus was concerned with the tendency for classical economics to become preoccupied with full employment states. He developed the idea that the level of output and employment were determined by the level of aggregate demand in the economy, rather than supply conditions. The important implication was that economies could consistently operate below full capacity, if demand were below the full employment level; unemployment was not a temporary, self-correcting phenomenon. The principle of effective demand lived on through various writers including the underconsumptionists like Hobson, but was only developed into a general theory by Keynes and Kalecki. The resulting strand of post-Keynesian economics has most in common with the school defined here as Keynesian economics.

Ricardo pioneered the formalization of economic theory, requiring a more abstract, ahistorical, static analysis. Methodologically, Ricardo paved the way ultimately for the precursors of modern neoclassical economics. But his focus on the size and distribution of the surplus of value of production over costs, as the main determinant of growth, has spawned an element of post-Keynesian economics (commonly referred to as neo-Ricardianism) which owes more to Keynes's contemporary, Sraffa, than Keynes himself (who disliked Ricardo's analysis). Sraffa's Ricardian model contributes to post-Keynesian understanding of effective demand, at the same time as providing a logical critique of neoclassical economics. But the Sraffa model requires an analysis outside historical time, and an analysis of the long run independent of the short run, both methodologically antipathetic to post-Keynesian economics. The neo-Ricardian strand of post-Keynesian economics must therefore be regarded as marginal to mainstream post-Keynesianism.

Marx's theory of crisis too has its influence; the theory of cyclical instability constitutes a bridge between the radical and post-Keynesian schools. Marx's study of the laws of motion of capitalism, driven by the accumulative motive, provides an explanation for the periodic emergence of crisis. The influence of Marx on post-Keynesians most commonly comes through the work of Kalecki. Kalecki had independently arrived at the same conclusions as Keynes about the normality of unemployment, the cyclical nature of capitalism, and the failure of market mechanisms to correct either. But he did so using a Marxian class framework, distinguishing between workers and capitalists, and without the degree of business competitiveness assumed by Keynes.

Post-Keynesians, then, are primarily interpreters and developers of Keynes, but also of Kalecki and, to a lesser extent, Sraffa. Most post-Keynesians are indebted to at least two of these three. The founding post-Keynesians were influenced by all three, being also contemporaries of theirs at Cambridge. It is for this reason that the school is sometimes referred to as the 'Cambridge school'. Of this group of contemporaries at Cambridge, Joan Robinson is most clearly the founder of post-Keynesian economics, her influence ranging over a variety of subject areas and fora. Her work combined the Keynesian theory of effective demand with Kaleckian imperfect competition and the Sraffian critique of neoclassical theory. Joan Robinson is important for her leadership among post-Keynesians, and for her efforts to communicate their ideas to neoclassical economists. She drew together the different threads of influence on post-Keynesian economics and in turn inspired different future developments.

Other founders, each of different aspects, of post-Keynesian economics are Kahn, Tarshis, Weintraub, Shackle, Kaldor and Dobb. Aside from his particular contribution of the concept of the income multiplier, Kahn was a prominent figure in the 'circus' at Cambridge which fostered and further developed the ideas of Keynes's *General Theory*. Tarshis and Weintraub both kept alive and further developed the neglected Keynesian focus on aggregate supply as well as aggregate demand. (Keynesian economics has popularly but erroneously been presented as 'demand-side' economics as if containing no 'supply-side' economics.) Tarshis made more use of the Kaleckian assumption of imperfect competition, while Weintraub emphasized more the Marshallian notions of competition underlying Keynes's own theory. Shackle too has been an important interpreter of the *General Theory*, his main contribution being the analysis of decision making under uncertainty at the level of the individual firm. His work has built a bridge between post-Keynesian and neo-Austrian economics.

Kaldor's work, like Joan Robinson's, shifted the emphasis to the long period, with an analysis of the determinants of economic growth. Some ascribe the primary influence on post-Keynesians to study growth to Harrod. However, methodologically, Harrod and Keynes were not altogether in tune, particularly in their use of the equilibrium concept. But Keynes had written only sketchily on the long-period implications of his theory; the development of growth models has been one distinctive feature of post-Keynesian economics. The concern with long-run processes has also been influenced by Marxian analysis, through the work of Dobb, and also of Meek. (As we shall see below, much subsequent work in the long-run has taken a different tack, following Sraffa, in effect abstracting from historical time.)

The current representatives of post-Keynesian economics can be seen to group around these various founders. Joan Robinson has been presented here as the primary founder because she succeeded in combining all elements of what we now call post-Keynesian economics. Accordingly, the archetypal current representatives are those who have followed this lead: Geoff Harcourt at Cambridge and Jan Kregel at Johns Hopkins, Bologna. While not specifically Robinsonian, Victoria Chick at University College London has developed post-Keynesian theory across a wide spectrum of issues. The UK and Italy are also the primary sources of the neo-Ricardian, or surplus, approach within post-Keynesian economics: John Eatwell at Cambridge, Ian Steedman at Manchester, Luigi Pasinetti at Milan, Pierangelo Garegnani, Sergio Parinello and Alessandrio Roncaglia at Rome, Krishna Bharadwaj at Jawaharlal Nehru University and Heinz Kurz at Graz are also significant contributors.

The Marxian tradition was translated into post-Keynesian economics by Hyman Minsky, with his financial theory of the cycle. The financial aspects of Keynes's theory have been built up notably by Paul Davidson, now at Tennessee, but without Minsky's Marxian perspective. Money is also the focus of a group in France led by Alain Parguez of ISMEA in Paris, who combine Keynesian and Marxian analysis in their theory of the monetary circuit. Davidson's late colleague at Rutgers, Alfred Eichner, developed rather a Kaleckian theory of the firm. He also instigated econometric testing of post-Keynesian results for the US; Philip Arestis has done likewise for the UK. Kaleckian theory has also been developed further by Tom Asimakopulos at McGill, Malcolm Sawyer at Leeds (England), Peter Reynolds at North Staffordshire Polytechnic and Peter Kriesler at New South Wales. Meanwhile Shackle has inspired a behavioural approach to analysis of the firm, further developed by Brian Loasby at Stirling, Peter Earl at Tasmania, and Neil Kay at Strathclyde.

There is so much new work being done in post-Keynesian economics in so many countries that it is hard to feel that any list of current representatives is adequate. This growing community of post-Keynesians has been fostered by several important institutional developments. The most explicit was the creation by Sidney Weintraub and Paul Davidson of the *Journal of Post Keynesian Economics* in 1977. But in addition, several explicitly non-mainstream journals have propagated the ideas, notably the *Cambridge Journal of Economics*, edited collectively, *Thames Papers in Political Economy* edited by Philip Arestis and Thanos Skouras, *Australian Economic Papers* while Geoff Harcourt was an editor, and the *Monnaie et Production* series of *Economies et Sociétés*, edited by Alain Parguez. In 1989 a new journal explicitly set out to publish post-Keynesian material, along with other forms of political economy: the *Review of Political Economy*, edited by John Pheby. In addition various conferences have been particularly hospitable to post-Keynesian ideas, notably the US Eastern Economic Association and the History of Economics Association. There are also explicitly post-Keynesian conferences: one following the Trieste Summer school (which is run by Sergio Parinello, Jan Kregel and Pierangelo Garegnani), one at Tennessee run by Paul Davidson and Jan Kregel, and one at Great Malvern, England, run by John Pheby, which spawned the *Review of Political Economy* and one in Australia. In addition, Victoria Chick and Philip Arestis have set up, since 1988, an ESRC Study Group in Post Keynesian Economics; similar groups meet in the Netherlands and in Australia.

METHODOLOGY

Looking at the work of any one post-Keynesian, we generally find elements which belong also to other schools of thought: no person is an intellectual island. But at the level of methodology it is more straightforward to identify boundaries, particularly between neoclassical and non-neoclassical economics. The non-neoclassical schools have some common methodological views: it is ideology which must then be considered (in addition to methodology) to distinguish between them, as we do in the next section.

Methodology is the study of scientific method. It is sometimes used in the narrow sense of 'study of technique'; here we use it in the broader sense of corresponding to a paradigm, as introduced by Kuhn. A paradigm is an approach to a discipline adopted by a community of scientists. It involves shared assumptions about fundamentals, so that scientific activity within the community revolves around problem solving (or 'normal science') given the fundamental theoretical framework, or methodology. The paradigm thus consists not only of technical procedures, but also of a world view which determines the types of questions asked, the way in which objective reality is perceived, and the method of analysis which is generally acceptable. We leave aside for the moment the important ideological content of the post-Keynesian world view, and concentrate on the view taken of how economic scientific activity should be conducted.

We have already departed from a neoclassical view of methodology, which is restricted to the study of technique. Non-neoclassical economists tend to be methodologically conscious because they find themselves out of sympathy with the implicit methodology of orthodox economics. So the methodological content of post-Keynesian writing tends to be high. This contrasts with the minimal attention paid to methodological issues in a textbook like Begg, Fischer and Dornbusch (1984, 1987). But, in any case, the post-Keynesian view of methodology as ranging from ideology through to technique requires that it be continually raised as an issue.

A key feature of the post-Keynesian view of methodology is that economic theory is not seen as necessarily evolving in a more or less continuous way to generate ever 'better' theories; there may be 'wrong turnings', and important elements of economic theories may inadvertently be swept aside. The neoclassical approach in contrast is to regard present theory as containing all that is good from past theory. Thus, for example, Begg, Fischer and Dornbusch's occasional attention to different traditions in economics sits ill at ease with the unquestioning application of neoclassical techniques in the body of the textbook. But for post-Keynesians, there is nothing inherently progressive about the shift from one paradigm to the next. Paradigms are what is called 'incommensurate': there are no universal criteria by which to judge all paradigms, only criteria internal to particular paradigms. Thus post-Keynesianism is regarded as one paradigm which its followers advocate *by post-Keynesian criteria*; but it is accepted that others will apply different criteria in adopting other paradigms. Further, this approach allows for differences within post-Keynesian economics as well as between post-Keynesianism and other schools of thought. It should already be clear that there are disparate traditions within the paradigm which attract different allegiances among post-Keynesians.

It follows from all this that the history of economic thought is important to post-Keynesian analysis. It is important since post-Keynesian methodology presumes that theory can undergo paradigm shifts which may not be regarded as a progression, and lessons may still remain to be learned from the past. It is also important for conveying the breadth and depth of the post-Keynesian paradigm, or some subset of it, to identify and explore historical roots. Both of these aspects are evident in the blossoming of post-Keynesianism following the publication of Keynes's *Collected Writings*. This material has proved to be a goldmine of ideas on subjects ranging from philosophy to economic policy, and has shed light on how Keynes's ideas were subsequently interpreted.

Keynes's work in mathematics and philosophy provides a foundation for the emerging understanding of the methodology of post-Keynesianism. Although Keynes did not refer to it, the philosophical work of Adam Smith provides another foundation, relatively isolated in the history of economics. For both Smith and Keynes, the process of theorizing and the assessment of theories are sociopsychological, rather than logical, processes. Both were conscious of the power of persuasion, the sociology of knowledge, and the psychological element of perception. While scientists may aim to understand the 'true world', there was no one best theory or style of theorizing. This view of theorizing was interdependent with their view of knowledge acquisition by economic agents. Both incorporated fundamentally in their analysis the irreversibility of historical processes, and thus the evolutionary nature of economics (as of knowledge and theorizing). Both too had a sophisticated view of human nature as being moulded by the sociopolitical environment as much as by self-seeking behaviour.

As a result, post-Keynesian methodology, drawing in varying degrees on these traditions, can be characterized as having the following features:

Absence of Dualism

Dualism involves the use in theorizing of definition according to two all-encompassing mutually exclusive categories with fixed meanings. This is a key feature of classical logic as applied within the formal expression of neoclassical economics. But post-Keynesians allow first for phenomena which are unknown and thus not amenable to inclusion in an all-encompassing definition. In particular, Keynes's analysis of probability demonstrated that numerical probabilities could only very rarely be assigned to predictions with complete certainty.

The evolutionary nature of historical processes means that surprise is endemic and we cannot categorically cover all possibilities in any definition or prediction. Second, economic phenomena seldom fall into either–or categories; it is unhelpful, for example, to define behaviour as being either purely rational or purely irrational, or to categorize evidence as being either known or not known. Third, even if either–or categories were helpful for theorizing, i.e. abstracting from reality, it is unhelpful for the meanings of categories to be fixed. Thus, for example, what is rational in one context may more helpfully be defined as irrational in another; or the notion of competitive markets may be seen to take on different meanings in different historical contexts; most notably within post-Keynesian economics, equilibrium may be given different meanings for different purposes.

By rejecting dualism, post-Keynesian theory has two important characteristics, as listed below.

The Absence of a Normative/Positive Split

As do most textbooks, Begg, Fischer and Dornbusch drew the dualistic distinction between analysis of what is (positive economics) and analysis of what ought to be (normative economics). This presumes that it is possible to conduct value-free analysis. But post-Keynesians regard both perceptions and theorizing as being necessarily conditioned by the environment in which the economist functions: what constitutes unemployment, for example, is a value-loaded concept. (In theory the basis of data can continually be brought to the surface as conditioning the analysis, but in practice some standard definition of unemployment is usually taken for granted.) It is regarded as laudable to make the value basis of theory as clearly visible as possible. But if values cannot be eradicated, the notion of a normative/positive split in economics is a misleading fiction.

The Absence of a Micro/Macro Split

All introductory textbooks, and Begg, Fischer and Dornbusch are no exception, separate material into macroeconomics and microeconomics. This is sensible only if the two levels of analysis reflect a distinction in reality. But if human nature is regarded as being social as well as individual, then the macro and micro levels of analysis are inextricably interrelated in a fundamental way. But the two levels are interrelated in the concern with the macro and micro implications of the unintended consequences of human actions. What are the implications, of disappointed expectations for the level of output and employment, and how do individuals react? The micro–macro distinction is retained by post-Keynesians for some purposes, but not as a dual as defined above.

Organic rather than Atomistic Analysis

The avoidance of a macro–micro dual stems also from the organic view of economic processes, which can be contrasted with the atomistic view of neoclassical economics. Atomism treats all elements of the economic structure as separable and unchanging (the structure is non-evolutionary). It is thus amenable to reductionism, which involves reducing all processes to their smallest constituent parts, i.e. to the behaviour of individuals. (If taken to its extreme, reductionism would break down individual behaviour into biological and/or psychological components.) The neoclassical individual is 'economic man', a pleasure-maximizing, pain-minimizing machine. An organic view of the economic process takes a more complex view of human nature and of individual behaviour, seeing individuals as social beings. In particular, individual behaviour conforms to habits and conventions determined at the social, or group, level. Thus, for example, investors are influenced in their expectations by the mood, or general view, of their associates. Expectational shifts explain much of the volatility of stock markets, and of capital expenditure plans. But the importance of group connections for expectations formation more generally promotes stability. Further, and more fundamentally, individual motivation is not regarded as solely self-interested, nor behaviour mechanistic. Here again the tradition derives from Adam Smith and his complex notion of sympathy as being a powerful determinant of human behaviour. More generally, an organic approach is non-axiomatic; it is not regarded as helpful in trying to understand economic processes either in different contexts, or in the full complexity of any one context, to try to tie them all down to a common set of axioms (like the axioms of rational individual behaviour).

Open Theoretical System

Post-Keynesian theory as a whole constitutes an open theoretical system. The axiomatic approach of neoclassical theory lends itself to building up a system of simultaneous equations: a closed system. This in turn allows deterministic answers to comparative–static questions like 'how does output compare under two different rates of income tax?' The equation system provides no information on a process occurring over time, i.e. a change in income tax and its consequences. Post-Keynesians however are concerned with processes and are more concerned to predict tendencies and chains of possible events, than to make definitive predictions which ignore process: 'It is better to be roughly right than definitely wrong'.

Viewed organically, the economy's reaction to an increase in tax rates will be complex and non-deterministic. The change may be so large as to promote institutional and behavioural change which would not be reversed if tax rates were to be reduced; increased resort to moonlighting would be an example. Alternatively, the change might not be large enough, or visible enough, to affect behaviour at all, other than reducing disposable incomes. The question could well be addressed simultaneously by means of a range of approaches to add weight to the final conclusion: looking at all questionnaire evidence, historical evidence, formal labour theory, for example. An open theoretical system is adopted where it is regarded as impossible to capture in one formal model all relevant aspects of an economic process; some aspects will require other methods. This makes post-Keynesian theory more difficult to tie down than neoclassical theory; closed formal systems have an aesthetic appeal, and are easier to teach and to learn.

Interdisciplinary Approach

It follows from the openness of the post-Keynesian system that it will be open also in a disciplinary sense. Thus sociology, history, psychology, business studies and politics may all provide input to particular chains of reasoning. Indeed much of the work going on at the frontiers of post-Keynesian economics is aimed at drawing on these other disciplines, particularly in developing rich alternatives to the limiting characteristics of rational, selfish, individualistic economic man.

Realism

This choice of methodology by post-Keynesians reflects a realist approach to economics, where realism means a concern to understand causal processes. These processes will take particular forms in particular situations (times, places); while general statements are made about the capitalist process, predictions on specific issues will be contingent on context. In so far as general predictions are made they are more predictions of tendency than precise predictions. Within a closed, formal theoretical system like that employed by neoclassical economists, realism can only be very limited: it can refer to whether or not assumptions are realistic, and to whether predictions are confirmed by the evidence. Predictions are precise, but their significance is limited by the all-important *ceteris paribus* assumption.

   The distinction between the two approaches is most evident in the context of econometric forecasting, which requires that economic structure does not change. But such change is the focus of post-Keynesian economics. Econometrics can identify such change after it has occurred, and help to explain what has happened. But if econometrics is to forecast successfully during a period of changing economic structure, there must be an accompanying analysis of evolutionary processes. For example, US econometric exercises in predicting the demand for money in the 1970s were hopelessly wrong, and it took considerable effort to identify after the fact the behavioural and institutional changes that had encouraged the lower demand for money that had actually transpired. This 'case of the missing money' seems remarkable to post-Keynesians, who naturally focus on the possibility of behavioural and institutional change in banking practice, for example, as a result of sharp increases in interest rates. No definite prediction could have been made of the extent to which the demand for money would be reduced, but there was alertness among post-Keynesians to the likely tendency. 'Testing' theories in post-Keynesian economics is thus a more open process than comparing definite forecasts with definite out-turns; it is again a more open process of comparing predictions of processes with actual processes as observed according to a variety of methods. Much of this description of post-Keynesian methodology is held in common with other non-neoclassical schools of thought. We turn now to discuss ideology to allow us to define post-Keynesianism more fully.

IDEOLOGY

Post-Keynesian methodology, as described above, lacks a set of principles governing the selection of methods to address particular issues, the selection of the issues themselves, and the underlying perception of reality. These are all provided by post-Keynesian ideology.

In political terms the majority, but by no means all, of post-Keynesians are left of centre. This is reflected in the predominant issues addressed by post-Keynesians: unemployment, income distribution, the distribution of power and economic instability. It is also reflected in the range of cures suggested for economic problems many of which involve state intervention in some form. Underlying all this is a particular view of the economic process within capitalist economies. Capitalism is understood as part of an evolutionary process, whereby the motive of financial accumulation generates an unstable cyclical pattern in economic activity, and an unbalanced distribution of income and power at all levels (individual to international). The state's role is to counteract this instability and uneven distribution by stabilization policy, particularly in the form of government capital expenditure and curbing the power of large business and the financial sector.

Post-Keynesianism inevitably attracts economists with some significant ideological differences. This should not be surprising given the diverse ideologies of the main influences on post-Keynesianism, notably Keynes who was a Liberal and Kalecki who was deeply influenced by Marx. Thus there are differences of opinion as to the degree of state intervention that is regarded as appropriate. Post-Keynesians are reformist in that there is no conception of a complete takeover of the private sector by the state; there is thus scope for considering different public sector/private sector mixes in a mixed economy. One specific dispute over the merits of a wage controls form of incomes policy is seen by some as being ideological: between those in favour, who see wage claims as a primary causal factor in the inflationary process, and those against, who see market power among producers as a primary causal factor.

The following is a statement of ideology by a leading post-Keynesian, which serves as a benchmark for understanding the ideology of the school. It is a particularly apposite statement, in that it demonstrates the interrelationship between methodology and ideology, and indeed the fundamental role of ideology in the work of any economist. In the previous section it was pointed out that post-Keynesians avoid the normative/positive split of neoclassical economists; this is precisely because of the inability to separate economics from ideology.

> [The purpose of economics is] to make the world a better place for ordinary men and women, to produce a more just and equitable society. In order to do that, you have to understand how particular societies work and where the pockets of power are, and how you can either alter those or work within them and produce desirable results for ordinary people, not just for the people who have the power. I see economics as very much a moral as well as a social science and very much a handmaiden to progressive thought. It is really the study of the processes whereby surpluses are created in economies, how they are extracted, who gets them and what they do with them. All economies have created surpluses in one way or another. Capitalism does it in a particular way and that is the process in which I am most interested because I live in capitalist economies. At the same time, I would like to help to create a society where the surplus is extracted and used in a way quite different from that of a capitalist society. (Harcourt, 1985, p. 5)

CONTENT

The methodological perspective outlined earlier helps us to understand the apparent diversity within post-Keynesian economics, of which this section provides an account. Individual post-Keynesians generally specialize in particular aspects of post-Keynesian economics, and employ particular ranges of methods. Thus the work of growth theorists like Kaldor differs significantly from that of post-Keynesians influenced by Shackle's work on expectations and uncertainty. But the point of post-Keynesian methodology is that no single theory can capture the complexity of the economic process, so that a richer understanding is provided by adopting a range of approaches simultaneously. What guides the choice and combination of approaches is a common ideology.

As a result, an account of the content of post-Keynesian economics cannot look like a Begg, Fischer and Dornbusch textbook account of neoclassical economics. Neoclassical economics employs a unitary methodology which allows all aspects of economics to be combined within a single formal mathematical system, which is equally applicable to all contexts. Thus the theoretical basis for Begg, Fischer and Dornbusch, written for the UK market, is identical with that of Fischer and Dornbusch (1983) written for the US market. Data and institutional detail referred to in the text differ, but the theoretical analysis is regarded as universally applicable. A post-Keynesian text of a similar detailed coverage which went beyond some basic principles would need to be rewritten fundamentally to apply to different countries' situations. However since we limit ourselves here to general principles, an overall guide to post-Keynesian economics is possible.

Monetary Production Economy

Money and production are regarded as being so fundamentally interrelated in the functioning of capitalist economies that it is rarely helpful to separate the two for analytical purposes. The driving force of capitalism is the desire to accumulate financial assets. This started, at the time of the agricultural revolution in England, with the efforts of serfs either to save enough or to borrow enough to acquire land, but accumulation has since become an end in itself. Not that human nature in general is depicted by post-Keynesians are entirely selfish and greedy; the motivation of all individuals is regarded as complexly interwoven with the institutional structure of society. (Thus, for example, Keynes pointed out that workers may be more concerned with relative wages than absolute wages. Similarly, entrepreneurs may be more motivated by the goal of personal fulfilment, than by profit seeking *per se*.) The importance of the goal of financial accumulation is that it is pursued by the main investors in financial markets, and it is their power within capitalist economies which makes their motivation and behaviour the driving force. The importance of this factor for post-Keynesian economics should become apparent as we proceed.

Principle of Effective Demand

Keynes and Kalecki re-established Malthus's Principle of Effective Demand as the key determinant of the level of output and employment in a modern economy. It states that output and employment are determined by the level of aggregate demand, as defined by the sum of consumption, investment, public sector demand and net foreign sector demand. The full employment level of output is only one of any number of possible levels of output determined by demand. In probabilistic terms, the normal situation would be one of less than full employment.

This principle is counterposed to Say's Law, which reverses the causal process: according to Say's Law, the supply of factors of production, including labour, determines the level of output and income, which in turn generates the demand to take up the output. In particular, all withdrawals from the expenditure stream in the form of saving return to the stream in the form of investment demand. The successful operation of Say's Law is conventionally regarded as ensuring full (and efficient) employment of resources. It requires that the markets in labour, capital and products all be perfectly competitive; it is the free movement of the real wage which makes the amount of labour supplied equal the full employment level, the free movement of the interest rate which equates saving and investment, and the free movement of the product prices which ensures that the composition of output is what the market wants.

The post-Keynesian assertion of the Principle of Effective Demand involves arguing that at least one (and in fact all) of these mechanisms fails to work properly. Thus, if the level of aggregate demand is below the full employment level, we cannot fall back on Say's Law to restore full employment. Put briefly, modern labour markets are incapable of generating the market-clearing wage; the interest rate clears the money market, not the market for loanable funds; and (although this is not a necessary feature of the Principle of Effective Demand) product markets are predominantly imperfectly competitive, so that the pattern of output is distorted in relation to the pattern of market demand. We shall elaborate on each of these points in our discussions below of the labour market, money, and the structure of production. But it is important to note at this stage that the general critique is an evolutionary one: it refers to how particular markets actually function in modern economies, and allows for differences as between contexts. Thus, for example, a successful incomes policy might increase control over the real wage. Say's Law *may* have been justified as a general theory by the institutional arrangements of the eighteenth century France and England in which it was developed. But to apply Say's Law automatically to modern economies is to adopt the inappropriate neoclassical method of assuming that theories have universal application.

Aggregate Demand and Aggregate Supply

Keynesian economics is often characterized as 'demand-side' economics, because of the Principle of Effective Demand. And indeed the inattention of post war Keynesians to supply considerations can be blamed for some of the problems that arose with Keynesian policies in the 1970s, and the rise of supply-side theory. But such a characterization imposes a neoclassical dual (demand versus supply) on Keynes's theory which incorporated both demand *and* supply; Keynes emphasized demand to counteract lack of attention to it in the existing literature. Keynes and post-Keynesians argue that supply is determined by given technology and the inherited capital stock, but also by expected demand. Investment and production plans are made on the basis of the expected market for the output. Actual private sector demand is determined by the income generated by previous production and earned by consumers, and by producers' investment with respect to the expected demand for their products in the future. There is thus an independent aggregate supply curve which, in combination with aggregate demand determines actual output and employment. But the two are fundamentally interrelated over time. The basis of actual output and employment is effective demand, the level at which firms' production plans, based on expected demand, and actual demand conditions, coincide. Supply is of course also governed by considerations of technology, bottlenecks in the supply of inputs, and so on. We turn to these aspects of supply when we consider economic growth below.

Business Cycle

Aggregate demand, output and employment follow a cyclical pattern which is inherent in capitalist economies; exogenous shocks like wars and technological breakthroughs can cause instability, but this is overlaid on an endogenous instability. (This contrasts with neoclassical theory's depiction of the cycle as being caused by government intervention or other exogenous forces, without which output and employment would be stable.) The instability of capitalism arises from the motive of monetary accumulation: the desire of producers and financial investors to amass wealth for its own sake. It must be said that this motivation is more muted for producers, particularly owner-managers. But for the large publicly owned corporations the goals of management must be tempered by the desire for increased profits on the part of the shareholders.

Post-Keynesian business cycle theory up to a point shares with other forms of Keynesianism a multiplier–accelerator theory as a cause of instability, but not as the sole cause. Thus the cycle in output and employment follows an investment cycle. The upturn starts as firms embark on replacement investment, and then new investment as the marginal efficiency of capital increases. The accelerator amplifies the resulting expansion in effective demand, encouraging increased supply in the short period and also further investment to increase supply further in the long period. Similarly in the downturn, the accelerator amplifies the cutback in production plans, in incomes, in consumption and in investment. The upturn is associated with the effects of more optimistic profit expectations, and the downturn with the effects of more pessimistic expectations. The accelerator model provides a mechanistic explanation for expectations to follow a cyclical pattern.

Post-Keynesian business cycle theory, under the influence of Kalecki and Minsky, is less mechanistic on two counts. First, long-period and short-period expectations are regarded as being potentially highly volatile, although conforming normally to conventional patterns. The long-period profit expectations of business people were called by Keynes 'animal spirits'. Second, financial markets undergo a cycle which has profound effects on the production cycle. The cycle can be explained in terms of investment, whereby the expected rate of return on the investment (the marginal efficiency of investment) is compared to the cost of capital (the interest rate). But post-Keynesian theory emphasizes the process by which the two are interrelated.

The interest rate is the compensation for parting with liquidity, for postponing decisions on expenditure on goods or financial assets. Other things being equal, the interest rate will be high (low) if liquidity preference is high (low) relative to the supply of liquidity. The supply of liquidity (in the form of the liquidity of existing assets, and the availability of new credit) in turn depends on two main factors: the level of activity in markets for non-monetary assets (which determines how easily these assets can be exchanged for money), and the availability of credit (how far bankers are willing to lend money). Both of these factors, together with liquidity preference, follow a cyclical pattern. As an upturn gets underway, expectations of returns on non-monetary assets become more optimistic: the desire for liquidity is low, since the expected capital gains from going illiquid are high, while markets become more active and bankers become more willing to lend. The demand for credit rises to finance new projects (although not for money to be held liquid). This latter factor may put upward pressure on interest rates, but the other factors ensure that the interest rate is low relative to expected returns on other assets, further encouraging investment.

As the accelerator slows down the production expansion towards the peak, it is financial assets and non-reproducible assets (old masters, land, etc.) which attract investors, rather than new capital goods. A speculative bubble may then build up, even though output and employment are already weakening. The financial system becomes very vulnerable to lower than expected returns on the one hand and relatively high interest costs on the other: forced asset sales to cover higher interest costs further depress asset prices. The process then goes into reverse, with liquidity preference increasing while markets become less active and banks become less willing to extend credit: the outcome is higher interest costs, and reduced credit availability, which serves to accelerate the contraction in output and employment. Financial markets play a key role in the cycle, therefore, since *their* estimation of the marginal efficiency of investment relative to the returns on other assets governs the cost and availability of credit to business. Lately, firms themselves have been engaging in these direct comparisons: as their estimate of marginal efficiency of capital deteriorates, they have been engaging more and more in financial investment. The cycle then arises from the search for profits, not only by producers, but also by financial investors.

Growth

The relationship between economies in the short period (following a business cycle pattern) and in the long period (following a growth path) is a source of some difference of opinion among post-Keynesians. As post-Keynesianism is being presented here, the long period is regarded as a cumulation of short periods; in other words, growth is not independent of cycles. The timing of turnarounds, i.e. the length of upturns and downturns, determines whether growth is slower or faster. For example, if a speculative bubble diverts finance from production well before full employment is reached, and if the downturn is so well entrenched that animal spirits take a long time to recover, growth will be relatively slow. It is primarily neo-Ricardians who regard the type of business cycle analysis presented above as inadmissable because they regard financial markets as being peripheral to the production process; for them it is the long-period trends in output which are of exclusive interest, so that economic theory is identified with growth theory.

The problem of the relationship between long period and short period is partly a methodological one, and can be illustrated with reference to Harrod's growth model, which is often identified as the origin of post-Keynesian growth theory. Harrod (1939) considered the implications of Keynes's theory of investment for production capacity. In particular, if animal spirits were depressed and investment were low relative to planned saving, incomes would fall until the two were equal. But at the same time, the depressed capital stock would limit the capacity of the economy to produce output. Alternatively, optimistic animal spirits would accelerate growth by increasing effective demand, but also by increasing capacity. The common interpretation of this model is that economies are destined to a cumulative process of expansion or contraction, which is hard to sustain in the face of the evidence of a much more uneven growth process. In fact, Harrod's model was not set in historical time, but referred to tendencies to expansion or contraction at a point in time; in historical time there would be the adjustments to saving behaviour and technology which formed the basis of his business cycle theory. The issue for post-Keynesian growth theory is whether relationships such as the propensity to save and the capital requirements of production follow a long-period pattern independent of cyclical variations, so that conclusions can be reached about long-term trends in the rate of growth of output, i.e. a systematic theory is at least partially identified.

An important focus of post-Keynesian growth theory has been the significance of income distribution, using the stylized fact that the propensity to save out of profits is much higher than the propensity to save out of wages. The rate of profit, which is a main determinant of investment, in turn determines a propensity to save; income adjusts to bring actual saving into equality with actual investment. Redistribution of income towards wage earners thus lowers the overall propensity to save, boosting effective demand. Income distribution is thus an important determinant of demand in the short run as well as the long run (emphasized by Chick 1983, Davidson, 1972, 1978 and Weintraub, 1966). Redistribution may bring the economy closer to full capacity output. But it is generally perceived that, to obtain a high rate of economic growth, investment and technological change are also necessary.

Post-Keynesian growth theory then explores the relationships between the rate of profit, investment planning, saving behaviour and technological change to establish the potential of growth of an economy, and to explain why it generally falls short of this potential. The crucial difference between post-Keynesian and neoclassical growth theory is that investment is regarded as being prior to saving. This priority is established where banking systems allow credit creation in response to the need to finance investment. Then it is investment which determines output and income and thereby saving; except in the absence of credit-creating capacity, actual saving can only constrain output if it affects expectations of demand and thus returns on investment. A further fundamental difference from neoclassical theory, outlined earlier, is that economies may or may not operate at full capacity; full employment equilibrium is at best a benchmark for analysis, certainly not the end-result of a process in mechanical time, as it is in neoclassical theory.

Key factors in investment behaviour are industrial structure and pricing behaviour, and the markets for labour and capital. These are dealt with in turn in the following two sub-sections. The independence of finance for investment from saving is also important, as is liquidity preference; these are addressed in turn.

Industrial Structure and Pricing Behaviour

The influence of Kalecki is most keenly felt in this aspect of post-Keynesian economics. Keynes presumed that industry was competitive, not in the neoclassical sense of perfect competition, but in the Marshallian sense of free competition. The latter allows for uncertainty in decision making, and unintended consequences of actions, both of which prevent the definition of supply curves. But at any rate most modern post-Keynesians take as a starting point, as did Kalecki, that a high proportion of production (constituting the core industries) is organized in oligopolistic markets. However, without free competition, far less perfect competition, supply curves certainly cannot be defined. One corollary is that prices are determined not by marginal utility, as in neoclassical theory, but by the structure of industry, and the technical conditions of production.

The predominant model of pricing in the short run is that of the mark-up: firms charge a given mark-up on costs of production. The mark-up clearly cannot be entirely independent of demand; but demand in turn is not regarded as independent of the conditions of production. Oligopolistic industries can create, through a variety of means, a market for their products, so that it is debatable how far product demand curves may be defined. Pricing behaviour results from interrelationships between firms and other conventions: oligopolistic behaviour is notoriously difficult to analyse formally as a result so that the notion of a mark-up provides a reasonable stylization.

The mark-up is greater the less competitive the industry, i.e. the greater the degree of monopoly. But for individual firms its size also depends on the need for internal financing of investment. As a corollary, prices will be higher, the greater the degree of monopoly, the greater is investment demand, and the less external funds are available to finance it. To the extent that these variables follow a cyclical pattern, there may be a cyclical pattern to inflation: the degree of monopoly increases in a recession as small firms face bankruptcy, and as the availability of external finance becomes more limited. Planned investment is strongest in the upturn, but an investment boom in an upturn can be externally financed. Even with weak investment plans in a downturn, there may still be strong demand for internal funds to finance takeovers and mergers. The tendency therefore may be for mark-ups, and thus inflation, to be pushed up even in a recession. The traditional post-Keynesian approach to the cycle has focused on output and employment responses rather than price responses; oligopolistic pricing is much more stable than in the perfectly competitive model. But a deep recession which forces a significant number of bankruptcies, takeovers and mergers will cause the type of price adjustment outlined above in addition to the output and employment response.

In times of inflation, the costs to which the mark-up is added are just as important as the mark-up itself. In the next sub-section we consider the factors of production, land (or raw material inputs), labour and capital.

But before moving on, we must make reference to the theory of long-run pricing, which is potentially incompatible with the mark-up model of short-run pricing. Sraffa (1960) was concerned with the relationship between prices, income distribution and the rate of profit in a long-run stationary state (the role of demand being notably absent): predetermination of any one of the three ensured that the other two are jointly determined. The rationale for, and methodological underpinnings of, the Sraffa model (and its development by the neo-Ricardians) are very different from those of the mark-up model. The latter conforms more to what is generally recognized as 'post-Keynesian'. Nevertheless Reynolds has pointed to ways in which the two theories may be rendered compatible, with the timeless Sraffian stationary state being translated into a long-run tendency.

Factors of Production

Just as for current production, the markets for the factors of production are regarded as being predominantly imperfectly competitive. The returns to each factor are the result of a struggle over income shares. Traditionally, raw material markets have been the most competitive, the result of which has been unstable export earnings and deteriorating terms of trade for developing countries heavily dependent on raw material production. The inflation of the 1970s was fuelled by a successful struggle on the part of oil producers to combine in order to increase their income share, and the unwillingness of oil consumers to yield that increase by accepting a fall in real incomes.

Wages generally constitute the highest proportion of production costs, and are identified by many post-Keynesians as being the main cause of inflation, reflecting the struggle of labour for its income share. As effective demand rises in an expansion, unemployment falls, increasing the market power of workers in their wage demands. In a contraction, money wages generally fall back relative to prices due to reduced worker power. Even if the labour market were competitive, Keynes showed that a further relative fall in money wages could not cure unemployment, because it would further weaken aggregate demand. Indeed it is the fluctuations in effective demand which are of primary significance; they would be aggravated rather than counteracted by the neoclassical cure of real wage adjustment. But for most post-Keynesians, the labour market is not regarded as competitive in any case, so that the neoclassical demand and supply analysis does not apply. The labour market, further, is particularly influenced by conventions, by historical experience, and by non-monetary considerations, all of which limits the scope for formal analysis and requires analysis to be context-specific.

The neoclassical literature often conflates the concepts of financial and physical capital, because their rates of return are equal in equilibrium. The two are clearly separated in the post-Keynesian literature, because they each play a different part in the economic process and because that process is the focus of attention more than equilibrium. We shall deal here with physical capital. Here the argument is parallel to that for labour: a fall in the cost of capital does not necessarily encourage more investment, since the overriding influence on investment, as on employment, is anticipated aggregate demand, which in turn determines the rate of return on investment. But in any case, the notion of the rate of return on capital is clouded by the fact that capital can only be valued in terms of its rate of return. Physical capital, and its return, only has meaning at the level of the firm, or possibly the industry. Just as in practice firms do not have free choice over the level of employment, so they are limited in their investment to a small number of 'blueprints', depending on the existing capital stock and labour force, and available technology.

Analysis of the market for physical capital, like the labour market, must thus be context-specific. With reference to growth, investment is regarded as key, and is determined by the technical conditions of production, as well as expected demand. While saving in general is not relevant as a constraint on the investment decision, availability of finance may be an effective constraint. If banks are unwilling to lend and other forms of finance are too costly, firms must rely on internal funds. Then, at the level of the firm, the capacity to generate saving (a function of market power) will be important. Thus, unless the supply of credit is elastic, growth requires exercise of market power to generate the saving to finance investment.

Money

The role of money as provider of prior finance for investment is inextricably tied up with the uncertainty surrounding investment planning. Production takes time, particularly when preceded by new investment. Expectations of demand, however well informed about the past, cannot be expressed even in terms of probability distributions with any precision. Money is the refuge of uncertainty; liquidity preference not only involves a desire to hold assets in as liquid a form as possible but also involves a wish to postpone investments and incur debt. But liquidity preference will be low if animal spirits overcome uncertainty with optimism about returns on investment. The pattern of liquidity preference over the cycle was outlined previously.

The availability of external finance is crucial to the argument that investment is not dependent on firms' own prior saving, and is the source of some difference of opinion among post-Keynesians. What is agreed is that money comes into circulation primarily as the counterpart of credit created by the banking system; it thus accompanies, rather than causes, an increase in expenditure.

While the scope for monetary control varies with the institutional environment, central banks in general are limited in their capacity to control credit creation. Direct credit controls are possible, but need to cover all sources of credit to be effective. The monetary authorities can indirectly control the supply of money by means of reserve ratios; but any attempt to do so would involve refusing to supply reserves to back up new credit created by the banking system. The banking system functions ultimately on confidence in the monetary authorities' willingness and ability to maintain the value of money (most importantly in the form of bank deposits). In general, to maintain this confidence, banks cannot be allowed to be insolvent or even illiquid on any significant scale. The remaining avenue of influence, which is most commonly employed, is the interest rate at which the monetary authorities will provide additional reserves.

The money supply is thus endogenous; it cannot be said to cause inflation since it is itself responding to demand, nor can it be controlled directly to cure inflation. The difference of opinion is over the degree of endogeneity. Some argue that it is purely endogenous; credit is available to meet all demand at the interest rate set by the monetary authorities. Others argue that banks themselves exercise liquidity preference; they will themselves choose to invest in securities rather than advances to industry if their (uncertain) expectations are of increased default risk due to failing aggregate demand. In terms of the business cycle, while banks fuel the expansion by their willingness to extend credit, showing optimism about returns on a wide range of assets, they can deepen the recession by an increasing unwillingness to extend credit.

The international debt crisis provides a case study of a massive expansion in bank lending as banks perceived relatively high returns on LDC debt, followed by a reversal as perceptions of default risk changed. This reversal in turn increased default risk by forcing downward income adjustment to meet high interest payments, and by encouraging private sector capital outflows from LDCs.

Policy

Post-Keynesian ideology suggests a strong role for the state in the economy. It also follows from the content of post-Keynesian theory that capitalist economies are inherently unstable, tend to operate at less than full capacity, and have inbuilt inflationary tendencies. All these tendencies are the result of a fallacy of composition whereby individual actions in private markets are incapable of producing the socially optimal outcome; reducing wages and increasing saving, if widespread, will simply aggravate unemployment, for example. Further, there is a prisoner's dilemma problem that the private sector does not always generate the institutions to promote cooperation even when fallacy of composition problems are absent; however the government can use legislation, and set up institutions, to promote cooperation.

The cure for unemployment, regarded as perhaps the most serious shortcoming of capitalist economies, is to boost aggregate demand. Investment is regarded as the key component of demand, not only because of its inherent instability, which becomes exaggerated by multiplier and accelerator effects, but also because it determines the long-term trend growth rate. Thus state expenditure can enhance private sector investment in four ways:

1.   Current expenditure can increase aggregate demand directly, increasing expected returns on planned investment.
2.   Current expenditure may increase productivity of labour through health, education and social welfare expenditure, and of capital through funding of research.
3.   Selective expenditures, e.g. through regional policy, may boost 'animal spirits'.
4.   The state may engage directly in capital spending where private sector investment cannot reliably be expected.

Monetary policy is also seen as a tool to stabilize total spending at a high level, with a high rate of investment. Financial stability is as important as the level of interest rates, not least because such stability discourages diversion of funds to speculation rather than purchase of new capital goods. Monetary policy is not seen as a vehicle for manipulating the level of aggregate demand and thereby inflation.

Inflation is regarded as the by-product of struggle over income shares, a struggle which would lose some heat if a high, stable rate of economic growth were to be attained. This would particularly be so in the context of a stable financial environment with adequate availability of external funds to finance investment. Some sort of long-term incomes policy is advocated by many post-Keynesians, in order to diffuse the uncertainty surrounding the wage bargain over what the resulting real wage will be.

CONCLUSION

The post-Keynesian school starts with a particular interpretation of Keynes's work which differs from the mainstream Keynesian interpretation which formed part of the neoclassical synthesis. The two hold in common the Principle of Effective Demand, which implies that unemployment can be cured by increasing aggregate demand. (The neoclassical synthesis however only allows demand a short-run role.) But the divergence from that point is, above all, a methodological one. Neoclassical synthesis Keynesian theory is mechanistic, assuming stable relationships in the economy. But post-Keynesian theory regards stability, where it exists, to arise from conventions and conventional behaviour, and focuses equally on the instability which is regarded as inherent in capitalist economies. Further, post-Keynesian macro-economics is integrated with a distinctive post-Keynesian microeconomics; together the two levels of analysis provide an explanation for stagflation, which draws on recent stages of evolution in industrial and financial structure.

Post-Keynesian theory overlaps too with several of the other traditions covered in this volume: the institutionalists regarding the role of conventions and their embodiment in institutions, and the evolutionary nature of economic processes; neo-Austrians regarding uncertainty and expectations, as well as institutions; the radical school regarding the theory of financial crisis and production crisis. But post-Keynesians are more willing to generalize beyond case studies than are institutionalists; they reject the extreme subjectivism of neo-Austrians and their critique of state interference; and they are reformist, unlike the radical school, in that scope is seen both for the state and for private sector institutional change, to counteract some of the ills of capitalist economies.

FURTHER READING

Several collections of papers by post-Keynesians have been published which, together with the editors' introductions, provide a good flavour of the scope and method of post-Keynesian economics: Eichner (1979), Arestis and Skouras (1985), Pheby (1989) and Arestis (1988).

The Hamouda and Harcourt paper in the Pheby volume provides the most comprehensive survey of the school. Coverage of a wide range of post-Keynesian economics can also be found in Reynolds (1987) and in the relevant sections of Dow (1985).

Further, influential post-Keynesian interpretations of Keynes and Kalecki can be found, respectively, in Chick (1983) and Sawyer (1985).

The closest thing to a post-Keynesian textbook in the conventional sense is Eichner (1987) and, at a more advanced level, Kregel (1973).

Finally, for those who wish to pursue particular topics, a collection of leading articles in post-Keynesian economics can be found in Sawyer (1988) or in the following journals (in alphabetical order):

Cambridge Journal of Economics
Eastern Economic Journal
Economies et Sociétés: Monnaie et Production
Journal of Post Keynesian Economics
Metroeconomica
Review of Political Economy
Thames Papers in Political Economy

SUMMARY OF THE POST-KEYNESIAN SCHOOL

World View

Capitalism is part of an evolutionary process, characterized by financial accumulation motive, which generates an unbalanced distribution of income and power at all levels (individual to international).
No single formal theory can capture the complexity of the process.
History of economic thought is very relevant, and conveys breadth and depth of the post-Keynesian paradigm.
Shifts in paradigms are not necessarily progressive.
The process of theorizing, and the assessment of theories, are socio-psychological, rather than logical, processes.
Economics cannot be separated from ideology. Value-free analysis is not possible.

Values (Ideology)

Economists' values should be made explicit.
Left of centre mainly, concerned with unemployment, distribution of income and power, and economic instability (cycles). Strong role for the state in a mixed economy, (reformist, not revolutionary), e.g. to curb power of large business and of financial sector.

Goals

Policy considerations in general override theoretical considerations; 'to make the world a better place for ordinary men and women, to produce a more just and equitable society . . . to understand how particular societies work, and where pockets of power are, and how you can either alter those or work with them'.

Methodological Practice

No real positive/normative distinction.
Micro- and macroeconomics integrated.
Organic rather than atomistic analysis – humans are social beings.
Open, dynamic, theoretical system, with non-deterministic tendencies, (not a unitary, formal, deterministic, closed, simultaneous-equation model).
Interdisciplinary approach.

Realism (searching for causal processes underlying evolutionary change).
A range of empirical methods employed.
Context-specific analyses, rather than universally applicable theories.

Hard Core

Realism:
– emphasis on causal mechanism,
– interaction between agency and structure.
Accumulation:
– laws of motion,
– (expanded) reproduction,
– firms rather than consumers as key agents.
Fundamental instability of market economies:
– fallacy of composition,
– divergence of private and social incentives,
– effective demand failures.
Importance of historical time:
– irreversibility,
– limited usefulness of equilibrium analysis,
– fundamental uncertainty.

Concepts

Effective demand.
Income distribution.
Equilibrium as tranquillity in historical time.
Interest rate as monetary phenomenon.
Monetary theory of production.
Uncertainty.
Conventions.

Positive Heuristic (Agenda)

Further integration of micro and macro.
Integration of growth theory and cyclical analysis.
Role of conventions, and of technical change.
Pricing behaviour.
Evolution of the financial system.
Comparative analysis which takes account of different institutions and histories.

Protective Belt Assumptions

Endogenous money supply.
Price and wage inflexibility.
Behaviour social rather than individualistic.

Themes

1. Monetary production economy:
   – driving force of capitalism is desire to accumulate financial assets.
2. Principle of effective demand:
   – key determinant of output and employment is level of aggregate demand = consumption + investment + public sector demand + net foreign sector demand.
3. Aggregate demand and aggregate supply:
   – supply is determined ultimately by expected demand.
4. Business cycles (short-period dynamics):
   – the cyclical pattern inherent in capitalist economies is due to the financial accumulation motive by producers, and especially by financial investors. Financial markets undergo a cycle which has profound effects on the production cycle via the inter-relationship of expected rate of return on investment and cost of capital (like radical school).
5. Growth (long-period dynamics):
   – Growth is the accumulation of cycles (for neo-Ricardians growth is independent of the cycles). Post-Keynesians explore the relationship between the rate of profit, investment planning, saving behaviour, and technological change.
6. Industrial structure and pricing behaviour:
   – high proportion of production is via oligopolies,
   – price = mark-up times costs of production,
   – mark-up is influenced by degree of monopoly, and could be cyclical,
   – demand is not autonomous of production.
7. Factors of production:
   – their markets are predominantly imperfectly competitive. Factors are responsive to expected aggregate demand, more than to factor prices.
   – returns to factors are the result of a struggle over income shares (inflationary).

8. Money:
   – money is the refuge in uncertainty,
   – money supply is endogenous, responding to credit creation by banks, given interest rate set by monetary authorities. Banks help to fuel expansion and contract recession.
9. Policy:
   – strong role for the state in a mixed economy: government expenditure, especially to enhance private sector investment, to boost aggregate demand, to lower unemployment;
   – dispute re merits of long-term incomes policies to combat inflation;
   – monetary policy for a stable financial environment, and hence counteract instability (cycles).

Evidence

Questionnaire evidence, historical evidence, 'stylized facts', econometric testing.

Conclusions (Examples):

Stagflation can be explained by micro and macroeconomics, together with the evolution of modern institutions.
Capitalist economies:
– are inherently unstable (cycles),
– tend to operate at less than full capacity (e.g. unemployment),
– have inbuilt inflationary tendencies, due to struggle for income shares.

8. The Institutionalist (Evolutionary) School

John Foster

Institutional economics has been one of the principal schools of non-orthodox economic thought, particularly in the US, in the twentieth century. It has had a much more 'economic' character than that other great engine of radical ideas in economics, Marxism, which has been wedded to interdisciplinary social science and identified with a social movement (see Chapter 9). It predates the post-Keynesian school, simply because it existed long before Keynes wrote the *General Theory* in 1936 (Chapter 7). Although the two schools have a number of comparable features, the relationship between them has continued to be an uneasy one. This has been due, first, to the fact that some institutionalists have argued that much of Keynes's analysis was already within the institutionalist tradition. Second, the connections between post-Keynesianism and neo-Marxism have led to some reluctance by institutionalists to accept the full range of ideas which have been classified as post-Keynesian.

Institutional economics reached its high point in the interwar period in the US when, contrary to impressions gained in some histories of economic thought, it was the principal school of economic thought. It was widely taught and exerted a strong influence on policy. For example, the New Deal was the product of institutionalism. It was not until after the Second World War that neoclassical economics began to replace institutionalism as the mainstream of American economics. From then on, the aspirations of economists to be seen as scientists led to rejection of the normative priorities of institutional economics in favour of the apparent positivism of mathematical logic as embodied in, for example, Paul Samuelson's *Foundations of Economic Analysis*. This trend led to a steady decline in the number of institutional economists over the postwar period. By the 1980s they were to be found mainly in schools and institutes of agriculture and commerce, where an institutionalist perspective was seen as indispensable to proper interdisciplinary research and teaching.

Antipathy towards the supposedly unscientific, normative and descriptive character of institutionalism grew to such an extent that some practitioners did not make their association with modern institutional thought very explicit. Both Kenneth Boulding and John Kenneth Galbraith, for example, built their substantial postwar reputations, as critics of neoclassical economics and proponents of alternatives, by drawing extensively on institutionalist principles, while working relatively independently of institutionalists of their time. Thus the institutionalist tradition has lived on through the work of a wider range of economists than simply the relatively small group who have used the label of institutional economics to describe their work.

However, this small group and the *Journal of Economic Issues*, which has been the focal point of their research endeavours, have had a vital role to play in preserving and developing the fundamental principles laid down by the founding fathers of institutionalism. Today, interest in institutions and how they evolve has, once again, become fashionable, as neoclassical microeconomics and macroeconomics have become widely perceived as analytically deficient (see Chapters 4 and 6). Although this renewed interest has led to a resurgence in institutional and evolutionary approaches in economics, much of this new work does not draw on established institutionalist thought in any direct way.

The 'new' institutional label has been attached, most notably, to Oliver Williamson on account of his *The Economic Institutions of Capitalism*, published in 1985, where he presents a picture of institutional development driven by the existence of transactions costs. Despite the fact that the transactional approach was developed much earlier by John Commons, a prominent institutionalist, Williamson's analysis is founded on a neoclassical view of economic behaviour. The 'new' evolutionary label has been taken by by economists who have adopted the mathematics and statistics of non-linear dynamics (or chaos) into the subject but largely within a Schumpeterian, rather than an institutionalist, perspective. Despite understandable protests from institutionalists concerning lack of acknowledgement of relevant contributions in their tradition, it must be recognized that these new developments constitute large steps away from neo-classical economics towards institutionalism. Too few economists have had sufficient respect for the history of economic thought, but it is undeniable that institutional economics is once again on the agenda of contemporary economics. It is, therefore, timely to examine its history and prospects.

In the next section we shall investigate the origins of institutional thought from the turn of the century on. The following section will present the fundamental propositions of institutional economics. Then the most successful employment of institutional ideas in the postwar period, by John Kenneth Galbraith, will be discussed, followed by a look at the concept of evolutionary dynamics which has been espoused by institutionalism from its beginning. After this we shall consider the emergence of the 'new' institutional economics and its relationship to the old, and finally assess the future of institutional economics.

THE ORIGINS OF INSTITUTIONAL ECONOMICS

Institutional economics has traditionally offered critiques of both neo-classical and Marxian economics. The alternative conception of the economy presented is, in part, a continuation of the German and English historical schools of political economy which existed in the nineteenth century. This historical tradition has been widely associated, in more recent times, with the writings of Max Weber. However, his work has received much more attention in mainstream sociology than in economics. This mirrors a common reaction to institutionalism, which gathered force with the spread of neoclassical economics, that it is 'not really economics'. Indeed, inasmuch as economics is now a modern specialism dominated by neoclassical economics, rather than political economy with its interdisciplinary perspective, then such protests may have some validity.

Institutional economics was born out of criticism of the neoclassical approach when the latter was in its infancy at the turn of the century. Its identifiable beginning is in the writings of Thorstein Veblen, particularly his *The Theory of the Leisure Class: An Economic Study of Institutions*, published in 1899. Veblen followed with a number of books and articles attacking most aspects of neoclassical thought as they stood in his time. He foreshadowed the critiques of rational economic man (REM) which were to be written half a century later. The neoclassical economic agent was, to Veblen, 'a lightning calculator of pleasures and pains' who operated in a static and timeless world.

However, Veblen did not merely argue that the assumptions which determine the behaviour of REM are unrealistic. He understood well the role of abstraction in logical analysis but argued that REM was inadequate as a useful abstraction even for simple thought experiments in economics. He could not see how an abstraction which was expressed in static terms in non-historical time could ever capture the essence of economic processes. He saw the critical driving force in economic behaviour as creativity but could find no theory as to how and why invention and innovation take place in neoclassical economics; therefore, to Veblen, neoclassical economics was vacuous. Furthermore, he could not see how economic analysis could proceed without explicit inclusion of the variety of institutional arrangements surrounding economic behaviour because, to him, institutions inhibited the progressive force of creativity.

This conflict between the developmental force of individual creativity and the repressive force of institutions formed the basis of Veblen's characterization of evolutionary tension. The dynamic process which he outlined was one where this tension operated through status emulation, which was viewed as motivationally central to individual economic behaviour. The result was fluctuating economic development, as old institutions broke down and new ones were created. The process described, although historical in a way comparable to the evolutionary vision of Karl Marx, was distinctly un-Marxian in content. The emphasis on creativity was Hegelian in spirit, in sharp contrast to dialectical materialism. Status emulation within the context of technological progress was Veblen's engine of economic development, rather than a deterministic struggle between narrowly defined social classes exhibiting solidarity.

Veblen's institutionalism was further developed by Clarence Ayres, in the 1940s, particularly in his *The Theory of Economic Progress*, and came to constitute one of the two main strands of institutionalism. The other strand comes from the writings of John R. Commons, most notably in *Institutional Economics*, where he took a much more favourable view of the role of institutions than Veblen or Ayres. He saw some institutions as facilitating collective action which would lead to economic development. In other words, he saw organizational development as a vital force as well as technology. Thus, Commons's depiction of evolution relies less on continual conflict between creativity and institutional inertia and more on the application of creativity to the design of institutions themselves.

These two distinct strands of institutionalism have existed side by side, enjoying amicable and constructive discourse. The difference concerns the relative emphasis on technology and institutions in economic development, but based on a considerable common core. Certainly this difference was not the cause of the decline in popularity of institutionalism since the 1930s in the US. It has much more to do with the contents of the common core, which can be loosely described as non-materialist, and to which we now turn.

THE FUNDAMENTALS OF INSTITUTIONALISM

Mainstream economists view the central economic problems as resource allocation, the determination of income, output and prices, and the distribution of income. In contrast, institutional economists see the organization and control of the economic system as the central problem. Thus, power relations take precedence over the price mechanism as the force governing economic outcomes. The 'market' is seen as comprising a number of different types of institutions coordinating economic activity. The auction market, which is synonymous with the market construct in much of neoclassical economics, is viewed as a special case from the institutionalist perspective. Furthermore, the interactive links between market institutions and other institutional arrangements in society, such as those embodied in law, custom and ethical behaviour, are considered explicitly in institutionalist analysis.

The fundamental institutionalist proposition is that it is the whole organizational structure of the economy which effectively allocates resources and distributes income, not just the market mechanism. The role of the market mechanism is not denied by institutionalists, as a part of the transmission mechanism from power structure to ultimate distributive and allocative outcomes. What they insist is that a broader set of explanatory variables than those normally included in demand and supply analysis is necessary to understand such outcomes.

Because power structure is strongly affected by legal rights, the role of governmental agencies in defining such rights is viewed as an essential ingredient in analysing economic problems. Neoclassical notions concerning market mechanisms without government are viewed as untenable because government is a core institution which forms an indissoluble part of the economic system.

The questions of interest to neoclassical economists are also of interest to institutionalists, but the primary interest of the latter is the organization and control of the economy. Thus, institutionalists are interested in, for example:

- the formation of institutions
- the changing relationship between economic and legal systems
- the relationship between power and belief systems
- the effect of technical change on institutional structure.

All these examples illustrate the emphasis placed on the dynamics of structural change. The concept of static equilibrium and associated optimality criteria in neoclassical analysis are firmly rejected as unhelpful abstractions which do not provide any insights about real economic phenomena.

Institutionalists regard the mainstream's search for deterministic technical conditions which yield stable equilibria as a goal that seriously obscures the true character of economic behaviour. Indeed, the use of mathematical formalism, for example, to derive optimal solutions is regarded as empty logic. Unquantifiable factors, such as ethics, customs and power relations, are seen by institutionalists as being ignored or downplayed by mainstream economists in such formalism. The institutionalist assigns a much higher priority to accurate description of the system in question and its historical evolution. Correspondingly, analysis tends to be more qualitative in emphasis. Furthermore, neoclassical formalism often involves reductionism whereby, for example, the representative agent is modelled and aggregated from micro to macro. The holistic nature of institutionalist thought necessarily precludes this type of aggregation.

Institutionalists generally reject the idea that economics should be methodologically 'positive' in the mainstream sense (see Chapter 2). First, they argue that even within the scientific boundaries set by mainstream economists, the interaction of value systems and economic behaviour must be understood in all economic situations. Second, they argue that mainstream economists are themselves influenced by implicit value systems and, therefore, a clear statement of value judgement is an essential preliminary step in any economic analysis. Building on these criticisms of the conventional positive/normative distinction, institutionalists are the only group of economists who have made a serious attempt to incorporate values directly into economic analysis.

Over a period spanning several decades, they have drawn on the inspiration of the American philosopher John Dewey's (Dewey, 1910) theory of instrumental logic and social value to develop the instrumental value principle. Marc Tool, a leading contributor to such development in its contemporary form defines it as: 'to do or choose that which provides for the continuity of human life and the noninvidious re-creation of community through the instrumental use of knowledge' (Tool, 1985). It is intended as a three-element, guiding principle for institutional economists to apply in coming to grips with real world economic problems. Tool goes on to say:

> The instrumental principle is wholly a cultural product. It rests not at all on non-experiential, non-evidential, or non-reasoned sources of information. It has no recourse to, neither does it depend on, spiritualistic visions, mystic intuitions, extra-sensory perceptions, supernatural beings, metaphysical

forces, natural laws, autogenic market phenomena, or geographical or psychological determinisms. (Tool, 1985, p. 6)

Although the principle becomes somewhat elusive on close inspection, what seems to be intended is explicit recognition of the evolutionary character of the economy and the society which it serves. Certainly, the welfare criteria applied in mainstream economics lack any kind of evolutionary dimension. Tool's words emphasize that institutionalists see the principle as a 'hard-headed' one which looks *at* a culture and doesn't merely project a researcher's favoured belief system. However, there is reluctance to specify the principle too precisely and controversy exists amongst institutionalists as to whether quantitative measures should be devised to measure instrumental value in specific cases. There are a number of examples in the institutionalist literature where the principle is applied to, for example, problem areas such as unemployment, macro instability, welfare programmes, industrial policy, foreign economic policy and public utility regulation.

Specific cases where instrumental value plays an unquantified role are frequently cited, particularly in the case of price formation, given its pivotal role in critiques of neoclassical economics. Institutionalists see prices as being set administratively rather than through the interaction of notional demand and supply constructs. It is argued that prices are set in a way which reflects instrumental value criteria. Low tuition costs in public higher education, taxes on alcohol and tobacco, parity price systems in agriculture and mortgage interest tax relief are some examples. In all these cases institutionalists argue that it is the direct application of values derived from culture which are in operation. To attempt to explain them entirely within the context of neoclassical utility theory, institutionalists argue, is to misunderstand completely the interaction of values and economic behaviour.

Institutionalists often refer to their methodological position as instrumentalism. However, this can be confusing because Milton Friedman has accepted this label, with encouragement from Lawrence Boland in his *The Foundations of Economic Method*, as more appropriate to his favoured methodological position rather than positivism (see Chapter 2). Poles apart though the institutionalists and Friedman may be, there is a common intent to take a pragmatic approach to empirical economics, to assign a high priority to the perceived needs of policy makers and to attempt to keep the ideological and metaphysical viewpoints of researchers and other 'irrational' factors from biasing their conclusions. Friedman is concerned with the predictive worth of a theory rather than with assessing the validity of its assumptions. The

institutionalists, rejecting theoretical abstraction in favour of empiricism, prefer to focus on the extent to which inductive empirical investigation can assist policy makers to implement the collective values of
a particular culture.

How does an institutionalist actually set about designing, implement-
ing and evaluating empirical research? This is an important question
because one of the main thrusts of mainstream economists' criticism
of institutionalism has been against what they regard as descriptive,
'naive empiricist' research. Central to the institutionalist's empirical
strategy is to obtain a good initial understanding of the relevant institutional structure and its historical development. This seems reasonable and certainly a serious omission in many mainstream studies.
However, the next step is more controversial. The institutionalist now
sets about attempting to identify the configuration of institutional
norms which emanate from the institutional power structure which
exists.

The approach adopted is to engage in extensive questioning of
relevant institutional representatives. Examples often cited are the
studies of cartel practices in the US, through insider disclosures in the
early years of the Second World War, in Walter Hamilton's *Price and
Price Policies* (1938) and Myron Watkins's *Cartels in Action* (Stocking
and Watkins, 1946). Assessments of the role of cultural and social
factors will also be made from such investigations. Both interviewing
and questionnaire surveys are recommended to obtain such information. Personal skill in obtaining information in this way is highly
valued. Although statistical work is not ruled out, orthodox econometric work, particularly on secondary source data, is regarded as
anathema to a proper understanding of economic questions.

A good recent example of an institutionalist empirical study is that
of Jack Guttentag and Richard Herring in 1985 concerning international debt provision to developing countries. They compiled a list
of the institutionalized behavioural norms which caused bankers to
over-extend lending in the 1970s and 1980s. The study draws on the
discipline of psychology and the concept of cognitive dissonance to
explain why bankers disregarded hazards to maintain their share of
banking business. Holistic analysis is used to explain why, although
each loan seems safe when looked at in isolation, systemic linkages,
identifiable by covariance analysis, mean that the risk is much higher
than is realized.

There is little doubt that such a study offers important insights into
the unfolding of a particular historical process and that it is far from
'naive empiricism'. Indeed, to ignore the institutional analysis pre-

sented and to forge ahead with regression analysis, based on some banking portfolio model, would seem to be much more naive. However, the problem with many institutional empirical studies is that they tend to be unfalsifiable, subject to observational equivalence and difficult to evaluate in conventional scientific terms (see Chapter 2). Of course, institutionalists would protest that they do not subscribe to scientific criteria imported from the natural sciences and that orthodox empirical research is usually guilty of the same charges, despite looking 'more scientific'.

In concluding our look at the fundamental features of institutional economics it is useful to reproduce the list presented recently by Warren Samuels, an authoritative commentator on and contributor to institutional economics, in the *New Palgrave: a Dictionary of Economics*. He identifies evolutionism and holism as the core features of institutional thought and the principal themes as, to quote:

1. A theory of social change, an activist orientation towards social institutions, through focusing on both the substantive impact of institutions on economic performance and the process of institutional change, treating institutions not as something to be taken as given but as man-made and changeable, both deliberatively and nondeliberatively.
2. A theory of social control and collective choice, or a theory of institutions, a focus on the formation and operation of institutions as both cause and consequence of the power structure and societized behaviour of individuals and subgroups, and as the mode through which economies are organized and controlled. Instead of focusing on opportunity sets, a focus on the formation of opportunity sets; instead of a focus on unfettered markets, a focus on the total, complex pattern of freedom and control, that is, on the formation and operation of the system of control through which both actual opportunity sets and freedom are formed.
3. A theory of the economic role of government, as a principal social process through which both itself and other institutions of economic significance are in part formed and revised. Instead of treating government, law and the system of as given either/or exogenous, these are treated as both dependent and independent, and always critical, not merely aberrational, economic variables.
4. A theory of technology, as defining and determining the relative scarcity of all resources, as a principal force in the evolution of economic structure (including the operation of institutions) and performance, and as the basis of the logic of industrialization

marking the mentality as well as the practices of modern economies.

5. The fundamental principle that the real determinant of resource allocation is not the market but the organizational-institutional, power-structure of society.

6. An emphasis on facets of the value conception which transcend price, on the values represented in and given effect by the habits and customs of social life, on the pragmatic, instrumental values ensconced in the transcendental notion of the life process of man and society, and on the constructive values latent within and given effect by the working rules of law which are both the foundation and the product of the power structure of society. Included are attempts to understand the process whereby values are changed, in contrast to the orthodox assumption of given values; that is, to consider within economics such questions as where the values come from, how they are tested, and how they are changed.

These six central themes of institutional economics have been developed by many authors. In addition to those already mentioned as playing an influential role, John Maurice Clark (1926) provided an analysis of the social control of business; Wesley Mitchell (1937) emphasized the centrality of monetary and financial institutions in economic development; Selig Perlman (1928) analysed the capacity of labour unions to promote institutional change; and Edwin E. Witte (1932) devised ways of creating institutions to protect new creative interests and methods of channelling social conflict potential into creative channels. Charles S. Peirce (1955) and William James are identified by many institutionalists as providing the pre-institutionalist philosophical basis for pragmatism and instrumentalism as elaborated by John Dewey (1910) and Clarence Ayres (1944).

JOHN KENNETH GALBRAITH

A closely knit group of modern institutional economists exists in the US. They are identifiable by their contributions to the *Journal of Economic Issues* and their membership of the Association for Evolutionary Economics. A list of well known figures, in addition to Marc Tool and Warren Samuels, would include John Adams, Daniel R. Fusfeld, Wendell Gordon, Allan G. Gruchy, David B. Hamilton, F. Gregory Hayden, Philip A. Klein, Anne Mayhew, Gardiner C. Means, Philip Mirowski, Walter C. Neale, Kenneth Parsons, Wallace Peterson, A. Allan Schmid, Robert Solo, Paul Straussman and Harry M. Trebing. No attempt will be made in this chapter even to summarize their various contributions to modern institutional thought. A useful common source containing contributions from most of these economists, plus others unmentioned here, is the two-volume *Evolutionary Economics*, edited by Marc Tool and published in 1988.

In addition to this group, there have also been leading figures who have practised institutional economics in a less direct sense, interacting with institutionalists to a very limited extent. Sometimes by sheer force of personality or by catching the imagination of much wider audiences than professional economists and their students, these figures have managed to mount important critiques and to present institutionalist alternatives to mainstream economic ideas. The 1974 Nobel prize winner Gunnar Myrdal and Kenneth Boulding are two examples of highly respected economists who have drawn heavily on the institutionalist tradition in their extensive writings. Both have commanded respect from their mainstream protagonists for the brilliance of their work. It would be fair to say that neither managed to alter the course of mainstream thinking in economics to any significant extent, but they do demonstrate that institutionalism can offer a serious challenge.

However, the strongest institutionalist challenge to mainstream economics in the postwar period came from John Kenneth Galbraith who offered the best known contemporary version of institutional economic analysis. Such was the respect of mainstream economists for his work that he, like Boulding, was elected president of the American Economic Association. It is instructive, therefore, to focus attention on Galbraith's institutionalism, not just because of its relative success, but also because the application of institutionalist principles is best illustrated by focusing attention on the work of a particular economist.

Galbraith's institutionalism is inspired by the writings of Veblen in a very direct sense. He exhibits little interest in post-Veblenians such as John Commons. Similarities with Veblen are numerous. Both were non-American incomers who taught at the prestigious Harvard University. (Veblen was of Norwegian parentage and Galbraith of Scots–Canadian.) Galbraith's abrasive, irreverent personal style is reminiscent of Veblen. However, Galbraith is no mere clone of the founder of institutionalism. He updated and revised the Veblenian vision to deal with the postwar US economy. In particular, he emphasized the message of John Maynard Keynes's *General Theory* to a much greater extent than other institutionalists, who seem to be content in the knowledge that they had already taken on board Keynes's policy message and translated it into the New Deal in the interwar period.

The result is that Galbraith is looked on by many economists as a Keynesian rather than an institutionalist. He has not discouraged this labelling and, indeed, was happy to fight for the Keynesian cause in televised debates with Milton Friedman, the monetarist.

It was this willingness of Galbraith to relate to the prevailing Keynesian orthodoxy in macroeconomics in the 1950s and 1960s which allowed him to gain exposure for his institutionalist alternative to neoclassical microeconomics. Galbraith never supported the orthodox 'neoclassical synthesis' interpretation of Keynes, derived from the famous 1937 paper in *Econometrica* by John Hicks and Alvin Hansen's *A Guide to Keynes*, (1953), preferring the post-Keynesian view, emanating from Joan Robinson and her associates in Cambridge, England (see Chapter 7). To Galbraith, mainstream economics was not about the search for 'truth' but, rather, he sees it as mainly concerned with the presentation of belief systems which favour existing power structures. He refers to mainstream economists as 'high priests' of a capitalist belief system.

Galbraith clearly views orthodox Keynesian economics as a belief system which received assent from postwar interventionist governments and took full advantage of the opportunity afforded by their receptivity to him as a Keynesian to promote his institutionalist economics. He made his institutionalist mark with a trilogy of books: *American Capitalism: the Concept of Coutervailing Power* in 1952, *The Affluent Society* in 1958 and *The New Industrial State* in 1967. Of course, he has written much more but these three books capture most of his Veblenian institutionalist vision of the postwar US economy. In each he demonstrates his ability to write with great skill to an audience wider than economists and to invent phrases which have become part of the language of economics such as 'countervailing power' and 'conventional wisdom'. It was his success in attracting a large popular readership in the 1960s, particularly with the second and third books of the trilogy, which forced mainstream economists to take him seriously.

American Capitalism focuses on the new institutional relationship between firms and the state which had grown out of the experience of the Second World war. It calls into question the conventional view that large corporations must be exploitative merely because they are large. Galbraith provided a vivid evolutionary analysis of how countervailing power can grow to nullify exploitative potential and lead to the creation of large productive structures. Such structures have long planning horizons and can design sophisticated organizational arrangements capable of fast technical progress and product development. He urged policy makers to abandon anti-trust legislation based on illusory goals of perfect competition and to focus, instead, on measures to facilitate countervailing power. The institutionalism in his arguments was less Veblenian than that which was to follow in later writings, presumably because Galbraith is optimistic about the potential of the US economy in the immediate postwar period.

By the time *The Affluent Society* was written, the Veblenian flavour had become much stronger. The pursuit of status through material consumption was emphasized. The success of the corporations, promoting mass produced goods through advertising and product differentiation is leading, in Galbraith's view, to overconsumption and 'public squalor' because of neglect in the provision of public goods. Material priorities were emphasized increasingly and the shift in economics itself, towards market-oriented, hedonistic, neoclassical economics, away from traditional institutionalism, is seen as a complementary shift in beliefs.

The book struck a chord with the general public and became immensely popular, elevating Galbraith to national prominence in the US. It undoubtedly played some political role, however indirect, in the rise of the Kennedy administration with a commitment to increased public goods provision. It is also likely to have been one of the first books to be read by the young campus activists of the 1960s, helping to form their anti-materialist stance. Popular impact was one of the goals of ex-journalist Galbraith, and his use of powerful Veblenian institutionalism, combined with his talent for writing, proved to be more than adequate for this purpose.

The New Industrial State constitutes a much more systematic institutional picture of the US economy. The development and perpetuation of cultural and social institutions of an adverse kind is explained much more carefully than in *American Capitalism*. In this third book of the trilogy, he moves closest to Veblen and, in particular, *The Theory of Business Enterprise* (1904) and *Absentee Ownership* (1923). The massive success of planning within large industrial organizations is seen as repressing any kind of individual creativity which did not serve and promote the interests of the industrial system. The brutal vision of the evolutionary process, so emphasized by Veblen, is depicted in the context of corporate power in the 1960s. However, Galbraith did not pass judgement on the process which he claimed to have revealed. Indeed, he admired the high degree of efficiency it had produced. It is the purposes which the process is seen as serving which he questioned, using a criterion similar to the instrumental value principle of the modern institutionalists in forming his judgement.

Despite his impact at popular and political levels, the institutionalism of Galbraith did not turn the tide in economics. Neoclassical methodology continued to tighten its grip and, in macroeconomics, orthodox Keynesianism gave way to monetarism in the late 1960s and, ultimately, to neoclassicism as well (see Chapter 5). Mathematical formalism continued to extend into the subject at the expense of qualitative approaches. In Galbraith's terms, the core belief system abandoned its brief flirtation with interventionism and was fully behind the market system again. The critical schools such as institutionalism and post-Keynesianism were squeezed to the extreme margins of economics to such an extent that neoclassical economists could jokingly refer to them as 'sociology'.

As Keynesianism declined in popularity in the 1970s, so did interest in the kind of institutionalism presented by Galbraith. The institutionalist school itself became unknown to large numbers of students of economics. Despite this, critiques of neoclassical economics, almost indistinguishable from those in unread institutional writings, kept on appearing. In this indirect sense, the spirit of institutionalism survives in unexpected places. Apart from the predictable criticisms of rational economic man, the 1970s witnessed growing dissatisfaction with the lack of sensible dynamics in neoclassical economics. To operationalize neoclassical hypotheses in the real world of historical time, it was necessary to introduce additional *ad hoc* translating hypotheses, such as partial adjustment and error-learning mechanisms. The fact that there is serious difficulty with such a 'disequilibrium dynamic' approach to economic behaviour was even highlighted by neoclassical economists themselves in the wake of the application of the rational-expectations hypothesis. However, this did not pave the way for a resurgence of institutionalism but, rather, a retreat to pre-Keynesian, neoclassical logical propositions based on a strong belief in market clearing (see Chapter 5).

EVOLUTIONARY DYNAMICS

A striking feature of economics in the twentieth century has been the consistent tendency for mathematical formalism to become increasingly popular in mainstream economics despite its difficulty in addressing real world economic problems. Galbraith argues that this formalism has grown in popularity, mainly because mainstream economics is largely about beliefs. The strongly pro-market Austrian school and the related contributions of Joseph Schumpeter are, arguably, more appealing programmes than neoclassical economics upon which to hang capitalist beliefs. What all these 'alternative' schools have in common is an underlying vision of dynamics which is evolutionary in character and, in each case, we find that the school in question has difficulty in formalizing these dynamics in mathematical terms. Indeed, it could be argued that the popularity of mathematical formalism in the mainstream stems from its aesthetic and more tractable character rather than from any denial that evolutionary dynamics exist.

Since evolution necessarily involves structural change, which is difficult to specify, conventional mathematical modelling and simulation are precluded in most cases. The neoclassical school's mathematical representations of dynamic economic behaviour rely on the proposition that periods of disequilibrium exist between equilibrium states. Institutionalists have frequently pointed to the unsatisfactory nature of this approach to dynamics in an evolutionary world. Rejection of mathematical formalism on these grounds is a subsidiary part of their overall unease with this and other abstractions, such as rational economic man, which are presumed to have general applicability.

This question of incorporation of evolutionary dynamics into economics was raised at the beginning of institutionalism in Veblen's article entitled: 'Why is economics not an evolutionary science?' in the 1898 volume of the *Quarterly Journal of Economics*. Veblen's view of how evolution worked in the social process involved a competitive selection process. Indeed, Veblen was not alone in seeing the potential of applying evolutionary dynamics to economics. Alfred Marshall, an early promoter of marginalism in formal neoclassical economics, stated, also in the 1890s, that 'the Mecca of the economist lies in economic biology rather than in economic dynamics' (Marshall, 1890, 8th ed., p. xii) and went on to caution that: 'The Statical theory of equilibrium is only an introduction to economic studies . . . Its limitations are so constantly overlooked, especially by those who approach it from an abstract point of view, that there is a danger in throwing it into definite form at all' (Marshall, 1890, 8th ed., p. 382).

Neoclassical economists ignored these dangers and developed the formal apparatus provided, largely in footnotes, in Marshall's *Principles of Economics* (1890). In contrast, the institutionalists' detailed descriptions of institutional structure and its historical development continually paid lip-service to evolutionary dynamics without any formal mathematical representation of the actual mechanisms at work. Evolutionary processes have been regarded traditionally as comprising two components:

1. 'The survival of those species which are best adapted to their

habitats', which is what Charles Darwin meant by his shorthand phrase 'the survival of the fittest' (this involves a selection process).

2.   The mutation of genes.

Kenneth Boulding, whose prolific writings on this subject are summarized neatly in his *Evolutionary Economics*, published in 1981, argues that the first component is only applicable to limited areas of adaptation and that the main thrust of evolution involves symbiosis between genetic types. He cites Peter Kropotkin's *Mutual Aid: a Factor in Evolution*, of 1902, as an early, much overlooked, example of this view. Boulding sees evolution as involving positive sum, rather than zero sum, games, as new 'niches' become available and provide evolutionary opportunities.

Although Boulding cites Veblen, his depiction of evolution is more compatible with the institutionalism of Commons. Furthermore, his technical presentation of the evolutionary process at work is much more formally specified than in previous institutional writings. The notion of systems avoiding entropy through evolution, as presented by Nicholas Georgescu-Roegen in his *The Entropy Law and the Economic Process* published in 1971, provides the basis for Boulding's evolutionary mechanism. The introduction of a more technical representation of the cooperative aspects of evolution by Boulding represented something of a turning point for institutionalism. The conflictual view of evolutionary dynamics had always been regarded with suspicion by economists who espoused the 'free market' view because of its association with Marxism and its appearance in Fascist propaganda. Its combination with the more cooperative aspects of evolution by Boulding in his systems approach offered institutionalism a new and appealing dimension.

Boulding's institutionalism focuses more on the nature of economic processes in historical time and less on the details of institutional complexity. An abstract characterization of evolutionary dynamics, designed to be applied in a wide range of situations, is presented. In a sense, this development signals a shift from institutional economics, where evolutionary dynamics are implicit, to evolutionary economics, where institutional structure influences the character of evolutionary dynamics. This subtle but vital shift brings institutionalism closer to other schools which also emphasize evolutionary dynamics as a replacement for the static equilibrium perspective of neoclassical economics.

Although the Schumpeterian view of evolutionary dynamics seems to be close in some respects to that of some of the institutionalists, Joseph Schumpeter has never been regarded as an institutionalist, since his work is founded in the Austrian tradition of von Mises and von Hayek (see Chapter 3). His depiction of evolutionary dynamics is close to that of Marx and, to further confound matters, he expressed great admiration for Walras's system of general equilibrium and dismissed the work of Keynes. Clearly, there was little in Schumpeter for institutionalists to relate to. However, in developing his 'theory of creative destruction', Schumpeter provided a dynamic picture of the rise and fall of firms which Veblen would no doubt have admired in some respects. The emphasis is on creativity, and competition is about the technological qualities of products. Like Veblen, Schumpeter portrays powerful firms as repressive forces, perpetuating their economic rents.

Probably because of the Austrian tradition from which he came, in his early writings Schumpeter emphasized the view that economic progress depended on individual inventors and the rise of individual entrepreneurs with innovative ideas. However, by the time he published his best known book, *Capitalism, Socialism and Democracy* in 1942, he had shifted his ground to a position where such creative activity was predominantly undertaken by large firms. Thus, the communality with institutionalist views was extended. But Schumpeter did not have institutionalist priorities. He was primarily interested in understanding business cycles within the overall process of capitalist development and the relationship between interest rates and profits at different cyclical positions. However, his interdisciplinary and non-technical method of achieving this objective yielded similar insights to institutionalists almost by default.

Schumpeter's lack of an institutionalist perspective is betrayed in his prediction that capitalism will give way to socialism. He does not rely on the 'inner contradictions of capitalism' as in the case of Marx but, instead, the erosion of the values and traditions, inherited from the pre-capitalist era, which he saw as facilitating capitalism. Few institutionalists would have such an inflexible and backward-looking view of the 'ideal' value structure or such a deterministic view of the future. However, when we turn to the neo-Schumpeterians of recent times such as Richard Nelson and Sidney Winter, whose ideas are well represented by their *An Evolutionary Theory of Economic Change* published in 1982, we find a greater degree of flexibility.

Nelson and Winter take a Lamarkian view of evolution in the sphere of economics, whereby organic units can pass on newly acquired adaptations through heredity. In biology, Lamarck's non-conflictual mechanism of adaptation has been consistently rejected by Darwinists and the debate continues to rage on. However, no matter how implausible Lamarkianism may be in biology, it is clearly the case that institutions can pass on technical adaptations, often copied from other institutions, without the need for a continuous conflictual struggle amongst random mutants. Nelson and Winter argue that habits and routines play a crucial role in permitting behavioural patterns to be passed from one institution to another.

This results in a view of evolution which is close to that of Boulding. However, Nelson and Winter do not explore the wider significance of their idea that routines act like 'genes' to pass on information and skills, either in terms of its compatibility with institutionalism or its implications for economic theory in general. They freely admit that there is difficulty in offering a general formalization which has empirical applicability beyond the kinds of simulation exercises which they conduct. A problem is that, in socioeconomic contexts, evolutionary processes tend to exhibit long periods of continuity interspersed with short periods of crisis and upheaval which are difficult to predict. In biology Nils Eldredge, in his book *Time Frames: Rethinking of Darwinian Evolution and the Theory of Punctuated Equilibria* (1985), also identifies this tendency for conflictual mutation to be compressed into very short periods.

The increasing overlap that occurred in the 1980s between what we might call neo-institutionalism and neo-Schumpeterianism is a direct result of a more sophisticated vision of evolutionary dynamics than that originally presented by Darwin for understanding change in the biological world. The presentation of historical time processes has, at last, taken on characteristics which permit the specification of the abstract principles of evolutionary dynamics and the mathematical formalization of special cases. It is this new view of economic dynamics which has come to offer a fundamental challenge to neoclassical economics and, at the same time, promises to revive interest in institutionalism.

THE NEW INSTITUTIONAL ECONOMICS

The new institutional economics tends to be associated with the work of Oliver Williamson but, in many respects, it is not new. In contrast to old institutionalism, it derives from a long tradition of classic liberalism, dating back to John Locke and John Stuart Mill. Indeed, it was this very tradition which Thorstein Veblen attacked so vehemently.

At a fundamental level, the old and the new are diametrically opposed since the latter espouses the notion of the abstract individual as the key decision-making unit.

New institutionalism and neo-Austrianism tend to be intertwined. Thus, any survey of it would include F.A. Hayek's *Law, Legislation and Liberty* (1982) and Andrew Schotter's *The Economic Theory of Social Institutions* (1981). New institutionalist works by Richard Posner, on the economics of law, Mancur Olson, on economic development, and Douglass North, on economic history, also have a strong classic liberal flavour but of a more neoclassical type. However, there is little doubt that the key figure in new institutionalism is Williamson, so we shall focus attention on his contributions.

In the 1960s and 1970s, Williamson was preoccupied with gaining an understanding of why there coexisted, in the economic system, internal hierarchical organization in firms to achieve economic coordination and external markets which used the price mechanism to coordinate. Williamson is not an institutionalist and prefers to search for an explanation which is founded in neoclassical maximizing behaviour. The explanation which he came up with is largely derived from Ronald Coase's well known paper, published in *Economica* in 1937 and entitled 'The nature of the firm'. The essence of the argument is straightforward: hierarchically organized firms exist because of the presence of significant transactions costs in market trading. Williamson also appealed to Herbert Simon's *Models of Man: Social and Rational* (1957) to support his propositions concerning the existence of individual behaviour within organizations which is non-maximizing in the conventional sense because of various institutional constraints. However, it is clear that there is some confusion in Williamson's mind concerning Simon's work since the implication of the latter is that the neoclassical model of behaviour is untenable, yet he persists with a rational, cost-minimizing model of the behaviour of agents driven by opportunistic self-interest. Simon's 'bounded rationality' and consequent 'satisficing' behaviour is clearly the product of information constraints and not, as Williamson implies, due to transaction costs.

Given that Willimson's new institutionalism boils down to a neoclassical model of behaviour with transactions costs, then institutional variation across the economic system and the evolution of a given institution over time depend critically on the technology of transacting. Small as it may seem to old institutionalists, this does represent a significant advance beyond conventional neoclassical economics. In particular, his attempt to deal with conventional optimization within an explicit transactions cost framework, offers a fundamental challenge to the neoclassical practice of simply adding in transaction costs in an *ad hoc* way to translate hypotheses from abstract to historical time.

Furthermore, Williamson's new institutional economics does echo old institutionalist ideas. The transactional analysis of Commons is similar, albeit from a different intellectual perspective, and Williamson's emphasis on opportunism as a central element in individual behaviour is not unrelated, in practice, to Veblen's emphasis on status seeking. The difference between new and old seems to be one of emphasis, with the former emphasizing institutions and evolution and the latter holism and instrumental valuing. Each has its analytical and empirical advantages and disadvantages but what is more important is that Williamson provides a dimension to the neoclassical school which makes it possible for constructive dialogue with institutional economists actually to take place. This is very apparent in the special 1989 issue of the *Review of Political Economy* (vol. 1, no. 3) which deals with old and new institutionalism.

THE FUTURE OF INSTITUTIONAL ECONOMICS

During the 1980s, institutionalists have discovered that evolutionary economics is no longer their exclusive province. There now exist several schools whose methodology has become evolutionary. In 1988 alone, a neo-Austrian, Ulrich Witt, and a neo-Schumpeterian, Horst Hanush, each published a book entitled *Evolutionary Economics*. However, what is distressing about these developments, as far as institutionalists are concerned, is the virtual absence of any reference to institutionalist writings. So, although institutionalists welcome the increased emphasis in the literature on evolutionary and institutional perspectives, there is growing frustration as their school continues to be marginalized.

The reason for this lack of acknowledgement arises largely because the non-institutionalists have developed their ideas out of independent critiques of the neoclassical tradition from which many came. These economists have begun to consider processes in historical time and social/ecological space, with minimal exposure to institutional literature. Furthermore, it has not been a case of 'reinventing the wheel' because they have tended to have differing methodological priorities. We have already discussed this in the context of the development of Williamson's new institutionalism.

Another example, much closer in spirit to institutionalist thinking is the work of Herbert Simon as one of the founders of what has come to be known in recent times as behavioural economics. His approach is essentially that of attempting, like Tibor Scitovsky in his *The Joyless Economy* (1977), to bring psychological considerations into economics. However, although there are parallels between behaviouralism and institutionalism, the difference lies in the methodological stance of each. The former school has the clear goal of formulating a superior set of abstract general behavioural principles to replace rational economic man in the framing of empirically testable hypotheses. In other words, it lies much closer to the orthodox view of the role and formulation of theoretical propositions. Institutionalists have tended to be sceptical about the extent to which scientific testing is appropriate to the verification of formal behavioural hypotheses concerning economic behaviour.

The difficulty which institutional economics has faced in gaining acceptance in the postwar era relates directly to the old debate concerning historicism versus abstraction. Orthodox economists have always regarded with suspicion pleas to found economics only on power struggles in historical time where all general analytical principles vanish, being replaced by a multitude of situation-specific game-playing possibilities. Such a 'more realistic' economics becomes intractable as far as the economist interested in analysis and prediction is concerned. We are witnessing today an increasing interest in economics as a process, but the quest now is to discover analytical principles which are set in historical time, rather than to abandon abstract analysis.

This is evident in all the new branches of evolutionary economic thought. The neo-Austrian school sees evolutionary mechanisms as an integral part of the emergence of 'spontaneous order' in economic systems. The non-linear dynamics (chaos) sub-group in the neo-Schumpeterian school refer to the 'principle of self-organization', following Ilya Prigogine, as the evolutionary abstraction relevant to dealing with underlying socioeconomic processes in historical time. It is clear that the institutional configuration is crucial in determining how such abstract dynamic principles work out in real world situations. Such configurations are also seen as being relevant in the context of empirical application of these principles. In other words, these new evolutionary approaches admit influences from other social sciences much more directly than the neoclassical school's approach, while still retaining abstract principles.

Although there has been some reluctance amongst long-standing institutionalists to accept the formal content of the new evolutionary approaches, there have also been attempts to provide syntheses. For example, Geoffrey Hodgson, in his book *Economics and Institutions:*

a Manifesto for a New Institutional Economics (1988), argues that it is possible to derive a new and powerful institutional economics from a synthesis of institutionalism, post-Keynesianism, neo-Schumpeterianism and neo-Austrianism. He argues that all these schools embrace a concept of economic process in historical time which is distinct from the neoclassical view. Questions concerning the culture and beliefs of agents figure prominently in all of them. Each school essentially operates within the same loose paradigm and, therefore, can engage in meaningful debate with the others.

Hodgson's efforts to seek synthesis and paradigmatic agreement are echoed in my own *Evolutionary Macroeconomics* (Foster, 1987) and also in the pleas of Tony Lawson, in the *Economic Journal*, 1987, for us to accept that any kind of realistic economic analysis must accept that *both* individual *and* holistic behaviour exists. Also Amitai Etzioni, a leading American sociologist, attempts make similar points from a more microeconomic perspective in his book, *The Moral Dimension* (1988). He gives the synthesis a new name, socioeconomics, in an attempt to avoid the specific connotations of established school labels. Although institutionalists mostly demur, there are undoubted advantages in a new name in any bid to shift the paradigm position of mainstream economics. Should such a shift occur, then surely the best work in the institutionalist tradition would receive due recognition in the fullness of time.

Institutionalism lost its interwar dominance of economics because it could not meet the requirements of scientific precision demanded by the new generation of economists. With orthodox Keynesianism providing macroeconomics with real world context for policy makers, and Friedman's brand of instrumental empiricism, institutionalism lost its monopoly as the opponent of deductive theoretical economics. The postwar ideological dichotomy between free market capitalism and totalitarian communism also created difficulties for institutionalism. Neoclassical economics suited the former ideology well, as did Marxian economics for the latter. Keynesian economics survived because the neoclassical synthesis rendered it an extension of neoclassical economics. Institutional economics was a uneasy mixture of intervention and non-intervention, reflecting well the pragmatic manner in which politicians concocted policies but did not provide the simple economic principles that these same politicians wished to invoke for intellectual support.

Today the capitalist/communist dichotomy seems to be breaking down in world politics and, therefore, ideological forces are likely to be less of a handicap for institutionalism in the 1990s. However, it is unlikely that the 'common sense' institutionalism of old will be revived to any significant extent. Economists will strive to retain the distinctiveness of their subject through subscription to abstract behavioural principles capable of formal representation. Although these principles will be substantially revised the progression will be seen as away from orthodox economics. We have already witnessed the trend towards game theoretics and the espousal of evolution in, for example, Robert Axelrod's *The Evolution of Co-operation* (1984) and Schotter's *The Economic Theory of Social Institutions* (1981). So, although institutionalists may well see familiar landmarks on the new orthodox terrain, their preference for historicism over abstraction will ensure that they will remain a peripheral part of what we understand as economics.

However, for the more flexible neo-institutionalist such as, for example, Geoffrey Hodgson, these are likely to be exciting times. The mixture of non-linear dynamics, game theoretics and behaviouralism which will soon redefine mainstream economics is one where the neo-institutionalist is well equipped to provide an influential input, particularly in offering evidence as to the character of institutional structure and how it has changed in the course of history. Neoclassical economics has little need for such information, in contrast to these three emerging strands of mainstream economics alluded to above. For each, such information is essential in both empirical research and policy implementation. Institutionalism may not be the orthodoxy of the future but its more enlightened practitioners have a clear opportunity to make an influential impact on the future evolution of mainstream economic thought.

FURTHER READING

Boulding, K.E. (1981) *Evolutionary Economics*, London: Sage.
Clark, N. and Juma C. (1987) *Long-run Economics: an Evolutionary Approach to Economic Growth*, London: Pinter.
Foster, J. (1988) *Evolutionary Macroeconomics*, London: Allen & Unwin.
Gordon, W. and Adams, J. (1989) *Economics as a Social Science*, Maryland: Riverdale.
Hodgson, G. (1988), *Economic and Institutions: a Manifesto for a Modern Institutional Economics*, Cambridge: Polity Press.
Review of Political Economy, vol. 1, no. 3, 1989.
Tool, M.R. (1988), *Evolutionary Economics* Vol. 1 *Foundations of Institutional Thought*, Vol. II *Institutional Theory and Policy*, New York: M. E. Sharpe.

Veblen, T.B. (1899), *The Theory of the Leisure Class: an Economic Study of Institutions*, London: Macmillan.

SUMMARY OF THE INSTITUTIONALIST SCHOOL

World View

Holistic, organic, evolutionary.

Values

Non-materialistic.

Goals

Normative priorities; the direct implementation of the collective values of a particular culture.
Description of the organization and control of the economic system and its historical evolution.

Methodological Practice

Interdisciplinary.
Qualitative, non-technical, empiricists.
Inductive pragmatists; historicism.
Situation-specific, game playing.
Description.
Anti-abstraction, anti-analytical principles, anti-mathematical formalism.

Criteria

Many institutional empirical studies are difficult to evaluate in conventional scientific terms.

Hard Core

Institutions – variety – social complexity.
Evolutionary, disaggregated, processes – dynamics of structural change.
Historical time.

Concepts

Custom.
Power relations.
Value systems and ethical behaviour.

Positive Heuristic (Agenda)

To understand the formation of institutions;
– the changing interrelationship between economic and legal systems;
– the relationship between power and belief systems;
– the effect of technical change on institutional structure.

Protective Belt Assumptions

For example, pricing is an administrative procedure.

Themes (Warren Samuels, New Palgrave):

1. Social change, process of (man-made) institutional change, effect on economic performance.
2. Social control and collective choice, focusing on the formulation of opportunity sets and freedom.
3. Economic role of government – an indissoluble core institution.
4. Technology – creativity – invention and innovation – how and why?
    5. The organizational–institutional, power structure of society as the major determinant of resource allocation and income distribution.
    6. Value concept, where values come from, how they are tested, and how they are changed (instrumental value principle).

Evidence

Case studies.
Interview responses and questionnaire surveys.

Conclusions (Example)

Large corporations are not necessarily always exploitative of the consumer, but their planning process often represses any individual creativity which does not serve and promote the interests of the industrial system.

9. Marxian and Radical Economics

Andrew G. Scott

In recent years Marxian economics has experienced something of a renaissance. This revival was sparked in part by a growing conviction, particularly in the US, that mainstream economics could not adequately explain the profound and protracted global economic crisis that occurred during the 1970s. After almost two decades of more or less continuous economic growth, full employment and virtual price stability, from the late 1960s rates of unemployment worldwide began to rise dramatically and inflation soared to levels unknown in the postwar period. And as the initial recession was transformed into a prolonged bout of economic stagnation with the quadrupling of oil prices late in 1973, the decline in living standards accelerated and brought in its wake acute social problems. The failure of conventional countercyclical fiscal and monetary policies to restore order to what was a rapidly deteriorating situation, along with the inability of orthodox economics to offer an adequate account of the underlying dynamics and scale of the crisis, pointed to basic defects in the theoretical foundations of the entire Keynesian–neoclassical synthesis. And the crisis was not confined to individual countries. At the same time, the old international economic order was crumbling. By 1971 the fixed exchange rate system established at the Bretton-Woods Conference in 1944 was collapsing. Moreover, a wave of 'new protectionism' was threatening to undermine the principle of free trade enshrined by the 1947 General Agreement on Tariffs and Trade, while tensions in the economic relationships between the rich industrialized countries of the 'North' and the poorer, less developed, countries of the 'South' were beginning to appear. On the one hand, the new international division of labour was increasingly posing a challenge to the industrial dominance of the 'North', whilst on the other, the commodity-producing countries were showing a greater readiness to exploit the bargaining power offered by collective action to ensure that demands for an improvement in their terms of trade were met.

Marxists have generally interpreted this economic crisis as representing a turning point in the development of capitalism. However, there is less agreement among them on the precise nature of the crisis (Schwartz, 1977, Part III). Traditional Marxists maintain that the origins of the crisis lie in the internal contradictions that Marx had argued were characteristic of the dynamics of commodity production in capitalist economies, specifically a tendency for the rate of profit to fall. Other Marxists reject this interpretation, arguing instead that the crisis originates in the sphere of commodity exchange. In their *Monopoly Capital* (1966), Paul Baran and Paul Sweezy present a reformulation of Marx's original theory of capitalist dynamics which not only explains economic stagnation solely in terms of demand deficiency, but which also advances the controversial proposition that this stagnation results from the tendency of the rate profit to *rise* rather than *fall* under conditions of mature capitalism. According to this view, the crisis results from a failure of consumption spending to grow at the rate necessary to enable capitalists to 'realize' profits. Although Baran and Sweezy's 'crisis' thesis is intensely contested by orthodox Marxists on the grounds that it is closer to Keynes than to Marx, *Monopoly Capital* was elsewhere acclaimed as both a seminal contribution in the development of Marxist economic theory and as an important critique of Keynesian economics. In the event, the framework established by Baran and Sweezy formed the basis from which the so-called 'radical', or neo-Marxist, school of economic thought later developed.

This is not to suggest that controversy between Marxist theorists is in any sense a recent phenomenon. Mainstream Marxism has always been characterized by a number of competing interpretations of Marx, and disputes between Marxists have seldom been conclusively resolved. Here we concentrate on the main schools of thought in Marxian economics. The remainder of the chapter is organized as follows. The next section outlines the key elements in Marx's theory of historical change from which Marxian methodology derives its distinguishing characteristics. Then we focus on the dynamics of capitalism. In particular, we consider the transition from competitive to monopoly capitalism and the internal contradictions in the latter which, all Marxists maintain, will inevitably precipitate a crisis. This sets the scene for a discussion of some prominent themes in contemporary Marxian economics. Finally we consider the continuing relevance of Marxian economics.

THE FOUNDATIONS OF MARXIAN METHOD

Although best remembered as the author of *Capital* (1976), a thorough analysis of the dynamics and development of capitalism, Marx's early years were devoted to philosophical studies. It was during this period that he formulated a distinctive theory of society, *historical materialism*, that conditioned each stage of his analysis of capitalism which he subsequently presented in the three volumes of *Capital*. More than any of the great classical economic studies of the nineteenth century, the political economy of Marx cannot be fully grasped unless studied in conjunction with this materialist theory of society. In this section we outline the four elements that together comprise the methodological foundations of Marx's economics.

Historical Materialism

In its most rudimentary form, the doctrine of 'historical materialism' states that the development of human society is dictated by specific – and discoverable – laws of change which are grounded in the social provision of the material means of human existence. Historical materialism comprises two principal elements. First, it is historical in that Marx is advocating a theory of human history in which the future is fashioned by events in the past according to particular evolutionary laws. This should not be taken as implying that we are, at any moment, able to predict accurately the future on the basis of conditions in the present. Rather, Marx claims that at any moment in history, society can only be properly understood by examining the conditions in the past which constitute the framework within which present structures have evolved. The evolutionary force which 'directs' the development of human society is the dialectic. Second, it is a materialist account of history in that Marx maintains that societies are formed solely for the purpose of collective provision of the material means of existence. The origins of historical materialism are to be found in the writings of two nineteenth century philosophers, Hegel and Ludwig Feuerbach (Sowell, 1985; Bottomore, 1988).

Hegel belonged to the 'idealist' tradition in philosophy which claimed that society at any moment in time is a reflection of the particular stage reached in the continuous development of the human consciousness, or intellect, as it progresses towards perfection. The continuity of the progress of man's consciousness, the evolutionary law, and by extension the continuity in society's development itself, follow from the dialectic method in which intellectual advancement occurred. Dialectics state that to each idea or 'thesis' there corresponds a counterpoint argument in the form of the 'antithesis'. Human knowledge develops through successively higher stages as the debate between 'thesis' and 'antithesis' is resolved. But the 'idea' that emerges from this debate will itself now become the subject of dialectic transformation, with the process being repeated time after time. The dialectic thus constitutes the evolutionary law determining the development of man's consciousness. Despite the appearance of human history as being a series of unconnected events, it is in fact a continuously evolving process in which each stage – being a reflection of ideas that resolve intellectual conflict in the immediately preceding stage – contains the seeds of its evolution to the next, higher stage. Although Marx quickly rejected the 'idealist' claim that all institutions and agencies of social life are shaped by human consciousness, he became convinced that the principle of dialectic transformation – in which future conditions were determined in the present – was in essence correct. Marx adapted the dialectic method of analysis to his materialist explanation of the evolution of social formations.

Marx's conversion to the materialist tradition in philosophy, which was subsequently to become synonymous with Marxism, resulted from his reading of Feuerbach. Feuerbach, as an exponent of the materialist tradition in philosophy, had argued that the relationship between 'consciousness' and 'reality' was precisely the opposite to that posited by the Hegelian idealists. It is the material needs of mankind that determined their consciousness, and not the other way around. This forms the core of Marx's historical materialism. According to Marx, production for the satisfaction of man's material needs constitutes the foundation, the 'base', on which all societies ultimately rest. It is the social relations which are embedded in arrangements surrounding the production of commodities that determine individuals' 'consciousness', thereby establishing the framework within which all other aspects of human interaction subsequently evolve. In his Preface to *The Critique of Political Economy*, published in 1859, Marx (1970) sets out his clearest statement of historical materialism:

> In the social production of their existence, men inevitably enter into definite relations, which are independent of their will, namely relations of production appropriate to a given stage in the development of their material forces of production. The totality of these relations of production constitutes the economic structure of society, the real foundation, on which arises a legal and political superstructure and to which correspond definite forms of social consciousness. The mode of production of material life conditions the general process of social, political, and intellectual life. It is not the

consciousness of men that determines their existence, but their social existence that determines their consciousness.

Marx's attribution of causality in the progress of history exclusively to
events in the economic sphere has, since the *Critique* first appeared,
been the subject of considerable debate within the Marxist literature.
In particular, a number of writers in the tradition of Western Marxism
have contested what they regard as an overly mechanistic element in
Marx, namely that the political–legal superstructure, as represented
by the 'State', is simply a passive reflection of pre-existing conditions
in the economic sphere, exercising no independent influence on the
evolution of either society or conditions in the economic base itself.
In part, the problem lies in the abstract method of analysis which
Marx insisted was necessary if science was to go behind superficial
appearances and establish the 'essence of things'. Although the
superstructure, partially or wholly, might appear to be founded
on aspects of social interaction that are unrelated to the economic
base of society, historical materialism reveals that the ultimate source
of the changing social order originates with the changing arrangements
that surround commodity production; that is, in the mode of production.

The Mode of Production

The mode of production is the conceptual framework within which
Marx presents his materialist analysis of society. Marx identifies four
modes of production – ancient, feudal, capitalist and communist –
where each represents a unique stage in the evolution of society. The
mode of production consists of two elements. The first is the material
forces of production which comprise the physical means of production
– land, raw materials, machinery, etc. – and labour power. The second
aspect is relations in production which are defined by the distribution
of ownership over the productive forces between different groups or
'classes' in society. Historical materialism asserts that it is the independent development of productive forces that dictates history. This
occurs as man continually seeks out new techniques and practices, and
acquires new skills, which improve the process of production and so
increase the level of output. Thus each mode of production – slavery,
feudalism, capitalism and, ultimately, communism – corresponds to a
distinct stage in the *progressive* development of productive forces.
Relations in production, on the other hand, are prescribed by the
distribution of ownership over the material means of production. As

the nature of ownership rights changes as we move from one mode of production to the next, then so too do relations in production. It is relations in production that determine all remaining aspects of the entire social order – the superstructure. In conforming to relations within the prevailing mode of production, the superstructure reinforces and legitimizes these relations. In Marxian terminology, the superstructure reproduces in society as a whole those relations essential to the further development of the forces of production.

However, there are definite limits to the extent to which productive forces can develop within any particular mode of production. These limits are imposed by what Marx calls the 'contradiction of material life'. This refers to the conflict that Marx states will inevitably surface between the forces and relations of production as the former develop, and which will be resolved only by the transition to a new mode of production. In short, the production relations which initially encourage the development of the productive forces eventually become an obstacle to their further development. At this point, a new mode of production, embedding within it new relations in production which resolve the contradiction, overwhelms the prevailing mode. This is a momentous event, involving as it does the overthrow of the entire social order as the existing superstructure is forcibly dismantled and rebuilt to reflect relations in production that define the now dominant mode. It is important to emphasize that the continuity of history is clearly implicit in the *dialectic* manner in which the process of economic and social change proceeds. The production relations that define the new mode of production are always grounded in the conflict that unfolds in the relations defined by the preceding mode.

Classes in Society

Marx's theory of class and of class conflict remain the most controversial elements in his analysis of the development of the capitalist mode of production. As we have already noted, classes in society are defined according to their position in the production process. The distinction between classes revolves entirely around the ownership of the material means of production. In all class-based societies there is always one class which owns or controls the means of production, and another that does not. Individuals do not elect to become members of one class rather than another, nor can they aspire to membership of a different class through income or ability. In feudal societies, one is either a landowner or a serf; under capitalism, either a capitalist or a worker.

Social class is not simply a passive category to which individuals are assigned; quite the contrary. It is on the basis of class that the entire 'consciousness' of the individual – interests, ideas, aspirations, and actions – are fashioned. This is the essence of Feuerbach's materialism. However, in Marx it becomes the primary determinant of political action. For Marx maintains that relations between classes at all times and in all class-divided societies are antagonistic. This is true both for classes within a given mode of production, and between the classes defined by competing modes of production. Classes are united in their struggle, and their struggle is at all times a class struggle. Moreover, the class struggle, whilst founded by relations in production, will pervade all aspects of the social order. Class antagonisms in all instances arise from the exploitation of one class by another. Exploitation results from the power that the relations in production, i.e. property ownership, bestow on one class at the expense of the other. In feudal societies, the landlord dominates and the serf is exploited; under capitalism, it is the worker who is exploited by the capitalist. The importance with which Marx viewed class antagonism is clear from *The Communist Manifesto*, (Marx and Engels, 1948, 1967) where he proclaims, 'The history of all hitherto existing society is the history of class struggles.'

As Roemer (1988, p. 114), a leading contributor to the 'analytical' critique of orthodox Marxism, notes, Marx appears to be advancing two competing dialetic theories of social transformation: one in which societal development and transformation are determined by the development of the material forces of production, and one where it is the class struggle that dictates the progress of society. But, Roemer adds, 'A reconciliation is not so difficult to propose, if class struggle is assigned the role of midwife at the birth of the new economic structure.' In Roemer's account, the class struggle, which may be an ongoing feature of the prevailing mode of production, will not be sufficient of itself to effect a transformation in society. Instead, this occurs only when productive forces in society have developed to the extent that an alternative mode of production – one which promises to improve the material conditions of life – becomes viable. As Marx says in his Preface, 'No social order is ever destroyed before all the productive forces for which it is sufficient have been developed, and new superior relations of production never replace older ones before the material conditions for their existence have matured within the framework of the old society'. When this stage is reached, the class struggle within the prevailing mode of production is augmented by a struggle between the dominant classes defined by competing modes of production. Only with the resolution of this struggle will society be transformed to reflect production relations embedded in the new economic structure.

Roemer explains the transition from feudalism to capitalism as follows (see also Junankar, 1982, p. 19). Feudal landowners were confronted with an emerging capitalist economic structure which, by virtue of the technology used in production, was able to raise the level of labour productivity and consequently pay its workers higher real wages than landlords felt necessary to pay serfs. The fermenting revolt by serfs against landowners was given an added impetus by the emergence of this alternative economic structure as serfs now had the option of becoming workers in the factories of capitalists. As the defection of serfs from the land accelerated, capitalism replaced feudalism as the dominant mode of production bringing with it new relations in production which subsequently transformed the entire social order. Capitalism differed from feudalism not only in the structure of production relations; it differed too in its objectives. Under capitalism, the purpose of commodity production was exchange rather than direct consumption by the producers. A consequence of this, as we go on to discuss in the next section, was that the nature of exploitation in capitalist societies differed from that in feudal societies.

The precise role played by class conflict in the history of social development remains a matter of intense debate within the Marxist literature. Two categories of criticism are regularly advanced. The first surrounds the concept of 'class consciousness'. By what mechanism are individuals informed of their class consciousness, and what determines the development of consciousness over time? Obviously this cannot be fashioned by the agencies of superstructure, thus excluding education and culture as the informing mechanism, as these are themselves seen to be a product of the consciousness of the dominant class. Second, orthodox Marxists present no explanation of the mechanism whereby class interests are transformed into class actions (Levine and Wright, 1989). The dominant class will persistently seek to undermine the unity of the subjugated class, particularly during periods when the prevailing mode of production is under attack, yet we are given no insight concerning the mechanism whereby workers gain command of the resources, ideological or political, to retaliate.

Value and Distribution in Marx

It was Marx's view that exploitation is a feature of all class-based societies, and is the source of ongoing class conflict within those societies. 'Exploitation' has a precise meaning in Marxist economics and is derived from Marx's labour theory of value. In formulating this theory, Marx followed in the classical tradition of Smith and Ricardo. Although the idea that the value of a commodity is related to the labour time expended in its production is to be found in Smith's *The Wealth of Nations* (Smith, 1970), it was only in the 1820s, with Ricardo's *Principles of Political Economy and Taxation* (Ricardo, 1971), that a comprehensive statement of the labour theory of value first appeared. Ricardo proposed that a direct correspondence exists between the *exchange value* of a commodity, i.e. the ratio in which one commodity exchanges for another, and the labour input required for its production. Thus if commodity A requires twice as much labour to produce as commodity B, then one unit of A will exchange for two units of B. Of course Ricardo was aware, as was Marx, that for a commodity to have an exchange value, it must also have a *value in use*, i.e. it must impart utility to the buyer. However, not everything that has utility has an exchange value. For example, we derive obvious utility from the air that we breathe but as it is an example of a free good, by definition it has no value in exchange. Consequently, utility cannot form the basis of an economic theory of value.

Instead, the common element in all goods that has both value in exchange and value in use is labour; therefore, labour is the only source of value. Moreover, the labour content in production is both objective and measurable, determined by the number of hours of human labour necessary to produce, or reproduce, a commodity. Consequently, value is itself objectively determined. The labour theory of value will hold even where production involves the application of physical capital – equipment and machinery, factories, etc. – as physical capital is simply 'dead' labour and can, at least conceptually, be measured according to the number of hours or weeks of labour needed for its (re)production. The final magnitude we must introduce is market *price*, for it is the wedge that Marx drives between value and price that constitutes the basis of exploitation. Marx accepted that price would reflect not only the (labour) value of a product, but also the level of market demand. Prices were, therefore, determined in what Marx called the 'sphere of exchange' and not, as is the case for value, in the 'sphere of production'. But, nonetheless, market prices will reflect labour values in a systematic manner. Although it is commonly accepted that Marx failed to reconcile the observed structure of relative commodity prices with the respective labour input in their production (i.e. commodity values did not correspond to commodity prices), a number of solutions to this *transformation problem* have been subsequently advanced (Meek, 1977; Fine and Harris, 1979).

Armed with Marx's labour theory of value we can now examine the precise nature of exploitation. To recap – the production of commodities which are essential to human existence requires the application of labour to the physical means of production and, as we now know, the value of a commodity is determined solely by the labour effort, measured in hours, days or weeks, expended in its production. However, as we have seen, the ownership of the physical means of production in society is typically unequal, making the non-propertied class dependent on the propertied class for its survival. Marx's fundamental insight was to recognize that labour, or more precisely *labour power*, is properly to be regarded as a commodity whose exchange value, i.e. the wage rate, will be determined in precisely the same manner as any factor input to production, that is by its reproduction costs. Consequently, wages will be fixed at the level required to maintain the well-being of the current labour force and guarantee the supply of the next generation of workers. Marx argued, however, that of all the inputs to the production process, only labour has the ability to create value *in excess* of its subsistence or reproductive requirements. This is *surplus value*, and it is the appropriation of this by the dominant class that Marx defines as exploitation. The theory of surplus value is common to all class-based societies, although the precise manner in which exploitation occurs depends on the objectives of the dominant class, which are themselves defined by the prevailing mode of production. It should be obvious that the theory of surplus value is, at the same time, a theory of income distribution. This contrasts sharply with neoclassical economics where the distribution of income is determined according to marginal productivity theory.

We are now in a position to review Marx's account of the capitalist mode of production.

THE STRUCTURE AND DYNAMICS OF CAPITALISM

As in all pre-capitalist modes of production, capitalism is characterized by a class division that is determined in the economic sphere on the basis of differing relations to the means of production. The dominant class comprises capitalists who, by virtue of their money holdings, alone have control over the material means of production, and a working class, the proletariat, who – having no independent access to the means of production – are obliged to sell their labour power to capitalists to earn a living. The aim of the capitalist is to enlarge constantly his money holdings, i.e. to accumulate more capital. The capitalist uses money to purchase physical capital and labour power to produce a commodity. However, unlike in feudalism, the commodity is no longer produced for the capitalist's own consumption, but to be sold in the market place in return for money. The difference between the capitalist's total costs of production, including wages, and revenue derived from market exchange constitutes *profit*. And it is only by creating profits that accumulation – the enlargement of capital – can occur. An important distinction in Marx is between the source of the capitalist's profit, which he maintains lies in the 'sphere of commodity production', and the realization of profit which he recognizes depends on prevailing market conditions in the 'sphere of exchange'. The bulk of *Capital* is concerned with conditions in the sphere of production as it is here that Marx identifies what he calls the 'internal contradictions' which will ultimately undermine the capitalist mode of production.

The economic model of capitalism that Marx advanced in *Capital* involves the development of two abstract and complex analytical strands, each of which is influenced by the Hegelian dialectic. These are, first, a theory of capitalist exploitation and, second, a theory of the contradictory laws of motion of capitalism. We consider each of these in turn.

Capitalism and Exploitation

The source of the capitalist's profit is the appropriation of the surplus value of labour, i.e. that part of the value created by labour in excess of its reproductive costs. It is this exploitation that establishes the basis for the ensuing class struggle between capital in general and labour in general. As they strive to enlarge their capital, capitalists embark on a continual search for higher profits or surplus by increasing the rate of exploitation of labour. Workers, for their part, are powerless to resist their exploitation. At any moment, there will be a 'reserve army of the unemployed' ready to work for whatever wages are offered and this strips labour of the capacity for collective resistance to its individual exploitation. The rate of exploitation is precisely defined as the ratio of 'surplus value', (s), to 'necessary value', (v), where necessary value refers to that part of the total value realized by market sale which must be paid out as wages to maintain the reproduction of labour. The higher the rate of exploitation, the greater the quantity of surplus relative to necessary value created in production and is approximately equal to the rate of profit.

The rate of exploitation can be raised through two mechanisms: directly, through an increase in the surplus element in total value, or indirectly, by a reduction of the necessary element of labour time in commodity production. Marx termed the former *absolute* surplus value and this could be raised by increasing the number of hours of work performed by labour, i.e. by lengthening the working day. As long as there is no corresponding rise in the reproduction cost of labour, this will achieve an increase in the absolute surplus produced. For example, if in the course of a 12-hour working day the revenue from 9 hours of labour effort is sufficient to finance workers' consumption, the remaining 3 hours of labour effort will be freed to produce surplus value. If the length of the working day is increased to 15 hours, however, the element of surplus value rises to 6 hours' output equivalent. But, of course, there are physical limits to the scope for increases in absolute surplus value set by the number of hours of labour that workers are capable of performing in any one day before their performance suffers and their 'reproduction' is jeopardized.

However, capitalists are still able to raise the rate of exploitation through increases in *relative* surplus value by changing the conditions of production to reduce the 'necessary' labour time (v) required to produce any given value of output. There are three mechanisms to achieve this: by investing in labour-saving constant capital, i.e. machinery; by advances in production technologies embodied in constant capital; and by concentrating production in larger units and reaping the cost advantages associated with economies of scale. In this way, the pursuit of higher profits induces capitalists to adjust the technical conditions in production through additions to the stock of physical capital. Changes in the technical composition of capital alters what Marx calls the *value composition of capital* in production, i.e. the share in the value of total productive capital accounted for by constant capital, c, the value of the means of production, and variable capital, v, the value of labour power, respectively. Marx describes this as a rise in the *organic* composition of capital.

Capitalism is, therefore, characterized by the ongoing struggle between workers and capitalists over what conventional economists would depict as the distribution of income. However, this description is unacceptable to orthodox Marxists. The real conflict, they insist, originates with the appropriation by capitalists of the value created by labour in production. This is considerably more than a semantic distinction. Class consciousness is solely determined by relations in production, and class antagonisms exclusively revolve around the appropriation of the value created by the working class by the capitalist class. The ensuing struggle is absolute – it constitutes the dialectic which determines the evolution of capitalist society. Capitalists may be able to placate workers temporarily by improving wages at the expense of profits, but this does nothing to resolve the underlying conflict which is fought out in the value domain, i.e. the sphere of production. It is only under capitalism that workers ultimately become aware of their exploitation. The raising of their consciousness results from the internal laws of motion of capitalism.

Capitalism's Laws of Motion

Capitalists are compelled by the competitive nature of capitalism to raise the rate of exploitation. Profits, or surplus value, can only be realized by the sale of the produced commodity in competitive markets. From the perspective of each individual capitalist, accumulation compels him to constantly seek out new arrangements in production that cheapen the cost of commodity production, thus enabling him to lower prices and improve his competitive position. This can only be achieved by expelling labour from the process of production. At first glance, Marx appears to be advancing little more than an elementary cost-of-production theory of prices. And, from the perspective of the individual capitalist, this is indeed the case. With the substitution of 'men' by 'machines' the share of revenue that must go to labour falls and the share accruing as profit rises. In other words, the rate of exploitation has risen due to an increase in the organic composition of capital. But Marx maintained that the competitive forces that compelled capitalists as individuals to raise the organic composition of capital would induce a crisis in capitalism as a whole.

Marxists regard competition between different units of capital as executing the inner law of motion of capitalism. But this law is subject to an internal contradiction which provokes episodes of crisis in the capitalist system. This involves the impact that changes in the composition of capital have on the rate of profit over the longer term. As profits are directly related to surplus value, the rate of profit (r) can be expressed as $r = s/v+c$, that is the ratio of surplus value to the total costs of production expressed as the sum of the value of variable and constant capital. We can rearrange this to yield $r = (s/v)/(c/v)+1$. Clearly, if (c/v), the value composition of capital rises more quickly than (s/v), the rate of exploitation of labour, then the rate of profit, r, must be falling. Marx refers to this as the *tendency for the rate of profit to fall*, which he argues is an inevitable consequence of the dynamics of capitalism.

The thrust of Marx's argument can best be understood in terms of labour productivity. Investment in physical capital is undertaken because it increases the productivity of labour. Consequently, the necessary labour associated with a given level of output declines, and as the direct labour content in commodity production falls, so too will its value, thus forcing down market prices and rewarding the innovating capitalist with a competitive advantage over his rivals. But Marx argued that there is a limit to the extent to which machinery can substitute for labour in production and as this limit is approached, further additions to the stock of physical capital will be associated with ever smaller gains in labour productivity. Therefore the tendency is for surplus value to grow at an ever decreasing rate with successive substitutions of constant for variable capital, and although surplus value (s/v) may continue to rise in absolute terms, it will only do so at a slower rate than the value composition of capital (c/v). If the (c/v) is rising faster than (s/v) then the general rate of profit for capital as a whole, r, must be falling. Nonetheless, the competitive process compels individual capitalists to continue to invest in labour-saving physical capital even when the general rate of profit is declining as only in this way can they hope to increase their individual rate of profit. The outcome is that profits for all capitalists will tend to decline, providing yet a further spur for the individual capitalist to seek out new means of cheapening commodity values. The tendency for the rate of profit to fall, equivalent to a relative decline in the rate of growth of surplus value, occupies a central place in orthodox Marxist accounts of capitalist crises as it will eventually interrupt the smooth progress of capitalist accumulation. In Marxian terminology, conditions in the sphere of production come into conflict with those in the sphere of exchange.

However, although the tendency for the rate of profit to fall is inherent in capitalism, Marx identified five counteracting tendencies which will raise the surplus element in total value. These are:

- increases in the intensity of exploitation by lengthening the working day;
- a reduction in wages paid to labour;
- a decline in the value composition of capital by cheapening constant capital;
- an expansion of foreign trade to provide cheaper imports of

constant capital and consumer goods, the latter serving to reduce the costs of reproducing labour; and

- an increase in the population which, through competition for jobs, lowers wages.

For Marx, the combination of these counteracting influences is sufficiently significant to transform the 'law' of a falling rate of profit to the more modest status of a 'tendency'. Nevertheless, this tendency will be of sufficient strength to initiate crisis phases in capitalist economies, manifested by sharp cyclical downturns in economic activity, recovery from which will occur only when a sufficient number of firms has been forced into bankruptcy, so reducing the value of constant capital as to permit a rise in the general rate of profit and initiate a new period of accumulation.

The mechanics of the crisis are simple to understand. As the rate of profit tends to decline, so demand in the investment or producer goods sector of the economy falls. As producers in this sector are unable to realize their profit or surplus, some will cut back production and reduce their work forces, while others will simply go bankrupt. This downturn in activity soon spreads to the remainder of the capitalist system as demand deficiency gathers momentum throughout the economy with more and more workers losing their jobs. The separation of commodity buyer from commodity producer, inevitable when production is for exchange rather than for use, encourages this multiplier effect as producers, uncertain about the market for their produce, curtail their activities. In this manner, the crisis originating in a declining rate of profit is speedily transformed into what Marxists refer to as a *realization* crisis as the lack of demand, underconsumption, prevents capitalists from realizing, through commodity sales, the surplus value that has been produced. Clearly, there is a strong resemblance between the Marxian category of underconsumption and the concept of aggregate demand used by Keynes to account for the business cycle that appears in the *General Theory* (Keynes, 1973). However, in Marxian analysis, the underconsumption or realization crisis is only the manifestation in the sphere of exchange of an accumulation crisis in the sphere of production.

Marx's critics have comprehensively rejected Marx's falling rate of profit thesis as being both technically and empirically wrong. Their criticism revolves around Marx's argument that the value composition of capital (c/v) must rise over time. We recall that this is the consequence of successive investments in labour-saving physical capital which, by reducing the labour content in commodity production, enable individual capitalists to lower the selling price of their output and gain a competitive price edge over rivals. But precisely the same logic must apply with equal effect in the capital goods-producing sector itself. In other words, the value, and so price, of the physical means of production, constant capital, should itself be falling as producers there adopt production technologies that yield productivity gains. The conclusion, maintain the critics, is that there are no grounds for arguing that the value composition of capital (c/v) will be rising faster than (s/v), the rate of growth of surplus value, since there are no grounds for assuming that the value of constant capital itself will not be falling as labour is expelled from production in the capital goods sector. Therefore, only by making the untenable assumption that technological developments do not extend into the capital goods sector can the logic of Marx's claim for the falling rate of profit be sustained. Moreover, it has little basis in fact. The history of contemporary capitalist development shows quite clearly that the rate of profit has tended to rise over time rather than to fall. Although orthodox Marxists insist that this criticism is based on a fundamental misconception of Marx's usage of the term 'tendency', as we discuss in the next section, many Marxists now accept that capitalism has no developmental tendency to a falling rate of profit.

Before examining developments in contemporary Marxism, however, it is important to make a brief reference to Marx's prediction that the developmental laws of capitalism will ultimately herald the introduction of the communist mode of production. As in other episodes of social transformation, this will occur when further development of the productive forces is impossible within the prevailing capitalist relations in production. Marx argued that only under capitalism will workers become fully aware of their enslavement and exploitation as a class. Capitalism represents the ultimate stage of the exploitation and dehumanization of labour in the history of organized production. The laws of motion which guide capitalism demand the *proletarianization* of labour – the creation of a labour force *qua* labour force from which has been removed the last vestiges of direct association with the product of their endeavours. The skills of labour so essential to production in the early stages of capitalism become redundant as technological advances create machines that replace men and which demand not craftsmen but operators to perform routine and alienating mechanical duties. Increasingly detached from a direct relationship with production and imprisoned within the confines of a technological society, capitalism forces labour to that stage where it can recognize the ideological nature of the struggle in which it is engaged. Only then is the transformation of society possible, as only then has labour as a class been stripped of all 'false consciousness' and consequently has the capacity to propel society to a new enlightenment based on the common ownership of the means of production.

DEVELOPMENTS IN MARXIAN ECONOMICS

If we are to assess the state of health of a research programme by the breadth and intensity of the debates which it provokes, then Marxist economics today must be declared alive and well. In this section we review two general themes in contemporary Marxist economics. The first is the revision to Marx's theory of capitalist dynamics proposed by writers in the 'monopoly capital' school. Second, we consider some contributions in the so-called 'radical' tradition in economic thought which continues to challenge the conclusions of neoclassical orthodoxy over a range of contemporary economic and social issues.

Monopoly Capital

It is generally acknowledged that the publication in 1966 of Baran and Sweezy's *Monopoly Capital* represented a landmark in the development of Marxist economic theory. Taking *Capital* as their starting point, Baran and Sweezy reformulated Marx's theory of capitalist development in the light of changes which had occurred in the structure of capitalism since the nineteenth century. Acknowledging their debt to the work of Michal Kalecki, a Polish-born Marxist who effectively anticipated all the major findings of Keynes's *General Theory*, and Josef Steindl, Baran and Sweezy investigated the dynamics of capitalism where the prevailing market structure was imperfect competition, i.e. oligopoly and monopoly, and not the perfectly competitive markets that characterized early capitalism (Kalecki, 1971; Steindl, 1976). Although Marx had recognized that the competitive dynamics of capitalism would lead to capital being concentrated in fewer hands, Baran and Sweezy maintained that Marx had understandably failed to recognize that this would profoundly affect the dynamics of capitalist development. Specifically, they argued that as capitalism entered its monopoly phase, whereupon the 'degree of monopoly' increased, individual capitalists would become 'price makers' rather than 'price takers'. And, because capitalists no longer competed through successive reductions in product prices, the tendency of the rate of profit to fall would not be a characteristic of late capitalism. Instead, the exact opposite would tend to occur – that is, oligopolistic firms would tend to experience an increase in the rate of profit. The reversal of Marx's tendency for the rate of profit to fall was explained by the cost-saving nature of technological innovation. Firms would continually seek out techniques which lowered production costs. But rather than reducing prices as they were forced to do in conditions of perfect competition, they would now leave prices fixed and appropriate the rising difference between costs and revenues directly in the form of higher profits. Prices would be unaffected as it was in the interests of all firms to avoid disruptive, and ultimately suicidal, price wars.

This constituted a profound challenge to orthodox Marxist explanations of episodes of crisis in capitalist economies. If these did not result from a falling rate of profit, then where did they originate? Baran and Sweezy's crisis theory centres on what they call the *absorption* problem or, as it is more commonly called, *underconsumption*. What they argue is that as the share of profit or surplus in total income rises, then if total demand in the economy is to equal total supply, capitalists as a class must increase their spending by the whole amount of their increase in profits. Capitalists' spending comprises two components: consumption and investment. However, capitalists will be unlikely to increase their consumption by the full amount of this growth in profit for two reasons. First, not all the higher profits will be distributed to the owners of capital by way of higher dividends and, second, some part of any increase in dividends that is paid out will undoubtedly be saved. Therefore, although capitalist consumption might grow in absolute terms, it will fail to grow as fast as the growth of the profits, implying that the part of the surplus which has to be absorbed through capitalists' investment must be ever increasing. But, of course, this will not happen precisely because consumption demand is failing to grow sufficiently quickly. Thus we have a situation in which the growth in total demand in the economy is insufficient to meet the growth in total output. As a result, excess productive capacity will emerge provoking a decline in capitalist investment and thereby initiating a cyclical downturn in the level of output and employment. The crisis is a *realization* crisis in capitalism as capitalists are unable to realize the surplus value, or profit, that has been produced. And, as there is no reason to expect a dramatic upturn in capitalists' consumption, the economic stagnation produced by the crisis will continue as long as the 'investment-seeking' element of the surplus is unable to find investment outlets. Consequently, only when 'the amount of surplus-seeking investment is exactly absorbed by available investment outlets' (Baran and Sweezy, 1966, p. 68) will the recession be halted and an upturn begin. In the underconsumptionist argument, therefore, episodes of crisis are provoked not by a decline in the rate of profit interrupting capitalist accumulation, but by the inability of capitalists to absorb the ever higher share of national income accruing to them in the form of profits.

In response to underconsumption, capitalists will be forced to other means of realizing their surplus. Baran and Sweezy identified three mechanisms for this: first, each firm will aim to enlarge its share of the market at the expense of rivals by allocating more resources to the sales effort in the form of advertising; second, wasteful consumption will be encouraged by, for example, the built-in obsolescence of consumer products; and, third, monopoly capital will collectively engage in an active search for alternative 'markets', such as government spending, to utilize excess productive capacity. It is through this third route that monopoly capitalism brings its influence to bear on the development of the political and ideological structures in society, thereby re-establishing the Marxian relationship between base and superstructure. In this Baran and Sweezy model, then, the function of the superstructure is *not* to reproduce the class relations required by the capitalist mode of production, but to protect the *stability* of the capitalist system as a whole, first, by imparting to society that specific set of values consistent with the aims and behaviour of monopoly capital and, second, by ensuring that monopoly capital is able to realize its produced surplus.

Orthodox Marxists have been highly critical of Baran and Sweezy's reformulation of the laws of motion of capitalism on the grounds of its implicit rejection of Marx's theory of value. Without this theory of value, of course, the determining contradiction in capitalism, the class struggle based on the exploitation of surplus value, has no foundation. Instead, the interruption to the progress of capitalist accumulation is explained purely by an appeal to a theory of imperfect competition and is conducted entirely in the sphere of exchange. The eschewal of any reference to conflictual relations in production as the underlying cause of crisis in capitalism leads Bell (1977) to conclude that 'this theoretical work seems part of a different project. It reifies economic categories and is powerless to analyze the class forces that constitute the basis of accumulation.'

A more basic deficiency in the underconsumptionist theory is detected by Wright (1977):

The most serious weakness in the underconsumptionist position is that it lacks any theory of the determinants of the actual rate of accumulation. The falling-rate-of-profit theorists have a specific theory of the determinants of the rate of accumulation. In equating the rate of profit with the rate of accumulation, they see a combination of the organic composition of capital and the rate of exploitation as the basic determinants of the actual rate of accumulation . . . In the underconsumptionist argument, however, the rate of profit and the rate of accumulation cannot be equated. If they were, there would not be a tendency for underconsumption.

Wright argues that until the underconsumptionist school provides an explanation for investment and the rate of accumulation, 'the theory remains incomplete'. In the absence of this explanation, the underconsumptionist school has little option but to invoke Keynesian-type crises of expectations to explain the decline in the level of investment. Indeed, there does appear to be at least a family resemblance between the arguments advanced in *Monopoly Capital* and Keynes's *General Theory*. However, whereas Keynes never provided adequate microeconomic foundations explaining the tendency for capitalist economic systems to experience periods of demand deficiency, Baran and Sweezy firmly identify these as the distributional consequences of oligopolistic pricing policy.

Radical Economics

The development of the radical tradition in economics owes much to Baran and Sweezy. By freeing Marxism from what many had come to consider its anachronistic dependency on the ill-defined concept of 'class', it paved the way for economic and social theorists to develop explanations of economic problems outside the deterministic framework imposed by Marx's historical materialism. Therefore, although radical economists share a vision of society which is founded on conventional Marxian concepts, they reject many of the dogmas maintained by orthodox Marxists. Sherman in his *Foundations of Radical Political Economy* (1987) identifies ten points on which radicals part company with orthodox Marxists. Here we briefly review these under four headings. Students are strongly recommended to consult Sherman's text for a fuller account.

Historical Materialism

Radicals do not accept the doctrine of historical materialism which maintains that the structure of society is simply a passive reflection of technical conditions in the economic sphere, and thus dispute the contention that the state is nothing more than a servant to the dominant class. The relationship between 'base' and 'superstructure' that Marx advanced in the 1859 Preface – see above – maintained the primacy of the productive forces, whose development determined relations in production. By and large, the radical economics tradition has rejected what is widely seen to be the unacceptably deterministic element in historical materialism. Instead, society is seen as a reflection of the continual interaction between ideas and institutions originating in the superstructure on the one hand, and developments in the economic sphere on the other. Causation may run in either direction, and feedback loops are permitted, producing what Sherman refers to as a 'never-ending interaction between ideas and the economy' (Sherman, 1987, p. 7). Although the activities of the state may well reflect the objectives of capitalism, orthodox Marxists fail to recognize that in democratic societies there is a political process that regulates state actions, and from which the working class frequently wins concessions.

Distribution of Income

Radicals contest the orthodox Marxist position on the distribution of income. Rather than explaining distribution in terms of the labour theory of value, radicals argue that income distribution is the outcome of a class struggle within the bounds imposed by the prevailing distribution of power in society. However, because power relations in society can, and do, change, the pattern of income distribution can change independently of the arrangements surrounding commodity production. Therefore, although it is accepted by radicals that class exploitation is an innate feature of capitalism, the rate of exploitation at any moment cannot be determined solely by reference to the economic base of society. Social and political factors are equally important. Radicals point to the development of 'dual' labour markets in advanced capitalist economies as evidence of this. For example, in both the UK and the US it has been shown that wages are related both to ethnic origin and gender. The wages of black workers and women are frequently below those paid to white males doing the same job. Similarly, the incidence of unemployment and the educational attainment within the working class both display biases that can be adequately explained only if racial and gender factors are explicitly recognized.

Theory of Crisis

Radicals argue that crises are more likely to originate in the sphere of exchange than in the sphere of production. In part, this follows from their general rejection of Marx's view that the rate of profit tends to decline under capitalism, and here the radical position accords with other critiques of Marxist economics. At the same time, radicals maintain that, by insisting that crisis can never originate in the sphere of exchange, orthodox Marxists are implicitly accepting the principles of Say's Law, namely that supply will create its own demand. In advancing a theory of cyclical crisis which is caused by a deficiency in the level of aggregate demand, radical economists explicitly align themselves with the Baran and Sweezy 'underconsumptionist' school rather than with orthodox Keynesianism. But, unlike Baran and Sweezy, radicals acknowledge that rising costs of production also play an important role in economic cycles. This is especially true during the downswing phase of the cycle where workers' resistance to reductions in their money wage effectively raises the real wage. And, as the sphere of wages in total income rises, profits decline and investment is curtailed. In fact, the radical school is in this respect at least much closer to the orthodox Keynesian accelerator model of business cycles than to Marxist accounts of capitalist crises.

The Socialist Economy

Radicals dispute the viability of state planning over all areas of economic activity, preferring instead a 'mixed' economy model in which planning coexists with market forces. The roots of radicals' dissatisfaction with planning undoubtedly lie in the postwar experience of East European countries. Radicals claim that orthodox Marxists confuse socialism with statism, where the latter describes conditions of state ownership of the means of production. The Soviet Union has, until recently, been 'statist' and this has directly led to the subjugation of the workers by a small group of elite managers. Instead radicals define socialism as 'a set of productive relations and productive forces that are democratically run by workers or by citizens, so that it is impossible to have a class of exploiters and a class of exploited' (Sherman, 1987, p. 260). This can only be achieved if the ownership and control over the means of production is firmly in the hands of the workers themselves, and not controlled by the state which Marxists mistakenly depict as the servant of the working class in communist society. Elements of planning are accepted as essential for all socialist economies, but equal reliance has to be placed on market forces. Radicals point to the calamitous economic performance of the Soviet Union and other East European countries as confirming the limitations of economic planning.

CONCLUSION

In the course of this chapter it has become clear that the Marxist paradigm accommodates a wide range of competing explanations of the dynamics of capitalist economies. However, although different authors may favour particular interpretations of Marx, they have in common an approach to economic and social inquiry in which it is the economic nature of society that, in the final instance, determines events. This is because it is economic criteria which divide society into its distinctive groups. Many contemporary Marxists, however, dispense with Marx's dogmatic class-based analysis of groups in society. As we noted, race and gender have been identified by radical economists as more important determinants of income distribution and employment than social class. Others, in particular writers in the 'analytic school' of Marxism, have argued that whilst collective social action is undeniably a feature of capitalist economies, this can be adequately explained by conventional rational choice theory. In other words, individuals will consciously align themselves with other individuals for specific ends and are not bound in their actions by reason of 'class consciousness'. Elster, a leading exponent of analytical Marxism, insists that game theory – the theory of interdependent decisions – provides a framework within which rational individual choice can readily produce a situation in which individuals will group themselves together for the purpose of cooperating to achieve a common goal (Elster, 1985, 1989). Whilst the work of Elster and others has been criticized by orthodox Marxists, it constitutes an important stage in the development of a paradigm in social science which accepts the rationality and independence of the individual while, at the same time, recognizing and explaining the role that collective social and economic action has in shaping events.

FURTHER READING

Baran, P. and Sweezy, P. (1966), *Monopoly Capital*, London: Penguin Books.
Howard M.C. and King, J.E. (1985), *The Political Economy of Marx*, Harlow: Longman.

Sherman, H. (1987), *Foundations of Radical Political Economy*, New York: M.E. Sharpe.

SUMMARY OF THE RADICAL AND MARXIAN SCHOOLS

[Augmented via Klamer (1984), chapter 11 Backhouse (1985) Roemer (1988) Pheby (1988)]

World View

All aspects (political economy, history, and philosophy) of human activity and society (organic system).

Material evolution (conditions of production) determines evolution of people's ideas and economic and social relationships.

Capitalism has evolved – is not a universal system – this implies that there are different social relationships, institutional and social structures for each stage of evolution.

Capitalism (one class owning the means of production) extracts surplus from wealth-producing class (labour). (Exploitation.)

Asymmetric relationship between classes leads to contradictions (conflictual relationships) in capitalist mode of production, i.e. capitalists to increase the rate of exploitation, the workers to reduce it, – which would eventually lead to its downfall.

Values

To create a decent and just society of fulfilled human beings.

Goals

To combine scientific enquiry with political activity, i.e.:
– to analyse the contradictions (to explain and predict the evolution of capitalism as an economic system).
– to test the predictions.
– to apply the analysis in order to change society.

Not mechanistic causality, but *dialectical causality*, simultaneous and reciprocal; action, reaction and interaction (difficult to test empirically?)

Go beyond empty abstractions to simple and crucial relationships.

Bridge the gap between appearances and essences (basic organic relationships); e.g. ignoring social relationships leads to superficial analysis (appearances only).

Methodological Practice

Realist.
Reject inductivism, instrumentalism, and deductivism.
Dialectical materialism (three laws of dialectics):
1. Concerns thresholds (an accumulation of small quantitative changes can lead to a qualitative change).
2. Unity of opposites: contradictory nature of reality, therefore focus on the conflictual relationships which lead to change in a continuing organic process.
3. Negation of the negation; thesis, antithesis, synthesis.
Not universal, ahistorical models!
Interdisciplinary; holistic; organic processes.
Historical materialism (commitment to the idea of the inevitability of the evolutionary process) can lead to insights.

Earlier work sloppy, not analytical, but dogmatic (as in other schools). Latterly, uses analytical tools of scientific enquiry, and hypothesis testing.

Criteria for Assessment of Theories

Internal logical coherence.
Observational consistency.
Practical effectiveness.
(Is the evolutionary process inevitable?)

Hard Core

Potentially contradictory (conflictual) relationships and structures influencing historical development (institutional variations).

Complex relationships between material determinism and peoples' subjective appreciations of things like work.

Capitalists' primary motivation of capital accumulation.

There is a conflict of interests between capitalist and worker.

Concepts

Class; value (in use and exchange); surplus, s; profits $\equiv$ surplus; wealth; welfare.
Capital (constant, c, and variable (labour), v).
Output, $o = s + v + c$.
Organic composition of capital, $k = c/(c+v)$.

Rate of exploitation, $e = s/v$.

Rate of profit, $r = s/(c + v)$.

Commodity (the cell-form of the capitalist system).

Production.

Competition (more like warfare than mutually beneficial exchange).

Subsistence (social determined) = labour power (hours) necessary to produce the wherewithall to live and reproduce.

Different stages in evolution of capitalism (merchant, industrial, imperial, and monopoly).

Positive Heuristic (Agenda)

Expose the disadvantages of the capitalist (private property) system: conflictual non-harmonious operation, discrimination, inequality and injustices, alienation, inefficiencies, instabilities (periodic crises, business cycles) (i.e. causes are endogenous to system).

Start with the fundamental features of capitalism (e.g. labour power as a commodity, relationship between capitalism and wage labourer).

Relationship of commodities with prices and money comes at a much later stage.

Protective Belt Assumptions

Only living labour (variable capital) produces a surplus.

Profits are equal to the surplus.

Capitalists seek to accumulate increased profits via an increase in the organic composition of capital, k.

Themes

1. *Labour theory of value*: subsequently inadequate, and unnecessary, for explaining prices-out-of-equilibrium, or for explaining relationships between exploitation and profit.

Superceded by Sraffa's *Costs of production theory of value*.

2. *Theory of exploitation*: capitalist (monopolist) buys labour power at its cost of reproduction (socially determined subsistence); thus the surplus of their production is appropriated as profits.

Exploitation leads to surplus and thence to profits.

3. *Transformation problem* (How values are transformed into prices):

$$r \equiv (1-k)e$$

The above relationship implies that if the organic composition of

capital, k, varies across industries, then one cannot have a uniform
rate of exploitation and a uniform rate of profits.

Marx's solution: there are two parallel systems:
- of values, in which e is uniform, and
- of prices, in which r is uniform.

There are three stages in the process of determining prices:
  • e determines values, and s,
  • $r = s/(c + v)$,
  • competition establishes prices such that all capitalists earn r.
This is based on a 'labour theory of profits' (where profits $= s$),
because relative labour values no longer determine prices in any simple
way.

4. *Class analysis of income distribution.*

5. *Struggle between capital in general and labour in general.*

6. *Two-sector growth model:*
   Assume that:
   - products exchange at their values (arbitrary?)
   - r is same in both sectors (unrealistic),
   - all wages and part of s are consumed,
   - rest of s is used to accumulate capital,
   - supply of labour is completely elastic,
   - supply and demand of capital goods are in balance (strange invest-
     ment decision by producers!)
   - supply and demand of consumption goods are in balance.
   Marx showed that the economy could reach a balanced growth path
in these circumstances, both sectors growing at the same rate.
   (Compare with neoclassicals' methodological practice of defining
necessary conditions for some defined and desirable outcome.)

7. *Marx's predictions re the future of capitalism*
The nature of technological change is such as to lead to increased
mechanization. This will lead to the immiseration of proletariat. Work
will become increasingly a mechanical activity; work conditions will
deteriorate, and destroy the demand for skilled workmanship.

Capital will increasingly be substituted for labour. The organic composition of capital, $k = c/(c + v)$, will steadily increase. This will lead
to both an accumulation of capital, and an increasing reserve army of
the unemployed.

This will lead to an increase in output, o, which will either improve the conditions of the workers, or lead to crises (gluts).

It will also lead to an increase in the size of productive units, and an increase in the concentration of industry.

Given the identity, $r = (1 - k)e$, and a constant value of e if k increases, then r must fall. This leads to Marx's (heavily qualified) theory of the *Tendency of the rate of profit to decline* (criticized by both Joan Robinson and Paul Sweezy).

The fall in r leads to a fall in investment and a crisis in overproduction (i.e. goods remain unsold – even though workers needs remain unmet) (realization crisis). (Compare with Keynes's ideas about underconsumption!)

Thus, the endogenously generated conflicts and contradictions will lead to its ultimate negation and replacement by the opposite form of society – socialism, and then communism, since the tendency towards more and more severe crises will force the proletariat to unite and overthrow capitalism.

Marx indicated that there would be counteracting factors temporarily offsetting the tendency of the rate of profit to decline (by raising e). Capitalists will:
- increase the length of the working day (physical limits);
- introduce innovations which raise productivity without requiring increases in c;
- try to depress wages below the value of labour power (easier when unemployment is high);
- use foreign trade, and rapid expansion of overseas markets, to try to reduce the cost of constant capital.
- an increase in the population → competition → reduces wages.

Capital accumulation is uneven over time, because technological change and innovations occur at irregular intervals.

8. *Role of state in supporting capitalism.*

Evidence

Many of the logical implications and conditional predictions are susceptible to tests and many have been verified, e.g. industry has been concentrated increasingly into fewer and much larger hands, and periodic crises have become more severe (Mandel, via Pheby, 1988, p. 124).

Conclusions (Examples)

Steedman (1977): the physical conditions of production, the real wage, and the capitalist desires to accumulate, together determine r, the rate of profits, the rate of accumulation, the prices of products, and the social allocation of labour.

Differences between Radicals and Marxians

The Radical school started in the 1960s in the US in the protest movements opposing the American role in the Vietnam War. It is concerned about injustices, such as discrimination, sexual and racial inequalities, and exploitation of the Third World by the developed countries.

Development of the ideas about monopoly capitalism of Baran and Sweezy.

Union of Radical Political Economics in 1968; publishes the *Review of Radical Political Economy* (Bowles-Gintis-Reich-Edwards).

It combines academic analysis with political activism. It decries excessive technical specialization in analysis, and seeks to widen participation in economic discussion.

It criticizes conventional economic theory (Lindbeck 1971 via Backhouse 1985) because it:

1. avoids discussing distribution of incomes, wealth, and economic power.
2. takes tastes and resources as given (this is too restricted a view).
3. analyses small changes only, rather than large ones.
4. ignores quality of life.
5. ignores interactions of economic with social and political factors.
6. theorises about static equilibrium models only.
7. emphasises optimizing behaviour and the role of markets, rather than the development and role of institutions.

Bibliography

Allingham, M. (1975), *General Equilibrium*, New York: Wiley.
Arestis, P. (ed.) (1988), *Post Keynesian Monetary Economics: New Approaches to Financial Modelling*, Aldershot: Edward Elgar.
Arestis, P. and Skouras, T. (eds) (1985), *Post Keynesian Economic Theory: A Challenge to Neo-Classical Economics*, Brighton: Wheatsheaf.
Arouh, Albert (1987), 'The mumpsimus of economists and the role of time and uncertainty in the progress of economic knowledge', *Journal of Post Keynesian Economics*, vol. 9, no. 3, pp 395–423.
Arrow, K.J. (1951), *Social Choice and Individual Values*, New York: Wiley.
Axelrod, R. (1984), *The Evolution of Co-operation*, New York: Basic Books.
Ayres, C.E. (1944), *The Theory of Economic Progress*, Chapel Hill: University of North Carolina Press.
Backhouse, Roger (1985), *A History of Modern Economic Analysis*, Oxford: Blackwell.
Baran, P. and Sweezy, P. (1966), *Monopoly Capital*, London: Penguin Books.
Barro, R.J. (1977), 'Long term contracting, sticky prices and monetary policy', *Journal of Monetary Economics*, vol. 3, pp. 305–16.
Barro, R.J. and Grossman, H. (1976), *Money, Employment and Inflation*, New York: Cambridge University Press.
Baumol, W.J., Panzer, J.C. and Willig, R.D. (1982), *Contestable Markets and the Theory of Industry Structure*, New York: Harcourt Brace Jovanovich.
Begg, David, Fischer, Stanley and Dornbusch, Rudiger (1984, 1987), *Economics*, Maidenhead: McGraw-Hill.
Bell, Daniel, and Kristol, Iriving (eds) (1981), *The Crisis in Economic Theory*, New York: Basic Books.
Bell, P. (1977), 'Marxist Theory, Class Struggle, and the Crisis of Capitalism', in Schwartz, J. (ed.) (1977), *The Subtle Anatomy of Capitalism*, Santa Monica: Goodyear Publishing.
Benjamin, D. and Kochin, A. (1979), 'Searching for an explanation of unemployment in interwar Britain', *Journal of Political Economy*, vol. 187, pp. 441–78.
Bergson (Burk), A. (1938), 'A Reformulation of Certain Aspects of Welfare Economics', *Quarterly Journal of Economics*, vol. 52, pp. 310–34.
Blanchard, O. and Summers, L. (1986), 'Hysteresis and the European Unemployment Problem', *NBER Macroeconomics Annual*, vol. 1, Cambridge Mass. and London: MIT Press.
Blaug, Mark (1980), *The methodology of economics: or how economists explain*, Cambridge: Cambridge University Press.
Blaug, Mark (1985), *Economic Theory in Retrospect*, 4th ed., Cambridge: Cambridge University Press.
Blaug, Mark (1986), *Great Economists before Keynes*, Brighton: Wheatsheaf.
Bodkin, R.G., Klein, L.R. and Marwah, K. (1988), 'Keynes and the Origins

of Macroeconomic Modelling' in Hamouda, Omar F. and Smithin, J.N. (eds), *Keynes and Public Policy After Fifty Years, Vol. II: Theories and Method*, Aldershot: Edward Elgar, pp. 3–11.

Böhm-Bawerk, E. von (1884, 1889, 1950), *Capital and Interest*, translated by Huncke, G.D. and Sennholz, N.F., South Holland, Illinois: Libertarian Press.

Boland, Lawrence A. (1982), *The Foundations of Economic Method*, London: George Allen & Unwin.

Bottomore, T. (ed.) (1988), *Interpretations of Marxism*, Oxford: Basil Blackwell.

Boulding, K.E. (1981), *Evolutionary Economics*, London: Sage.

Caldwell, Bruce F. (1982), *Beyond Positivism: Economic Methodology in the Twentieth Century*, London: George Allen & Unwin.

Caldwell, B.J. (1988), 'Hayek's transformation', *History of Political Economy*, vol. 20, no. 4, pp. 513–41.

Callinicos, A. (ed.) (1989), *Marxist Theory*, Oxford: Oxford University Press.

Canterbury, R. (1980), *The Making of Economics*, Belmont, California: Wadsworth.

Chamberlin, E.H. (1933), *The Theory of Monopolistic Competition*, Cambridge, Mass: Harvard University Press.

Chick, V. (1983), *Macroeconomics After Keynes: A Reconstruction of the General Theory*, Oxford: Philip Allan.

Clark, J.M. (1926), *Social Control of Business*, Chicago: McGraw-Hill.

Clark, N. and Juma, C. (1987), *Long-Run Economics: an Evolutionary Approach to Economic Growth*, London: Pinter.

Clower, R. (1965), 'The Keynesian Counter-revolution: A Theoretical Appraisal', in Hahn, F.H. and Brechling, F.P.R. (eds), *Theory of Interest Rates*, London: Macmillan.

Coase, R.H. (1937), 'The nature of the firm', *Economica*, vol. 4, pp. 386–405.

Coddington, A. (1983), *Keynesian Economics: The Search for First Principles*, London: George Allen and Unwin.

Colander, David (1988), 'The evolution of Keynesian economics: from Keynesian to New Classical to New Keynesian', in Hamouda, Omar F, and John N. Smithin (eds), *Keynes and Public Policy After Fifty Years Vol. I: Economics and Policy*, Aldershot: Edward Elgar, pp. 92–100.

Commons, J.R. (1934), *Institutional Economics*, New York: Macmillan.

Cournot, A.A. (1838, 1929), *Researches into the Mathematical Principles of the Theory of Wealth*, translated from the French by N.T. Bacon, New York: Macmillan.

Creedy, J. (1986), *Edgeworth and the Development of Neoclassical Economics*, Oxford: Basil Blackwell.

Davidson, Paul (1972, 1978), *Money and the real world*, Basingstoke: Macmillan.

Demsetz, H. (1988), *Ownership, Control and the Firm*, Oxford: Basil Blackwell.

Dewey, John (1910), *How We Think*, New York: Heath.

Domar, E.D. (1946), 'Capital Expansion, Rate of Growth and Employment', *Econometrica*, vol. 14, pp. 137–47.

Dow, S.C. (1985), *Macroeconomic Thought: A Methodological Approach*, Oxford: Basil Blackwell.

Dow, S.C. (1988), 'What Happened to Keynes's Economics?', in Hamouda, Omar F. and Smithin, J.N. (eds), *Keynes and Public Policy After Fifty Years, Vol. I: Economics and Policy*, Aldershot: Edward Elgar, pp. 101–10.

Dugger, W.M. (1979), 'Methodological Differences Between Institutional and Neoclassical Economics', *Journal of Economic Issues*, vol. 13, no. 4, pp. 899–909.

Earl, Peter E. (1983), 'A Behavioural Theory of Economists' Behaviour' in Eichner, Alfred S. (ed.), *Why Economics is not yet a science*, London: Macmillan.

Earl, Peter E. (1988), *Behavioural Economics*, Schools of Thought in Economics Series, 2 vols, Cheltenham: Edward Elgar.

Earl, P.E. and Kay N.M. (1985), 'How Economists Can Accept Shackle's Critique of Economic Doctrines without Arguing Themselves out of Their Jobs', *Journal of Economic Studies*, vol. 12, 34–48.

Economist (1988), 'New Economists: The Cambridge tendency', 24 December, pp. 97–100.

Edgeworth, F.Y. (1881), *Mathematical Psychics*, London: Kegan Paul.

Edgeworth, F.Y. (1925), *Papers Relating to Political Economy*, London: Macmillan.

Eichner, A.S. (ed.) (1979), *A Guide to Post Keynesian Economics*, London: Macmillan.

Eichner, Alfred S. (ed.) (1983), *Why Economics is not yet a science*, London: Macmillan.

Eichner, A.S. (1987), *The Macrodynamics of Advanced Market Economics*, London: M.E. Sharpe.

Eldredge, N. (1985), *Time Frames: Rethinking of Darwinian Evolution and the Theory of Punctuated Equilibria*, New York: Simon and Schuster.

Elster, Jon (1982), 'Marxism, Functionalism and Game Theory: The Case for Methodological Individualism', *Theory and Society*, vol. II, pp. 453–82.

Elster, J. (1985), *Making Sense of Marx*, Cambridge: Cambridge University Press.

Elster, J. (1989), 'Marxism, Functionalism, and Game Theory: The Case for Methodological Individualism', in Callinicos, A. (ed.), *Marxist Theory*, Oxford: Oxford University Press.

Etzioni, Amitai (1988), *The Moral Dimension: Toward a New Economics*, New York: Free Press.

Fellner, W. (1979), 'The credibility effect and rational expectations', *Brookings Papers on Economic Activity*, no. 1, pp. 167–78.

Fine, B. and Harris, L. (1979), *Rereading Capital*, London: Macmillan.

Fischer, Stanley and Dornbusch, Rudiger (1983), *Economics*, Tokyo: McGraw-Hill.

Fisher, Robert M. (1986), *The Logic of Economic Discovery: Neoclassical Economics and the Marginal Revolution*, Brighton: Wheatsheaf.

Fleming, J.M. (1962), 'Domestic financial policies under fixed and floating exchange rates', *International Monetary Fund Staff Papers*, vol. 9, pp. 369–77.

Foster, John (1987), *Evolutionary Macroeconomics*, London: Allen & Unwin.

Friedman, J.W. (1977), *Oligopoly Theory*, Cambridge: Cambridge University Press.

Friedman, M. (1953), 'The Methodology of Positive Economics', in Friedman,

M. (ed.), *Essays in Positive Economics*, Chicago: University of Chicago Press, pp. 3–43.

Friedman, M. (1959), 'The demand for money: some theoretical and empirical results', *Journal of Political Economy*, vol. 67, pp. 327–51.

Friedman, M. (1968), 'The role of monetary policy', *American Economic Review*, vol. 58, pp. 1–17.

Friedman, M. (1970), 'A theoretical framework for monetary analysis', *Journal of Political Economy*, vol. 78, pp. 193–238.

Friedman, M. (1980), 'Memorandum to the House of Commons Treasury and Civil Service Committee', *Memoranda on Monetary Policy*, Cmnd 720, London: HMSO.

Friedman, M. (1986), 'Keynes Political Legacy', in *Keynes's General Theory: Fifty Years On*, Hobart Paperback no. 24, London: IEA.

Friedman, M. and Meiselman, D. (1959), 'The relative stability of monetary velocity and the investment multiplier in the US, 1897–1958', *Stabilisation Policies: Commission on Money and Credit*, Englewood Cliffs, N.J.: Prentice Hall.

Friedman, M. and Schwartz, A.J. (1963), *A Monetary History of the United States 1867–1960*, Princeton: Princeton University Press for the NBER.

Galbraith, J.K. (1952), *American Capitalism: the Concept of Countervailing Power*, Boston: Houghton Mifflin.

Galbraith, J.K. (1958), *The Affluent Society*, London: Hamish Hamilton.

Galbraith, J.K. (1967), *The New Industrial State*, London: Hamish Hamilton. Republished (1969), Harmondsworth: Penguin.

Gee, J.M.A. (1983), 'Marshall's Views on "Short Period" Value Formation', *History of Political Economy*, vol. 15, pp. 181–205.

Georgescu-Roegen, N. (1971), *The Entropy Law and the Economic Process*, Cambridge Mass: Harvard University Press.

Goodhart, C.A.E. (1975), *Money, information and uncertainty*, London: Macmillan.

Gordon, Wendell (1984), 'The Role of Institutional Economists', *Journal of Economic Issues*, vol 18, no. 2, pp. 369–81.

Gordon, W. and Adams, J. (1989), *Economics as a Social Science: an Evolutionary Approach*, Maryland: Riverdale.

Gravelle, H. and Rees, R. (1981), *Microeconomics*, Essex: Longman.

Guttentag, J.M. and Herring, R. (1985), 'Commercial bank lending in developing countries', in Smith, G.W. and Cuddington, J.T. (eds), *International Debt and the Developing Countries*, Washington: World Bank.

Hamilton, W. (1938), *Price and Price Policies*, New York: McGraw-Hill.

Hamouda, Omar F. and Smithin, J.N. (eds) (1988), *Keynes and Public Policy After Fifty Years, Vol. I: Economics and Policy*, Aldershot: Edward Elgar.

Hamouda, Omar F. and Smithin, J.N. (eds) (1988), *Keynes and Public Policy After Fifty Years, Vol. II: Theories and Method*, Aldershot: Edward Elgar.

Hansen, A.H. (1974), Keynes on Economic Policy in Harris S. *The New Economics*, New York: A.A. Knopf Inc.

Hansen, A.H. (1953), *A Guide to Keynes*, New York: McGraw-Hill.

Hanush, H. (ed.) (1988), *Evolutionary Economics: Applications of Schumpeter's Ideas*, Cambridge: Cambridge University Press.

Harcourt, G.C. (1985), *Controversies in Political Economy: Selected Essays of G.C. Harcourt*, edited by O.F. Hamouda, New York: New York University Press.

Hargreaves-Heap, S.P. (1980), 'Choosing the wrong natural rate: Accelerating inflation or decelerating employment and growth', *Economic Journal*, vol. 90, pp. 611–20.

Harrigan, F.J. and McGregor, P.G. (1989), 'Natural rates in an open economy model under imperfect competition', *Strathclyde Papers in Economics*, 89/6.

Harrod, R.F. (1939), 'An Essay in Dynamic Theory', *Economic Journal*, vol. 49, pp. 14–33.

Hayek, F.A. (1931), *Prices and Production*, London: Routledge.

Hayek, F.A. (1949), *Individualism and Economic Order*, London: Routledge and Kegan Paul.

Hayek, F.A. (1955), *The Counter-Revolution of Science*, London: Collier-Macmillan.

Hayek, F.A. (1982), *Law, Legislation and Liberty*, 3 volume edition, London: Routledge and Kegan Paul.

Hicks, J.R. (1937), 'Mr Keynes and the "Classics": a suggested interpretation', *Econometrica*, vol. 5, pp. 147–159.

Hicks, J.R. (1939), *Value and Capital*, Oxford: Clarendon Press.

Hicks, John R. (1982), *Collected Essays on Economic Theory, Volume II: Money, Interest and Wages*, Oxford: Basil Blackwell.

Hicks, John R. (1983), *Collected Essays on Economic Theory, Volume III: Classics and Moderns*, Oxford: Basil Blackwell.

Hodgson, Geoffrey M. (1988), *Economics and Institutions: a Manifesto for a New Institutional Economics*, Cambridge: Polity Press.

Howard, M.C. and King, J.E. (1985), *The Political Economy of Marx,*, Harlow: Longman.

Hume, David (1740, 1967), *A Treatise of Human Nature*, edited by L.A. Selby-Bigge, Oxford: Clarendon Press.

Hunt, E.K. (1979), *History of Economic Thought: a Critical Perspective*, Belmont: Wadsworth.

Institute of Economic Affairs, (1986), *Keynes's General Theory: Fifty Years On*, Hobart Paperback no. 24, London: IEA.

Jaffé, W. (1976), 'Menger, Jevons and Walras de-homogenised', *Economic Inquiry*, vol. 14, no. 4, pp. 511–24.

Jevons, W. Stanley (1871, 1970), *The Theory of Political Economy*, Pelican Classics, ed. R.D. Collison Black, Harmondsworth: Penguin Books.

Johnson, H.G. (1972), 'The Monetary Approach to the Balance of Payments', in H.G. Johnson, *Further Essays in Monetary Economic*, London: Allen and Unwin.

Junankar, P.N. (1982), *Marx's Economics*, Oxford: Philip Allan.

Kaldor, N. (1939), 'Welfare Propositions of Economics and Interpersonal Comparison of Utility', *Economic Journal*, vol. 49, pp. 549–52.

Kaldor, N. (1970), 'The New Monetarism', *Lloyds Bank Review*, no. 97, July, pp. 1–17.

Kaldor, N. (1983), 'Keynesian Economics After Fifty Years' in Worswick, D. and Trevithick, J. (eds), *Keynes and the Modern World*, Cambridge: Cambridge University Press, pp. 1–27.

Kalecki, M. (1971), *Dynamics of the Capitalist Economy*, Cambridge: Cambridge University Press.

Katouzian, H. (1980), *Ideology and Method in Economics*, London: Macmillan.

Keller, Robert R. (1983), 'Keynesian and Institutional Economics: Compatibility and Complementarity?' *Journal of Economic Issues*, vol. 17, no. 4, pp. 1087–93.

Keynes, J.M. (1930), *A Treatise on Money*, London: Macmillan.

Keynes, John Maynard (1936, 1973), *The Collected Writings of John Maynard Keynes, Volume VII: The General Theory of Employment, Interest and Money*, London: Macmillan for the Royal Economic Society.

Keynes, J.M. (1939), 'Professor Tinbergen's Method', *Economic Journal*, vol. 49, pp. 558–68.

Keynes, J.M. (1973), The General Theory and After: Part I, Preparation Volume XIII of *The Collected Writings of John Maynard Keynes*, London: Macmillan for the Royal Economic Society.

Keynes, John Neville (1891), *The Scope and Method of Political Economy*, London: Macmillan.

Kirzner, I.M. (1973), *Competition and Entrepreneurship*, Chicago: University of Chicago Press.

Kirzner, I.M. (1985), *Discovery and the Capitalist Process*, Chicago: University of Chicago Press.

Klamer, Arjo (1984), *The New Classical Macroeconomics: Conversations with the New Classical Economists and their Opponents*, Brighton: Wheatsheaf.

Klein, L.R. (1954), 'The Empirical Foundations of Keynesian Economics' in Kurihara, K. (ed.), *Post Keynesian Economics*, New Brunswick: Rutgers University Press.

Klein, L.R. (1966), *The Keynesian Revolution*, New York: Macmillan

Knight, F.H. (1937), 'Unemployment and Mr. Keynes' Revolution in Economic Theory', *Canadian Journal of Economics and Political Science*, vol. 5, pp. 100–123.

Knight, F.H. (1956), *On the History and Method of Economics*, Chicago: University of Chicago Press.

Koutsoyannis, A. (1979), *Modern Microeconomics*, Hong Kong: Macmillan.

Kregel, J.A. (1973), *The Reconstruction of Political Economy: An Introduction to Post Keynesian Economics*, London: Macmillan.

Kropotkin, P. (1902), *Mutual Aid: a Factor in Evolution*, New York: Doubleday.

Kuhn, Thomas S. (1962, 1970), *The Structure of Scientific Revolutions*, Chicago: University of Chicago Press.

Kuhn, W.E. (1970), *The Evolution of Economic Thought*, Cincinnati: South-Western Publishing.

Lachmann, L.M. (1986) *The Market as an Economic Process*, Oxford: Basil Blackwell.

Laidler, D. (1981), 'Monetarism: an interpretation and assessment', *Economic Journal*, vol. 91, pp. 1–28.

Laidler, D. (1984), 'The Buffer Stock Notion in Monetary Economics', *Economic Journal*, Supplement, vol. 94, pp. 17–34.

Laidler, D. (1985), *The Demand for Money: Theories, Evidence and Problems*, 3rd ed., New York: Harper and Row.

Lakatos, Imre (1976), *Proofs and Refutations*, Cambridge: Cambridge University Press.

Lakatos, Imre and Musgrove, Alan (eds) (1970), *Criticism and the Growth of Knowledge*, Cambridge: Cambridge University Press.

Latsis, Spiro (ed.) (1976), *Method and appraisal in economics*, Cambridge: Cambridge University Press.

Lavoie, D. (1985), *Rivalry and Central Planning*, Cambridge: Cambridge University Press.

Lawson, A. (1987), 'The relative/absolute nature of knowledge and economic analysis', *Economic Journal*, vol. 97, pp. 951–70.

Layard, R. and Nickell, S. (1986), 'Unemployment in Britain', *Economica*, vol. 53, pp. 121–69.

Leijonhufvud, Axel (1968), *On Keynesian Economics and the Economics of Keynes*, London: Oxford University Press.

Leijonhufvud, Axel (1969), *Keynes and the Classics*, Occasional Paper 30, London: Institute of Economic Affairs.

Lerner, A.P. (1936), The General Theory, *International Labour Review*, vol. xiv, pp. 148, 233.

Levine, A. and Wright, E.O. (1989), 'Rationality and Class Struggle', in Callinicos, A. (ed.), *Marxist Theory*, Oxford: Oxford University Press.

Lindbeck, A. and Snower, D.J. (1988), 'Union activity, unemployment persistence, and wage-employment ratchets', in Cross, R. (ed.), *Unemployment and the natural rate hypothesis*, Oxford; Basil Blackwell.

Lipsey, R. (1960), 'The relationship between unemployment and the rate of change of money wage rates in the UK, 1862–1957, – a further analysis', *Economica*, vol. 27, pp. 1–41.

Lucas, R.E. (1972), 'Expectations and the neutrality of money', *Journal of Economic Theory*, vol. 4, pp. 103–24.

Lucas, R.E. (1973), 'Some International Evidence on Output-Inflation Trade-offs', *American Economic Review*, vol. 63, no. 3, pp. 326–34.

Lucas, R.E. (1977), 'Understanding business cycles', in Brunner, K. and Metzler, A.H. (eds), *The Phillips Curve and Labour Markets*, Carnegie Rochester Conference Series on Public Policy, 5, Amsterdam: North-Holland.

Lucas, R.E. and Rapping, L.A. (1969), 'Price expectations and the Phillips Curve', *American Economic Review*, vol. 59, pp. 342–50.

Lucas, R.E. and Sargent, T.J. (1978), 'After Keynesian Macroeconomics', in *After the Phillips Curve: Persistence of High Inflation and Unemployment*, Reserve Bank of Boston, Conference Series, 19.

Lucas, R.E. and Sargent, T.J. (1981), *Rational Expectations and Econometric Practice*, Minnesota: University of Minnesota Press.

Luce, R.D. and Raiffa, H. (1957), *Games and Decisions*, New York: Wiley.

Lutz, Mark and Lux, Kenneth (1988), *Humanistic Economics: The New Challenge*, New York: Bootstrap Press.

Magee, B. (1973), *Popper*, London: Fontana/Collins.

Marshall, A. (1890, 1920), *Principles of Economics*, 8th ed., London: Macmillan.

Marx, K. (1970), *A Contribution to the Critique of Political Economy*, Moscow: Progress Publishers.

Marx, Karl (1976), *Capital*, Vols I, II, & III, Harmondsworth: Penguin Books.

Marx, Karl and Engels, Friedrich (1948, 1967), *The Communist Manifesto*, (this translation by Samuel Moore was first published in 1888), Harmonds-worth: Penguin Books.

Marx, K. and Engels, F. (1959), *Basic Writings on Politics and Philosophy*, New York: Anchor Books.

McCloskey, Donald N. (1986), *The Rhetoric of Economics*, Brighton: Wheat-sheaf.

Meek, R.L. (1977), *Smith, Marx and After*, London: Chapman and Hall.

Meltzer, A.H. (1981), 'Keynes's General Theory: A Different Perspective', *Journal of Economic Literature*, vol. XIX, pp. 34–64.

Menger, Carl (1871, 1981), *Principles of Economics*, ed. J. Dingwall and B.F. Hoselitz, New York and London: New York University Press.

Menger, Carl (1883, 1963), *Problems of Economics and Sociology*, ed. L. Schneider and trans. F.I. Knock, Urbana Illinois: University of Illinois Press.

Mill, J.S. (1843, 1965), *A System of Logic*, London: Longman.

Mises, L. von (1912, 1953), *Theory of Money and Credit*, trans. H.E. Batson, London: Jonathan Cape.

Mises, L. von (1949), *Human Action*, New Haven: Yale University Press.

Mises. L. von (1962), *The Ultimate Foundation of Economic Science: An Essay on Method*, Princeton: Van Nostrand.

Mitchell, Wesley (1937), *The Backward Art of Spending Money*, New York: McGraw-Hill.

Modigliani, F. (1944), 'Liquidity Preference and the Theory of Interest and Money', *Econometrica*, vol. 12, pp. 45–88.

Moggridge, D.E. (1976), *Keynes*, London: Macmillan.

Moggridge, D.E. (1988), 'The Keynesian Revolution in Historical Perspective', in Hamouda, Omar F. and Smithin, J.N. (eds), *Keynes and Public Policy After Fifty Years, Vol. I: Economics and Policy*, Aldershot: Edward Elgar, pp. 50–60.

Mundell, R.A. (1962), 'The appropriate use of monetary and fiscal policy under fixed exchange rates', *International Monetary Fund Staff Papers*, 9, 70–77.

Muth, J.F. (1961), 'Rational Expectations and the Theory of Price Movements', *Econometrica*, vol. 29, pp. 315–35.

Nash, J.F. (1951), 'Non-Cooperative Games', *Annals of Mathematics*, vol. 54, pp. 289–95.

Nash, J.F. (1953), 'Two Person Cooperative Games', *Econometrica*, vol. 21, pp. 128–40.

Nelson, R.R. and Winter, S.G. (1982), *An Evolutionary Theory of Economic Change*, Cambridge, Mass: Harvard University Press.

Newman, P. (1965), *The Theory of Exchange*, New Jersey: Prentice-Hall.

O'Driscoll G.P. (Jnr) and Rizzo, M.J. (1985) *The Economics of Time and Ignorance*, Oxford; Basil Blackwell.

O'Hear, A. (1980), *Karl Popper*, London: Routledge and Kegan Paul.

The New Palgrave: A Dictionary of Economics, (1987) London: Macmillan.

Patinkin, D. (1976), 'Keynes and Econometrics: On the Interaction between the Macroeconomic Revolutions of the Interwar Period', *Econometrica*, vol. 44, pp. 1091–123.

Pareto, V. (1906, 1971), *Manual of Political Economy* (translation), New York: Kelly.

Perlman, Selig J. (1928), *A Theory of the Labour Movement*, New York: Macmillan.

Pheby, John (1988), *Methodology and economics: a critical introduction*, London: Macmillan.

Pheby, J. (ed.) (1989), *New Directions in Post Keynesian Economics*, Aldershot: Edward Elgar.

Phelps, E.S. (1967), 'Phillips Curves, expectations of inflation and optimal unemployment over time', *Economica*, vol. 34, pp. 254–81.

Phillips, A.W. (1958), 'The relationship between unemployment and the rate of change of money wage rates in the UK, 1861–1957', *Economica*, vol. 25, pp. 283–99.

Pierce, Charles S. (1955), *The Philosophical Writings of Pierce*, edited by J. Buchler, New York: Dover Publications.

Pigou, A.C. (1920), *The Economics of Welfare*, London: Macmillan.

Pigou, A.C. (1936), 'Mr J M Keynes' General Theory of Employment, Interest and Money', *Economica*, vol. 3, pp. 115–32.

Popper, K.R. (1934, 1959), *The Logic of Scientific Discovery*, London: Hutchinson.

Popper, K.R. (1957), *The Poverty of Historicism*, London: Routledge and Kegan Paul.

Popper, K.R. (1963), *Conjectures and Refutations*, London: Routledge and Kegan Paul.

Popper, K.R. (1972), *Objective Knowledge*, Oxford: Clarendon Press.

Quine, W.V. and Ullian, J.S. (1970), *The Web of Belief*, New York: Random House.

Radcliffe (chair) (1959), *Report of the Committee on the Working of the Monetary System*, Cmnd 827, London: HMSO.

Reddaway, W.B. (1936), 'The General Theory of Employment, Interest and Money (Review)', *Economic Record*, vol. 12, pp. 28–36.

Reder, M.W, (1982), 'Chicago economics: permanence and change', *Journal of Economic Literature*, vol. 20, pp. 1–38.

Reynolds, P. (1987), *Political Economy: A Synthesis of Kaleckian and Post Keynesian Economics*, Brighton: Wheatsheaf.

Ricardo, D. (1971), *Principles of Political Economy and Taxation*, Harmondsworth: Penguin Books.

Rima, I.H. (1988), 'Keynes's Vision and Econometric Analysis', in Hamouda, Omar F. and Smithin, J.N. (eds), *Keynes and Public Policy After Fifty Years, Vol. II: Theories and Method*, Aldershot: Edward Elgar, pp. 12–22.

Robbins, L. (1932), *An Essay on the Nature and Significance of Economic Science*, London: Macmillan.

Robertson, D.N. (1926), *Banking Policy and the Price level*, London: P.S. King.

Robinson, E.A.G. (1947), 'John Maynard Keynes, 1883–1946', *Economic Journal*, vol. 57, no. 1, pp. 1–68.

Roemer, J. (1988), *Free to Lose*, London: Radius.

Rowley, R. (1988), 'The Keynes–Tinbergen Exchange in Retrospect', in Hamouda, Omar F. and Smithin, J.N. (eds), *Keynes and Public Policy After Fifty Years, Vol. II: Theories and Method*, Aldershot: Edward Elgar, pp. 23–31.

Russell, B. (1948), *Human Knowledge: Its Scope and Limits*, London: Allen & Unwin.
Salant, W.S. (1988), 'The Spread of Keynesian Doctrines and Practices in the United States', in Hamouda, Omar F. and Smithin, J.N. (eds), *Keynes and Public Policy After Fifty Years, Vol. I: Economics and Policy*, Aldershot: Edward Elgar, pp. 61–76.
Samuels, W.J. (1988), 'Institutional Economics', *The New Palgrave: a Dictionary of Economics*, pp. 864–6.
Samuelson, P.A. (1947), *Foundations of Economics Analysis*, Cambridge Mass: Harvard University Press.
Samuelson, P.A. (1954), 'Pure Theory of Public Expenditure', *Review of Economics and Statistics*, vol. 36, pp. 387–9.
Samuelson, P.A. (1955), 'Diagrammatic Exposition of a Theory of Public Expenditure, *Review of Economics and Statistics*, vol. 37, pp. 350–6.
Sawyer, M.C. (1985), *The Economics of Michâl Kalecki*, London: Macmillan.
Sawyer, M.C. (ed.) (1988), *Post Keynesian Economics*, Schools of Thought in Economics Series 2, Aldershot: Edward Elgar.
Schotter, A. (1981), *The Economic Theory of Social Institutions*, Cambridge: Cambridge University Press.
Schumpeter, J.A. (1934), *The Theory of Economic Development*, Cambridge Mass: Harvard University Press.
Schumpeter, J.A. (1936), 'The General Theory of Employment, Interest and Money', *Journal of the American Statistical Association*, pp. 791–5.
Schumpeter, J.A. (1942), *Capitalism, Socialism and Democracy*, US 1st ed. 5th ed. (1976), London: Allen and Unwin.
Schwartz, J. (ed.) (1977), *The Subtle Anatomy of Capitalism*, Santa Monica: Goodyear Publishing.
Scitovsky, T. (1941), 'A Note on Welfare Propositions in Economics', *Review of Economic Studies*, vol. 8, pp. 77–88.
Scitovsky, T. (1977), *The Joyless Economy*, Oxford: Oxford University Press.
Sen, A.K. (1970), *Collective Choice and Social Welfare*, San Francisco: Holden-Day.
Shackle, G.L.S. (1949), *Expectation in Economics*, Cambridge: Cambridge University Press.
Shackle, G.L.S. (1972), *Epistemics and Economics*, Cambridge: Cambridge University Press.
Sherman, H. (1987), *Foundations of Radical Political Economy*, New York: M.E. Sharpe.
Shubik, M. (1983), *Game Theory in the Social Sciences*, Cambridge Mass; MIT Press.
Simon, H.A. (1957), *Models of Man: Social and Rational*, New York: Wiley.
Smith, A. (1759, 1976), *The Theory of Moral Sentiments*, edited by D.D. Raphael and A.L. Macfie, Oxford: Clarendon.
Smith, Adam (1776, 1970, 1974), *The Wealth of Nations*, edited by Andrew Skinner, Harmondsworth: Penguin.
Smith, Adam (1776, 1976), *An Inquiry into the Nature and Causes of the Wealth of Nations*, edited by R.H. Campbell and A.S. Skinner, Oxford: Clarendon.
Smith, A. (1795, 1980), 'History of Astronomy', in Wightman, W.B. (ed.), *Essays on Philosophical Subjects*, Oxford: Clarendon.

Smith, Vernon L. (1990), *Experimental Economics*, Schools of Thought in Economics Series, Cheltenham: Edward Elgar.

Sowell, T. (1985), *Marxism, Philosophy and Economics*, London: Unwin.

Sraffa, P. (1960), *Production of Commodities by means of Commodities*, Cambridge: Cambridge University Press.

Stackleberg, H. von (1952), *The Theory of the Market Economy*, Oxford: Oxford University Press.

Steedman, Ian (1989), *Sraffian Economics*, Schools of Thought in Economics Series, 2 vols, Cheltenham: Edward Elgar.

Steindl, J. (1976), *Maturity and Stagnation in American Capitalism*, New York: Monthly Review Press.

Stewart, I.M.T. (1979), *Reasoning and Method in Economics*, London: McGraw-Hill.

Stewart, M. (1967), *Keynes and After*, London: Penguin.

Stocking, G. and Watkins, M. (1946), *Cartels in Action*, New York: Twentieth Century Fund.

Sugden, R. (1986), *The Economics of Rights, Co-operation & Welfare*, Oxford: Basil Blackwell.

Thurow, Lester (1983), *Dangerous Currents: The State of Economics*, New York: Random House.

Tinbergen, J. (1937), *An Econometric Approach to Business Cycle Problems*, Paris: Herman.

Tobin, J. (1970), 'Money and income: post hoc ergo propter hoc?', *Quarterly Journal of Economics*, vol. 84, pp. 301–17.

Tobin, J. (1983), 'Comment' on 'Keynesian Economics After Fifty Years' by N. Kaldor in Worswick, D. and Trevithick, J. (eds), *Keynes and the Modern World*, Cambridge: Cambridge University Press, pp. 28–36.

Tool, Marc R. (1985), *The Discretionary Economy: a Normative Theory of Political Economy*, Boulder, Colorado: Westview Press.

Tool, Marc R. (ed.) (1988), *Evolutionary Economics, Vol. I: Foundations of Institutional Thought*, New York: M.E. Sharpe.

Tool, Marc R. (ed.) (1988), *Evolutionary Economics, Vol. II: Institutional Theory and Policy*, New York: M.E. Sharpe.

Veblen, Thorstein (1898), 'Why is economics not an evolutionary science?', *Quarterly Journal of Economics*, vol. 12, pp. 373–97.

Veblen, Thorstein (1899), *The Theory of the Leisure Class: An Economic Study of Institutions*, London: Macmillan.

Veblen, Thorstein (1904, 1965), *The Theory of Business Enterprise*, New York: Kelley.

Veblen, Thorstein (1923), *Absentee Ownership and Business Enterprise in Recent Times*, New York: Heubsch.

Walker, D.A. (1989), 'A primer on Walrasian theories of economic behaviour', *History of Economics Society Bulletin*, vol. 11 no. 1, pp. 1–24.

Wallis, K.F. (ed.) (1988), *Models of the UK Economy*, Oxford: Oxford University Press.

Walras, Léon (1874, 1877, 1965), *Elements of Pure Economics, or The Theory of Social Wealth*, translated by W. Jaffé, London: Allen & Unwin.

Ward, Benjamin (1972), *What's wrong with economics?*, New York: Basic Books.

Weintraub, S. (1966), *A Keynesian Theory of Employment Growth and Income Distribution*, Philadelphia: Chilton.
Wicksell, K. (1898, 1936), *Interest and Prices*, trans. R.F. Kahn, London: Macmillan.
Wiles, Peter and Routh, Guy (eds) (1984), *Economics in Disarray*, Oxford: Blackwell.
Williamson, O.E. (1975), *Markets and Hierarchies: Analysis and Anti-Trust Implications: A Study in the Economics of Internal Organisation*, New York: Free Press.
Williamson, O.E. (1985), *The Economic Institutions of Capitalism*, New York: Free Press and London: Macmillan.
Winch, P. (1958), *The Idea of a Social Science and its Relation to Philosophy*, London: Routledge and Kegan Paul.
Witte, Edwin E. (1932), *The Government in Labour Disputes*, New York and London: McGraw-Hill.
Witt, U. (1988), *Evolutionary Economics*, Cambridge: Cambridge University Press.
Wonnacott, P. and Wonnacott, R. (1986), *Economics*, New York: McGraw-Hill.
Worswick, D. and Trevithick, J. (eds) (1983), *Keynes and the Modern World*, Cambridge: Cambridge University Press.
Wright, E.O. (1977), 'Alternative Perspectives in Marxist Theory of Accumulation and Crisis', in Schwartz, J. (ed.), *The Subtle Anatomy of Capitalism*, Santa Monica: Goodyear Publishing.
Yeager, L.B. (1986), 'The Keynesian Heritage in Economics', in *Keynes's General Theory: Fifty Years On*, Hobart Paperback no. 24, London: IEA.
Zeuthen, F.L.B. (1930), *Problems of Monopoly and Economic Warfare*, London: Routledge.

Index